THE BURNING

ALSO BY TIM MADIGAN

SEE NO EVIL

THE
BURNING

MASSACRE, DESTRUCTION,
AND THE TULSA
RACE RIOT OF 1921

TIM MADIGAN

THOMAS DUNNE BOOKS
ST. MARTIN'S PRESS ⚛ NEW YORK

THOMAS DUNNE BOOKS.
An imprint of St. Martin's Press.

www.stmartins.com

Library of Congress Cataloging-in-Publication Data

Madigan, Tim.
    The Burning: massacre, destruction, and the Tulsa race riot of 1921 / Tim
Madigan.—1st ed.
        p. cm.
    Includes index.
    ISBN 0-312-27283-9
    1. African Americans—Oklahoma—Tulsa—History—20th century.
2. African American neighborhoods—Oklahoma—Tulsa—History—20th
century. 3. Riots—Oklahoma—Tulsa—History—20th century.
4. Violence—Oklahoma—Tulsa—History—20th century. 5. Tulsa
(Okla.)—Race relations. 6. Racism—Oklahoma—Tulsa—History—20th
century. I. Title.

F704.T92 M33 2001
976.6'86052—dc21

                                                        2001041811

First Edition: November 2001

10 9 8 7 6 5 4 3 2 1

THIS BOOK IS LOVINGLY DEDICATED TO MY PARENTS,
MYKE AND LOIS MADIGAN, FOR WHO THEY ARE, ALL
THEY'VE DONE, AND ALL THEY CONTINUE TO DO.

AND TO THEIR SECOND SON, STEVE,
WHO TEACHES US STILL.

CONTENTS

ACKNOWLEDGMENTS

One afternoon early in this work, my brother, Steve, asked this question: When would I know when to end my book research and begin the process of writing? I thought for a second, then replied, saying something to the effect that "When you've done this sort of thing for a while, you just know." A look of relief and understanding crossed his face when I answered, which surprised me because it seemed to be such a small point. But looking back, I think he saw in that discussion a metaphor for the much more profound transition then awaiting him. When was it time to stop fighting the tumor that had taken away the use of his legs? When was it time to let go? "Yeah," Steve said that day in his hospital bed. "You just know."

And Steve knew. I know of no other person who faced the end of his life with more courage, grace, and wisdom than he. I was among his loved ones who held his hand on the sunny morning of August 3, 2000, when he passed from this life, and Steve has been holding my hand, almost literally, ever since, sustaining and inspiring me as I worked to complete this book. He is greatly loved and greatly missed.

Now back to the beginning. Julie Heaberlin, my editor in the features department of the *Fort Worth Star-Telegram*, first brought the tragedy of Tulsa to my attention, and assigned me to do a piece about the burning for the newspaper. Thus this journey began. It is fitting that it should have begun with Julie, for she is my friend, and it has been my great good fortune to work with her for several years. The support of colleagues in the features department has also meant much. For more than a decade, *Star-Telegram* editor Jim Witt has been a friend, mentor, and advocate. I thank him for his support on this book, and everything he has done for me in the years before. Bob Ray Sanders is a friend, mentor, and hero who has helped inspire my own awakening about race, and shared the journey of this book, as did *Star-Telegram* photographer Jill Johnson. *Star-Telegram* book editor Jeff Guinn was unfailingly generous with his advice and assistance.

Dallas literary agent Jim Donovan was the first to envision my newspaper piece as the basis for a larger work. In the months afterward, Jim guided me through uncharted waters with his advice, support, editing, and slightly warped sense of humor. He's a buddy now, and you can't have too many of those. I'm also grateful to agent B. J. Robbins, who worked with Jim to make this book a reality. My editor at Thomas Dunne Books, Peter Wolverton, signed on early, and shared my belief that this could be both a good book and an important one. I thank him for his editorial wisdom, and all the encouraging notes via e-mail that kept me moving forward. Writer friend Carlton Stowers, who has appointed himself my literary guardian angel, also had a role in getting this project off the ground, but will never admit to what it was.

It was my cosmic good fortune that this work would take me to Tulsa, where two of my dearest and oldest friends from my Minnesota childhood, Joel and Leslye Rood, had come to reside. During my trips to Tulsa, the Roods put me up in their guestroom, allowed me to raid the refrigerator, enthusiastically supported this work, and shared my grief over the loss of Steve. To their children, Timmy and Anneke, I was the "snortle monster," but that's another story.

My thanks once again to survivors Otis Clark, George Monroe, Eldoris Ector McCondichie, Veneice Sims, and Wilhelmina Guess Howell, living examples of grace and forgiveness, and to the white witnesses who were so generous with their time and memories, Philip Rhees, Clyde Eddy, Lee Cisco, Richard Gary, and Margaret Anderson. This is the appropriate place to add a special salute to Eddie Faye Gates, who has befriended so many of these elderly people, and always kept their best interests at heart.

Let me reiterate my gratitude to Oklahoma state representative Don Ross, Scott Ellsworth, Paul Lee, Dick Warner, and Ed Wheeler, who know this story better than anyone, and who I now call my friends. It was always a delight for me to talk to Roxanne Blystone in Don's office in the Oklahoma capital and to Frances Jordan, executive administrator of the Greenwood Cultural Center in Tulsa. Mary Warner, Dick's wife, was always gracious and accommodating on the several occasions I invaded her home. And a special thanks to Ruth Sigler Avery, whose heroic efforts to unearth and preserve the truth informs so many of these pages.

I always looked forward to my time in the Special Collections Department of the University of Tulsa's McFarlin Library, not only for the wealth of information there, but for the good nature and professionalism of Lori Curtis, the head of the department, Lisa Inman, and Milissa Burkart. Randy Kreihbel and Wayne Greene at the *Tulsa World* were also of tremendous help to me, and always took time from their own assignments to return my telephone calls and answer my questions. My additional thanks to the staff of the Tulsa Public Library, and Tulsa Historical Society.

I also owe a debt to the following: Beryl Ford, Jack Adams, Don Adams, Obera Mann Smith, John D. Mann, Nancy Little, Jenkins Lloyd Jones and Jenkins Lloyd Jones, Jr., Hannibal Johnson, Sherri Carriere of the Tulsa County Sheriff's Department, Red Phelps, Bob Hower, Alfred Brophy, and Ron Trekell.

Finally, there are no words to describe my love and gratitude for friends and family who shared these extraordinary months of my life. Chris and Kelly Molloy, Edmund Schenecker, Norval and Susan Kneten, all my good friends at Rivercrest, Dick and Janice Lord, Jim and Kathy Larsen, John and Cheri Seabers, Uncles Gordy and Vernon and their families, Mike, Patty, Carrie and Rob McMahon, Andy Martin, and Fred Rogers are all pilgrims on the same trek. They share this destination with me. A note to my players on the Wild: You guys helped me keep my sanity. It was a joy and privilege to be your coach.

As Steve's disease progressed, he urged those of us who loved him most to join hands and fight for life. My sisters Chris Madigan and Terri O'Neill, joined the battle, as did brothers Mike, Pat and Kelly, as well as their families and so many of their friends. Steve's wife, Cally, was the first among us to fight, with Steve's sons, Tim and Tyler, who are wonderful boys. Their dad is very proud of them, I know. My mother and father, Myke and Lois Madigan, inspired us all with their love, courage, stamina, and faith. This book is dedicated to them, and to Steve.

My life is dedicated to my wife, Catherine, and to my children, Melanie and Patrick. Their great sacrifices that made this book possible were made cheerfully. I know of no man who has a sweeter existence than I. They are the reason.

AUTHOR'S NOTE

I was oblivious to Tulsa's historic nightmare until that day in the winter of 2000 when Julie Heaberlin, my editor at the *Fort Worth Star-Telegram*, stopped by my desk in the Features Department. It was then that Julie handed me a copy of a short wire-service story about the Tulsa Race Riot Commission, which had been created a few years before to study a particularly deadly racial outbreak in 1921. As many as three hundred people had been killed in the catastrophe, the wire story said, most of the victims black. A uniquely prosperous community of African Americans, called Greenwood—thirty-five square blocks and literally thousands of homes, businesses, churches, and schools—had been obliterated by a white mob in Tulsa that numbered in the thousands.

When I read the story, my reaction was the same as my editor's had been. How could we not have known about such a thing? If the Tulsa Race Riot of 1921 was as horrible as the wire story seemed to suggest, surely it deserved a place among the watershed moments in American racial history, alongside events such as the assassination of Martin Luther King, Jr.; *Brown v. The Board of Education*; Little Rock; the March to Selma, and Rosa Parks' historic resolve. Instead, the riot had never been mentioned in any history book I had ever read.

Julie dispatched me to Tulsa a few days later. There I interviewed a handful of elderly African Americans, people who remembered the terrible hours of June 1, 1921, when the whites swarmed over the railroad tracks separating white Tulsa from black. On that first trip I also met Oklahoma State Representative Don Ross, a veteran African American legislator who had grown up in Greenwood, and talked by telephone with a white historian named Scott Ellsworth, a Tulsa native who, like Ross, had devoted much of his life to restoring the Tulsa catastrophe to its proper place in history. My own article ran in the *Star-Telegram* on January 30, 2000, beneath the headline TULSA'S TERRIBLE SECRET. The dozens of *Star-Telegram* readers who called or wrote afterward, both black and white, young and old, had much the same reaction as my editor and myself. How could we not have known?

In important respects, I was an unlikely candidate for such an assignment. I was born and raised in a small farming community in the north of Minnesota, where the only people of color were the Hispanic migrants who came up from Texas each summer to work in the sugar-beet fields. By and large, through the first twenty years of my life, television was the only place I saw a black face. Racial issues were wholly irrelevant to me then, and continued to be even after newspaper work took me to Texas, where I lived and worked for the first time with people from other cultural backgrounds. In retrospect, my lack of curiosity about those people and their experience in America was stunning. I will never forget my first night in Tulsa, having dinner with Don Ross in a quiet Chinese restaurant, and the look on his face as I asked questions such as, "What was it like for blacks after the Civil War?"

Ross was stunned at first, then angry. "How can you not know these things?" he demanded. Then, his voice rising to the point that others in the restaurant looked uncomfortably over at our table, he said, "And you're one of the educated whites. If we can't count on you to understand, who can we count on?"

For the rest of that night and for weeks thereafter, Ross called me "ignorant white boy." I am pleased to say that Ross and I are good friends today. When my newspaper article appeared, he went so far as to dub me "an honorary Negro." He has since retracted such blasphemy and in his more charitable moments, now calls me a "moderate" where racial issues are concerned. I'm not kidding myself, either. I am still ignorant. But after my recent journey into the darker corners of our past, one that began with my newspaper story and has continued with the research and writing of this book, I'm not nearly as ignorant as before. I will never be able to look at a black person the same way again. I think I'm beginning to understand.

Until that night with Don Ross, I had never heard of historian John Hope Franklin (a native of Tulsa, as it turned out) or his book *From Slavery to Freedom* (McGraw Hill, 1994). At Ross's suggestion, Franklin's book became the launching point for my crash course into black history, and I'm now of the opinion that it should be taught in every American high school. Until reading Franklin's book, I was only vaguely aware of the horrors of slavery. I was almost completely ignorant of the terror and hardship that came with emancipation—the murderous rides of the original Ku Klux Klan; the reign of Jim Crow; thousands of lynchings; racial hatreds that were not only tolerated, but widely condoned and endorsed at the highest levels of our society by people and institutions in the North and South alike; the revival of the KKK in the 1920s, and so on.

Not long into my research, I realized that what happened in Tulsa in 1921 was scarcely an isolated event. It might have been the worst incident of its kind in our history, but almost every month, American newspapers of that time carried new accounts of racial bloodshed in another town or city, new atrocities perpetrated against Negroes by mobs of whites. Rather than an exception, I learned, what happened in Tulsa was a metaphor for that period of our history, those particularly ugly years that followed World War I, and for the black experience in America in the century after the Civil War.

In addition to *From Slavery to Freedom*, several other books were especially helpful in my quest to understand that history and to place the burning of Greenwood in its proper context. Chief among them were Wyn Craig Wade's *The Fiery Cross: The Ku*

Klux Klan in America (Simon and Schuster, 1987); *Only Yesterday: an Informal History of the 1920s,* by Frederick Lewis Allen (Harper and Row, 1957); Joseph Cartwright's *The Triumph of Jim Crow: Tennessee Race Relations in the 1880s* (University of Tennessee Press, 1976); and *The Unknown Soldiers: Black American Troops in World War I,* by Arthur E. Barbeau and Florette Henri (Temple University Press, 1974). I also relied heavily on independent scholar Paul Lee, who is as knowledgeable and passionate about these matters as any individual I've encountered. I never failed to be inspired by our long telephone conversations, which often stretched far into the night.

Most of my research, obviously, focused on a particular moment in that wretched history, and my debt to those who helped me understand what happened in Tulsa cannot be overstated. Eddie Faye Gates, a member of the Tulsa Race Riot Commission, took it upon herself to befriend many of the more than one hundred survivors of the burning that the Commission identified after being created by the State Legislature in 1997. Gates was also my tireless intermediary with those elderly people, both blacks and whites, who were burdened with their awful memories. Nonetheless, in every instance, I found the black survivors and white witnesses to be charming, gracious, and wholly accommodating. My profound gratitude goes out to black survivors George Monroe, Otis Clark, Eldoris Ector McCondichie, Veneice Sims, and Wilhelmina Guess Howell, and to white witnesses Lee Cisco, Clyde Eddy, Philip Rhees, Richard Gary, and Margaret Anderson.

From our first telephone conversation, historian Scott Ellsworth has never been anything but generous with his time and accumulated wisdom. Ellsworth is chief among the handful of individuals, many of them white, whose courage and doggedness have helped wrest the burning of Greenwood from the shadows of history, and thus made this book possible.

Ellsworth's book *Death in a Promised Land: The Tulsa Race Riot of 1921* (LSU Press, 1982) was the first scholarly examination of the event ever published, and an essential road map in my own attempts to reconstruct what had happened. Equally valuable were taped recordings of Ellsworth's interviews, conducted more than twenty years ago, with riot survivors who were teenagers or young adults at the time. In almost every instance, those individuals are deceased. Their preserved recollections now reside on tape in the Special Collections Department of the University of Tulsa's McFarlin Library, where I spent several fruitful days following in Ellsworth's footsteps, eavesdropping on his conversations with survivors like Bill Williams, Seymour Williams, and Robert Fairchild. Also among the Ellsworth tapes was Wilhelmina Guess Howell's 1989 address to a Tulsa community group, a speech that included her own riveting account of the burning, and a tour through her remarkable family history, dating to the Civil War.

It is my great privilege to congratulate Ruth Sigler Avery for her attempts to discern and disseminate the truth about Greenwood's obliteration. In the spring of 1921, she was a little girl growing up in Tulsa in a wealthy white family. But she was old enough to be traumatized by what happened, and decades later, her lingering outrage inspired her to produce *Fear, The Fifth Horseman: A Documentary and Anthology on the 1921 Tulsa Race Riot*. Included in that unpublished work are transcripts of more than fifteen interviews that Avery conducted in the 1970s and early 1980s with riot survivors, white witnesses, and a Klansman, all of whom are now dead. Avery's work informs this book more than any other single source, having allowed me a glimpse into the life of Tulsa shoeshine-boy Dick Rowland, an insight into the prevailing attitudes of both whites and blacks, and having provided me with hitherto unknown details of the mind-numbing cruelty and horror.

I am similarly grateful to Ed Wheeler, whose 1971 magazine article broke Tulsa's half-century of silence where the burning was concerned. Wheeler was equally generous with his time and recollections.

My research went on to include dozens of conversations with descendants of Greenwood residents, most notably Jack Adams and his brother Don, and Obera Mann Smith, and J. D. Mann, who shared family stories that had been passed down for generations, stories so crucial to my understanding of some of this book's most prominent characters. My reporting also included an exhaustive review of the Tulsa newspapers of that time, as well as publications such as *The New York Times* and other major national newspapers and periodicals that covered the burning in the days and weeks after it happened. A graduate-school thesis written about the burning by Loren Gill in the 1940s was similarly valuable; as were several magazine articles; National Guard duty reports of that time; hundreds of pages of court transcripts and legal depositions, and the final report of the Tulsa Race Riot Commission, which was presented to Oklahoma Governor Frank Keating and the Oklahoma Legislature on February 28, 2001.

The story that follows synthesizes what I learned over the course of a year from hundreds of sources. In most cases, descriptions and dialogue that appear in the book are taken directly from the recollections of survivors and witnesses, from newspaper accounts, or legal documents. In some cases, I have taken the license of approximating dialogue for the purpose of maintaining the narrative. These instances are totally consistent with the character of the people involved as my research revealed them to be, and wholly true to the events as they unfolded in 1921.

For me, work on this book has been a life-changing odyssey. Early in the process, I began to suspect that a crucial piece remained missing from America's long attempts at racial reconciliation. Too many in this country remained as ignorant as I was. Too many were just as oblivious to some of the darkest moments in our history, a legacy of which Tulsa is both a tragic example and a shameful metaphor. How can we heal when we don't know what we're healing from? I hope this book contributes in some small way toward that broader understanding. Such is the spirit in which it is written.

—TIM MADIGAN
March 2001
Arlington, Texas

THE BURNING

PROLOGUE: LIKE JUDGMENT DAY

For the rest of her life, and she lived a very long time thereafter, Eldoris Ector McCondichie remembered the exact words of her mother.

"Eldoris, wake up! We have to go!" Harriet Ector shrieked to her daughter on that beautiful spring morning of June 1, 1921. "The white people are killing the colored folks!"

The cloudless sky outside was still pink from the dawn, but with those words, Eldoris's drowsiness was gone in a blink, rendering her fully awake and trembling by the time she tossed aside the covers. The nine-year-old girl threw a dress over her head as her mother rushed her along, with scarcely time for shoes and socks, and followed her parents and older brother as they hurried toward the front door of their small home on Iroquois Avenue.

White people? Killing the coloreds? Eldoris waited to shake free from the nightmare, but she couldn't. She turned her mother's words around in her young mind, trying to fit them together in a way that would make sense, but that didn't happen, either. The days before had been so peaceful, boys and girls antsy because the end of the school year was just a few days away, but nothing else seemed amiss whatsoever.

And white people? Eldoris never had reason to fear them before. Every morning since she could remember, her father had set out on foot, walking south through the black quarter where her family lived, the place called Greenwood. Then he crossed the Frisco railroad tracks at the edge of the Negro community, stepping into the dream world of tall buildings and streetcars and big new stores and huge schools and fancy homes where the whites of Tulsa, Oklahoma, lived. Every day Eldoris's father clipped those white folks' lawns and weeded their gardens, and the rich whites brought her father cold drinks on hot afternoons, and gave him a ham at Christmas, and otherwise treated her father fine, at least as far as his young daughter knew. But most important, they also paid her daddy a nice wage. Eldoris was old enough to know that the salary Howard Ector earned across the tracks was the reason his family had their little house on Iroquois. It paid for their food, and fifteen-cent movies at the Dreamland Theater on Greenwood Avenue, for her dresses, even for a doll or two.

And Eldoris knew the story was the same in almost every Greenwood household—Negroes toiling for white folks across the tracks, thousands of men and women joining Howard Ector on that same trek south to work as maids, or as mammies who suckled the white infants, or as chauffeurs, elevator operators, ditch-diggers, landscapers, or shoeshine boys, taking the burden from white Tulsans who got rich from the oil wells gushing just south of the city.

Many Negroes disappeared into white Tulsa for days on end, swallowed up in the affluence like Jonah by the great whale, living in servants' quarters on the south side. Greenwood didn't see them until Thursday, the maids' day off, when the servants rushed back home over the tracks and donned their fanciest clothes to stroll the two-block section of Greenwood Avenue where it ran into Archer Street—Deep Greenwood, as it was called. The maids and chauffeurs and gardeners and mammies ambled around for hours, past the sturdy brick drugstores, beauty parlors, newspaper offices, meat lockers, restaurants, jewelry stores, fine hotels, jazz joints, barbershops, skating rinks, and pool halls, all of them owned and run by blacks—past the offices of the lawyers and doctors, all of whom were Negroes, too. The heavenly aromas of fried chicken, barbeque ribs, and collard greens filled the air, mixing with the notes of jazz and blues that poured into the street. Promenading. That's what they called the activity of those wondrous Thursday nights—walking and flirting, pausing to spend some of their hard-earned money on an ice cream cone, or a glass of lemonade or a new hat, or on a snootful of bootleg liquor, then walking some more. Young men fought as the nights wore on and the moonshine flowed, and shot their guns into the air and sometimes at each other. But by and large, those nights were happy times, celebrations of what seemed possible for Negro people in America less than sixty years after the Civil War.

So on those Thursday nights in particular, the Negroes could forget about the new brick skyscrapers, fancy cars, and big homes that belonged to the whites on the south side of the tracks. They could forget that blacks, whose sweat was certainly welcome there, couldn't shop in white stores, or see movies at white theaters, or ride in white railroad cars. They could forget that new laws had caused even the telephone booths in Oklahoma to be segregated. They could forget that whites had larger, nicer, newer schools with all the latest textbooks for their children. They could overlook all these things because of the promise of those Thursday nights—because Greenwood Negroes, probably more so than blacks in any other place in the nation, had everything they needed on the north side of the Frisco tracks. As far away as Chicago, blacks said the Greenwood community in Tulsa, Oklahoma, was the top of the mountain for people of their race, a remarkable little city within a city, remembered over the decades as the "Negro Wall Street of America." And even a child knew the money that Negroes like Eldoris's father earned from the whites made it all possible.

But then, on that rosy dawn of June 1, 1921, it all disintegrated with her mother's early morning words. *The white people are killing the colored folks!* and in the second that Eldoris poked her head out the front door, she knew it was true.

She turned her head south as she stepped outside looking toward Deep Greenwood, the scene of all those festive Thursday nights. A massive black cloud of smoke billowed there now, nearly obliterating the rising sun.

As her father pulled her from the house by the hand, she heard a terrible noise from the sky and looked up to see airplanes buzzing low. The little girl had seen the flying machines only a time or two before, and they were ominous creatures even then, but now as they roared above them, she heard the dull thuds of bullets hitting the ground around her feet like fat raindrops, and she realized that she and her family were being shot at from the air. She yanked free from her father then, racing in panic to a nearby chicken coop and pulling open the door. The terrified eyes of several Negro adults already crowded inside stared back at her from the shadows. Chickens cackled nervously at the intrusion. Eldoris pushed her way through the grown-ups and crouched in a corner of the coop and would have stayed there forever if her father hadn't appeared at the door, pulled her back outside and dragged her off to the north to join all the others.

For her family was certainly not alone in their flight. A great column of black people was hurrying north with them along the Midland Valley railroad tracks that ran past her house, a sorry procession of thousands that stretched as far as Eldoris could see. Some were dressed only in bathrobes or nightclothes, having been flushed from their homes in the middle of the night by white mobs in the grip of the devil. "Come out, niggers!" members of the mob called to them in their Greenwood homes that night. "Come out or die!" So they rushed outside and headed north, many without shoes or socks. Women carrying wailing babies quietly wept to themselves. People hauled bundles of clothing on their heads. An old woman clutched a tattered Bible to her chest. A girl about Eldoris's age carried a little white dog beneath one arm. Some of the men cried, too, or stared off to a place far away, as if looking for answers there. Parents dragged their older children along after them, just as Howard Ector now dragged his daughter. The old people shuffled along as best they could. Many of them were old enough to remember slavery, but nothing from those times compared to the horror of what was happening on this morning.

The planes disappeared from the sky after a few minutes, so

now and then someone in the procession took a moment to ponder the growing wall of smoke to the south. Beneath that cloud, their homes and all their other earthly possessions were being incinerated. Back there, they had seen their neighbors tortured in the most hideous ways, or shot down in cold blood, or burned alive.

Why? The question hung over the procession like the smoke from the fires behind them. All anyone knew was that a few days before, a white girl had accused a black boy of assault, which somehow caused Greenwood to be swallowed up by rage, as if every ounce of enmity that had been building up in the whites since the Civil War had exploded on their doorsteps. *The white people are killing the colored folks!* An angry white mob clamored at their heels. So Eldoris and her family and the rest of the Negroes fled for their lives up the Midland Valley tracks toward the wooded hollows and rolling hills to the north of town, where they might finally be safe.

Looking around at the others, at the horror etched on the refugees' sunken faces, at the smoke behind her, Eldoris was reminded of something she had learned about in Sunday school. This was like Judgment Day! As she stumbled north with her family, she expected to see Jesus appear on his throne at any second, come to set everything right. But she never did.

Each member of Eldoris's family survived that day, but so did the horror—her mother's chilling words in the morning, the smoke, the crowds, the planes, the death and grief and destruction her family saw when they were allowed to return home a few days later. Somehow, their little house on Iroquois had survived, but most of the other buildings for thirty-five square blocks—almost every business, church, hospital, school, and home in Greenwood—had been reduced by the mob to ash and rubble. A few days after the burning, Eldoris walked to Detroit Avenue on the shoulder of Standpipe Hill, where so many of the black doctors and lawyers and businessmen and schoolteachers had their large, beautiful brick houses. Now only an occasional wall or chimney still stood. On one surviving wall, a wisp of white curtain dangled from a window, tossing in the breeze. Eldoris somehow took that as a sign of God's love and hope.

But the memories always stalked her, God's love and hope or not. The memories stalked everyone. In the decades to come, few Tulsans on either side of the tracks spoke out loud of the great burning, as though the catastrophe was a secret that both blacks and whites conspired to keep. Indeed, people who moved to the city only a few years later might never have known that it happened at all. But whether it was discussed or not, no one who witnessed the events of those historic days in Tulsa could ever forget. Seventy-nine years later, seventy-nine years later almost to the day, on a cloudy spring morning in the year 2000, Eldoris Ector McClondichie shuffled to a bookcase in the living room of her tidy Tulsa home, not far from the place on Iroquois where she grew up. She was an elderly widow now. She pulled two tissues from a box on the bookcase and sat down on her sofa, smiling weakly.

"By now, I know better to talk about that day without holding a few of these," Eldoris said.

CHAPTER 1

BEYOND HATRED'S REACH

On a warm May night in 1913, in the shadowy lamplight of Greenwood's First Baptist Church, Mrs. Lucy Davis read the audience a short essay on love, and the Rollison sisters nervously stepped to the altar to sing a lovely duet. Men wearing expensive suits and white gloves and women in their finest white dresses applauded politely. But those were only the quaint preliminaries to the primary attraction, one anticipated in the Greenwood community for days. Scarcely a spot in the pews was empty that night, for the principal speaker at the annual meeting of one of Greenwood's leading fraternal orders was none other than Captain Townsend D. Jackson—ex-slave, revered black lawman and militia leader in both Oklahoma and Tennessee, a man who had cast off the shackles of slavery and now looked the white governor of Oklahoma straight in the eye without blinking.

Or so Tulsa Negroes had heard. Just a few months before, Jackson and his family had moved to Greenwood from the Oklahoma town of Guthrie, preceded by Jackson's considerable notoriety, and his new neighbors were certainly anxious to hear for themselves the man's thoughts on the great racial questions of the day. That night at the church, they would finally get their chance.

He was impressive enough to look at—a stately, six-foot fellow whose short, dark hair had gone mostly gray. Jackson was also what Negroes called a "light," a mulatto whose creamy skin color gave rise to suspicions that he had been fathered by his Georgia slave owner in the 1850s, a common enough occurrence in those days. Little matter. As the Rollison sisters warbled their final note, Jackson rose and slowly stepped toward the pulpit, away from the front-row pew where his wife and youngest son, the handsome young physician Dr. Andrew Jackson, were sitting with him.

As he did, Andrew J. Smitherman removed a piece of paper and pencil from his breast pocket and leaned forward in his own pew near the front, poised to capture Jackson's every word. Smitherman, a bulldog-like man, was the irascible editor of the *Tulsa Star*, Greenwood's leading publication and its most authoritative public voice. In the eight years between that night in the church and the great burning to come, Smitherman doggedly chronicled all the local news, from street brawls to potluck dinners. But he also never missed a chance to rail in print against injustices perpetrated against his people, and had intervened personally in attempted lynchings in neighboring towns. An early banner headline summed up his belligerent disposition where race matters were concerned: YOU PUSH ME, the headline promised, AND I'LL PUSH YOU.

Seated next to Smitherman was John B. Stradford, a short, dapper, mustachioed man, the son of a Kentucky slave and an owner of a law degree in Indiana. He quickly had emerged as one of black Tulsa's most successful entrepreneurs, including among his ventures the famously luxurious, fifty-four-room Stradford Hotel on Greenwood Avenue, one of the state's largest black-owned businesses. But like his friend Smitherman, Stradford's overriding concern was the Negro's plight in America, and like the editor, Stradford wasn't shy about saying so. Just ask the white deliveryman Stradford had beaten to within an inch of his life for a racist remark made within earshot.

Others in the First Baptist audience that night were less inclined toward racial militance perhaps, but were no less noteworthy. John Williams and his wife Loula owned a drugstore, an auto shop, and a movie theater, and were the first Tulsa Negroes to purchase an automobile. O. W. Gurley owned Greenwood's first hotel and grocery store. Dr. R. T. Bridgewater was black Tulsa's first physician; Barney Cleaver, the towering fellow seated near the back, was the first Negro deputy. Lawyers and schoolteachers were in the audience, too, people who memorized Shakespeare and read Latin.

On the issue of race, some no doubt shared the confrontational notions of Smitherman and Stradford. Others preferred a quieter course. But each in his or her own way had put the lie to the prevailing theories of Negro inferiority with which the whites of that time continued to justify so much of their cruelty. Indeed, to visit First Baptist on the night of Jackson's speech was to observe Greenwood's gentry in its proud entirety—educated, literate, affluent Negroes packed into the sanctuary, estimable folks curious about Captain Jackson, just the latest in a series of remarkable success stories that continued to unfold in the place called Greenwood.

They were the children of slaves, or, in a few cases, had been born into slavery themselves. Some of the Greenwood gentry, in fact, remembered the dreary years after the Civil War, when four million Negroes were emancipated but without the skills, education, and experience in public life to guide them in their new freedom. In the decades after the war, tens of thousands of freedmen were thus obliged to work as sharecroppers or as tenants for their former owners for pitiable wages or no wages at all, earning a standard of living a slim notch above slavery itself.

Thousands of other emancipated blacks wandered confused and homeless from place to place, one step ahead of starvation, or they congregated in the cities, depending on handouts from the Freedmen's Bureau, which had been created by the federal government in the North to help tide them through.

But federal assistance was short-lived. Government policies during what was called Reconstruction, policies designed to protect the ex-slave and assist his transition into free society, evaporated within a decade after the Civil War. Federal troops assigned to keep order were recalled from the South, placing Negroes once more at the mercy of the whites, men and women embittered by their defeat by the North, people who typically believed Negroes a wholly inferior species—as much animal as human. Those whites thought Negroes childlike at best, bestial at worst, a threat to the safety and dignity of Southerners, and certainly incapable of meaningful participation in self-government. So when the North looked the other way, white state legislatures across the South quickly moved to make sure that blacks would not have the chance to participate in the democracy.

State after state effectively disenfranchised them with voting requirements most Negroes had no hope of meeting. Who knew how many windows there were in the White House? That was the kind of question Negroes needed to answer to obtain a ballot. In 1870, Tennessee passed the South's first "Jim Crow" statute, mandating segregation in every facet of social and public life, and the other members of the former Confederacy were quick to follow. In the years just after the Civil War, embittered Rebel soldiers joined the Ku Klux Klan by the tens of thousands and rained death and terror on Negroes and their Southern sympathizers. Over the decades, thousands of Negroes were lynched by white mobs, some for the crime of attempting to vote, or for tipping a hat to a white woman, or for failing to observe the "rituals of deference and submission," as one writer later put it.

But by that night in 1913, something had changed. No. The whites seemed as hateful as ever. That wasn't it. The change had come instead in the hearts and minds of the former slaves and their offspring, and nowhere in America was that transformation in greater evidence than in the community on the north side of the railroad tracks in Tulsa, Oklahoma.

Many there had embraced the teachings of men like Booker T. Washington, the famous educator and businessman who, beginning in the 1880s, preached that the path to white respect and ultimate equality ran through education and the acquisition of useful vocational skills.

As years passed, others in Tulsa began to subscribe to a far less accommodating philosophy that took hold after the turn of the century with a new generation of Negro leaders. One of them, the Harvard-educated writer W. E. B. Du Bois, was among the founders of the National Association for the Advancement of Colored People, a man whose beautifully strident prose ignited fires in the hearts of oppressed Negroes everywhere.

"We have cast off on the voyage which will lead to freedom or death," Du Bois wrote in those years. "For three centuries we have suffered and cowered. No race ever gave passive submission to evil a longer, more piteous trial. Today we raise the terrible weapon of self-defense. When the murderer comes, he shall no longer strike us in the back. When the armed lynchers gather, we too must gather armed. When the mob moves, we propose to meet it with sticks and clubs and guns."

Thus was the debate that went on every day in Greenwood barbershops, jazz joints, and confectioneries, as it did across Negro America. Were equality and respect to be earned or not? Was it to be the quiet achievement of Negroes, or sticks and clubs and guns? Was it the way of Booker T. Washington or of W. E. B. Du Bois? That spring night in 1913, the issue lingered in the air of First Baptist like smoke from the gas lamps that lit the sanctuary. Just where would the great Captain Jackson stand?

Jackson squinted in the dim light at the piece of paper upon which he had neatly copied his remarks. He paused and cleared his throat in the anxious silence, then bid his new neighbors a pleasant good evening. Otherwise, his first words were not of confrontation, but of modesty and humility, reminding his listeners of Jesus's instruction to enter his kingdom "like little children." He extolled the virtues of the Negro who "shakes thrones and dissolves aristocracies by his *silent example* and gives light to those who sit in darkness."

To think that those meek words came from a man who had spent the better part of his life as a black law officer, facing down white mobs.

"With money and property comes the means of knowledge and power," Jackson continued. "A poverty-stricken class or race will be an ignorant and despised class and no amount of sentiment can make it otherwise. If the time shall ever come when we possess in the colored people of this country a class of men noted for enterprise, industry, economy and success, we shall no longer have any trouble in the matter of civil and political rights; the battle against the popular prejudice shall have been fought."

What better example of his message could there be than the life of Jackson's own son, Dr. Andrew Jackson, who listened to his father from the front of the congregation? Dr. Andrew Jackson had rapidly become known as one of the finest black surgeons in the nation, respected by white and black alike. Whites even consulted the black doctor, seeking cures for their ailments. Would not such achievement be a shield against the mob? Would not such achievement disarm prejudice? That's precisely what Captain Jackson seemed to be saying.

The speech was a bitter disappointment to the Greenwood militants in his audience, and in the end, of course, the militants were right. No black achievement would appease the white hatred of that time. How naive Jackson's words would seem eight years later, on the terrible spring morning when Greenwood burned. Jackson's optimism must have seemed horribly ironic then. For in the great catastrophe of 1921, no one would lose more than Captain Townsend D. Jackson himself.

If anything, it was a wonder that Jackson's faith had endured until 1913, for Jackson, as much as any black, had experienced firsthand the bitter realities of racial hatred in America, dark passions that, in fact, had nearly killed him.

The story of his escape from Memphis survived in his family for generations. It was said that the trouble began on a day in 1889, when Townsend Jackson had the temerity to buy and smoke a cigar in a white store, the final insolent act to the many Memphis whites who hated him, one that begged to be dealt with in the traditional Southern way.

Jackson had always been uppity, those whites figured, had al-

ways insisted on standing apart from the rest of his colored brethren, going right back to slave days. His last days of slavery came
not on his owner's Georgia plantation, but on the smoky, mist-
dampened battlefield of Lookout Mountain near Chattanooga,
Tennessee. The husky mulatto boy was only seven when his fa-
ther/master first hauled him into battle, only nine two years later,
in the fall of 1863, when his owner's Rebel regiment withered
beneath a bluecoat assault up the mountain and was forced to
retreat.

What passed then between slave and master could only be
guessed at later. Was there genuine affection between them, feelings that perhaps derived from parentage? Did the white man
offer the boy any advice, any money? Did they embrace as they
parted? Or did the young slave simply escape? All that could be
known for sure was that shortly after the Rebel defeat at Lookout
Mountain, Townsend Jackson was free.

It was Jackson's habit in the decades afterward to minimize the
hardships and dangers he encountered then, and to downplay the
fortitude and resourcefulness required for the boy to survive
them. After all, he was not yet ten when he earned his freedom.
His world was still at war, his people still in bondage. But an
account of his life in the *Tulsa Star* years later, one based on an
interview with Jackson himself, described those postwar years in
just two sentences: "Secured his discharge after the battle of
Mount Lookout, and went to Memphis a short while thereafter.
Through correspondence, he found his mother at Trenton, Tenn.,
to which place she had immigrated after the war."

After the reunion, Jackson found work in Memphis as a waiter
at the famous Gayosa Hotel, serving the rich white man his grits
and freshening his whiskey. But Jackson's new servitude would
be brief. Another Negro waiter taught him to read, which allowed
him to attend night school to study math and history, literature
and Latin. He thus fortified himself for the affluent, intoxicating
swirl that was black Memphis, a city whose population in the
decades after the Civil War was nearly half Negro, a place where

every manner of black commerce sprouted from the brown-brick buildings on Beale Street, that Negro hub of business and entertainment known across the nation for its vibrancy and the variety of its temptations.

Jackson's ambitions, however, did not lie in entrepreneurship. He aspired instead to a career as a lawman, perhaps because of his early memories of military life. As a young man, he helped to recruit and organize a black militia, and in 1878, it was Jackson and his officers who stayed behind to maintain public order while white police fled a deadly outbreak of yellow fever that killed thousands in Memphis. When the fever abated, the bravery of Jackson and fourteen of his militiamen earned them permanent positions on the Memphis police force.

But such Negro prosperity was both illusory and fleeting in the South after the Civil War. Negro affluence invariably triggered escalating jealousies and fears among the whites, and in Memphis, one consequence was that Jackson and his Negro officers lost their jobs to a group of racist Irishmen. Then, in 1889, Jackson's cigar finally triggered the ire of a white mob.

A few years earlier, Jackson might have faced down the mob out of principle. He had done so many times before as a Memphis policeman, protecting Negroes accused of variously trumped-up charges. But a decade earlier, he had met and married another former slave, named Sophronia, and by 1889, he was the father to three fine children, two boys and a girl. Nothing was left for the family in the poisoned racial environment of Memphis in any event. When the mob arrived at their home in Memphis that night in 1889, they found it empty, Jackson, his wife and children, safely hidden in the homes of friends. A few days later, the family headed west aboard a car of the Rock Island Railroad.

At exactly noon on April 22, 1889, troopers of the U.S. Cavalry sounded bugles and fired their guns into the air, setting off a mad dash at the boundary of a Southwestern wilderness, which until that moment, had belonged to Indians. Thus began the Great Land Rush of 1889 in what would become the State of Oklahoma eighteen years later. Thousands of frenzied settlers, both black and white, people from every quarter of American life, rushed in on foot, by horseback, by wagon and railroad car, to stake a forty-acre claim to free land, needing only to register their claims in a crude wooden building hastily erected by the government on the prairie, the place where the town of Guthrie sprang up almost overnight.

Thousands of voracious new settlers contested every square inch of the free land, while thousands more poured into Guthrie hoping to capitalize in other ways. New stores, restaurants, hotels, and banks transformed the Guthrie landscape from one day to the next. Just four months after the land run, Guthrie was home to sixteen barbers, sixteen blacksmiths, two cigar makers, seven hardware stores, fifteen hotels, eighty-one lawyers, nineteen druggists, five photographers, thirty-nine doctors, forty restaurants, six banks, five newspapers, and at least one Negro jailer, Captain Townsend Jackson.

What a perfect place for that stubborn Negro optimist. Guthrie's chaos made Memphis seem tame by comparison. But a large percentage of the new arrivals were black, having fled Jim Crow of the South and the same racial hatreds that had driven Jackson and his family from Memphis. In this place, at least initially, the new arrivals of both races were too caught up in the promise of instant wealth, too distracted by the thrills of the raucous boom-town, to give bigotry much heed.

Negroes, in fact, assumed important positions in Guthrie's new territorial government, and Townsend Jackson was one who stepped into the new community's leadership void. In addition to his job as jailer, Jackson was elected justice of the peace. Within a few years, he was appointed to the Guthrie police force, and as in Memphis, he organized the territory's first black militia, thereby becoming a well-known local fixture to politicians of both races.

After statehood, the white governor of Oklahoma appointed Jackson to serve as an Oklahoma delegate to an important national conference on Negro education.

At home in Guthrie, his family also flourished. Jackson's oldest child, daughter Minnie Mae, met and married a bright young lawyer named H. A. Guess, soon to become one of the most respected Negro attorneys in the Southwest. But the proudest moment of Townsend Jackson's life undoubtedly came near the end of the century, when he and Sophronia embraced their youngest child, Andrew, standing with him on the crowded platform of the Guthrie train station. Andrew, always a quiet, solicitous, studious boy, held a ticket to Nashville and a spot in the freshman class at Meharry Medical College, the nation's finest medical school for Negro doctors. Tears poured down Townsend Jackson's face as he watched the train puff off, bearing his son to the east, remembering his own days of learning to read by candlelight and the long struggles to succeed that followed.

Yet Jackson's contentment was again impermanent. White hatreds caught up with the Negro in Guthrie, too. In 1907, when Oklahoma became the nation's forty-sixth state, the legislature passed its version of Jim Crow as one of its first acts. Five years later, the mayor of Guthrie ordered Townsend Jackson to limit his policing to the black sections of Guthrie. Jackson immediately resigned.

But the latest affront only briefly discouraged him. Jackson had survived slavery, the Civil War, and the dangerous years afterward. He had insisted on making a name for himself, first in Memphis, then in Guthrie. His son by then was a doctor. Jackson's stubborn hopefulness had become a habit. It would endure. He would continue to believe that resourcefulness would triumph over hatred in the end.

Just look at what was happening a hundred miles east, in the booming oil town of Tulsa. Jackson had heard that Negro prosperity without precedent was taking root there. Industrious blacks in Greenwood had finally succeeded in placing themselves beyond the reach of white malice. So in 1912, Townsend Jackson and his family boarded the train once more, this time for a shorter trip east, to the Promised Land. And on a warm May night a year later, Townsend Jackson's heart swelled as he stood at the pulpit, addressing new neighbors who had endured odysseys so similar to his, who had survived those struggles with optimism every bit as strong.

Those remarkable life stories were told again and again beneath the striped green awnings of the Greenwood barbershops and pool halls, at the church socials, and on wooden benches along Greenwood Avenue where men lingered to pass the days. Every man worth a nickel had a story.

Barney Cleaver, the tall sheriff's deputy who patrolled Greenwood's streets, recalled his birth to ex-slaves in Virginia, working on a steamer that chugged up and down the Ohio River between Charleston and Cincinnati, then toiling in the West Virginia coal mines, before his odyssey landed him in Oklahoma. John Stradford's journey had taken him from Kentucky to Ohio, to Missouri and Kansas, danger and hardship stalking him and his family at every stop. A fellow named Fairchild had a story similar to Townsend Jackson's, of escaping from his home in Arkansas only hours before angry whites appeared at his family's door. And so on.

But of all the tales, few reflected more ambition, luck, and timing, if not outright peril, than O. W. Gurley's. He was born to former slaves on Christmas Day, 1868, and later moved with them from Alabama to Pine Bluff, Arkansas, where he studied in a public school and worked on his father's farm. He taught school himself as a young man, then caught on with the U.S. Post Office, a coveted position for a Negro of the time.

But young Gurley was restless, his dreams vacillating between monetary wealth and political ambition, a hunger that led him to an Oklahoma land claim in 1893, which he soon abandoned to run for county treasurer in the town of Perry. He served as a school principal when defeated, then changed course again, opening a Perry mercantile store that thrived for almost a decade.

It was early in the new century when the familiar yearning seized him again. Gurley began to envision even greener pastures for himself in the little town fifty miles away, a place that until 1905 had been a no-account cattle outpost and Indian trading village. But on November 22, 1905, wildcat oil drillers, working the land of a man named Ida E. Glenn, hit the first gusher of what became the Mid-Continent Oil Field, the most bountiful producer of petroleum in the nation for years to come. Glenn Pool No. 1 gushed only fourteen miles south of the village called Tulsa, almost instantly transforming the place into an oil capital. White oilmen and speculators flocked there by the thousands, many becoming millionaires overnight. Gurley rightly reasoned that somehow, Negroes could also cash in.

So a year after the oil strike, Gurley and his family moved to Tulsa. With profits from Perry, he bought a strip of land and opened another mercantile store, this time along a muddy country road cut through empty rolling prairie north of the city limits. But neither the prairie nor Gurley's pockets remained empty for long. Blacks poured off train cars at the Frisco depot by the dozens every day, having heard of the Tulsa boom and hoping to capitalize on it themselves. The newcomers threw up crude shanties of scrap lumber and packing crates and had no choice but to buy their groceries from the man who had been there first. Within a year, Gurley added a boardinghouse to his holdings in Greenwood, the place so named after another Negro town in Arkansas.

Thus O. W. Gurley was the first Negro to profit from a remarkable symbiosis born between black and white in Tulsa. Blacks could not shop in white stores, but by 1910, virtually every white family middle class and above employed black chauffeurs, maids, mammies, gardeners, or laundresses. By 1921, a third of Tulsa's black population lived not in Greenwood, but in the servants' quarters of white Tulsa, and hundreds more made the daily commute south across the tracks on foot, mule, or horseback. In downtown Tulsa, where magnificent high-rise hotels and banks and office towers materialized like magic, black shoeshine boys, bellhops, and doormen—earning salaries of five dollars a week—routinely took home ten dollars a day in tips alone, twenty dollars a day on weekends, thereby earning more than some of the black lawyers and teachers. Negro bootblacks took to wearing twenty-dollar gold pieces from their watch chains to flaunt their new wealth.

Otherwise, the Negro shoeshine boys, chauffeurs, maids, and mammies took their money home to Greenwood to spend on haircuts, barbeque, booze, prostitutes, groceries, jewelry, movie tickets, bootleg liquor, visits to black doctors when they were ill, and on black dentists when their teeth hurt. Dozens of black entrepreneurs and professionals had arrived to meet the demands of those hungry consumers.

With a nearby brick factory supplying cheap raw materials, and skilled Negro artisans arriving by the score, impressive brown-brick buildings sprouted like dandelions around Gurley's store at 112 Greenwood Avenue. Just south of Gurley along Greenwood, there were the Tulsa Waffle House, the Bell and Little Restaurant, and C. L. Netherland's barbershop. North of Gurley on the first block alone were a dry cleaners, an undertaker, another restaurant, a shoeshine shop, and a lawyer's office. A tailor set up across the street, next to a café and Andrew Smitherman's newspaper office, which in turn adjoined a grocery store, cigar store, billiard parlor, and clothing store. When Captain Townsend Jackson arrived in 1912, he would have imagined himself back on Beale Street at the height of its Memphis glory. In 1913, an organizer for a national Negro business association described Greenwood as "a regular Monte Carlo." And O. W. Gurley had started it all—Greenwood's first entrepreneur, who quietly tucked his earnings into white banks across the tracks.

So how the blood must have rushed into Gurley's cheeks when he heard the engine rumble up the street outside his store one morning in 1911. He was used to being first. But here was this young black man behind the wheel, that fellow John Williams in his new Chalmers, proudly inching his way down Greenwood Avenue with the ragtop conspicuously down. Until then, even the wealthiest blacks relied on horse and buggy to get from here to there. But now came Williams, with his wife Loula sitting next to him in front, and young son Bill alone in the backseat of black Tulsa's first car, and O. W. Gurley could have spit.

John Williams had a story, too, one equal to anyone's on the north side of the Frisco tracks. He was born in Pittsburgh, and drifted to Memphis as a teenager to work as a fireman on the Illinois Central Railroad. There he met Loula, a teacher and college graduate, and the couple soon moved to Arkansas and Mississippi, where Loula taught and John worked on steam engines, until the growing threat of the white lynch mob that always shadowed such industrious blacks drove them out of the Deep South to Oklahoma.

Williams worked on a paving crew when he arrived in Tulsa, then as a boiler operator for the white-owned Thompson Ice Cream Company on First Street, earning a salary sufficient to buy the new Chalmers, a purchase that caused his new neighbors to sit up and take notice.

But the surprises were just beginning where Williams was concerned. For John Williams not only managed to buy a car, he taught himself to repair its engine, a skill that quickly endeared him to Tulsa whites desperate for help with their balky new machines. The engine trade was so lucrative that he quit his job at the ice cream company and opened Williams' One Stop Garage on Archer Street, which enjoyed the patronage of Tulsa's leading white entrepreneurs and oilmen.

Such was the beginning of a remarkable Greenwood metaphor. As if by magic, the garage begat the three-story Williams Building at the prime corner of Greenwood Avenue and Archer Street. The family lived on the second floor of Greenwood's tallest build-

ing and rented the third for attorneys' offices. But the Williams'
Confectionary on the ground floor was what became the heart of
Greenwood's social life: a spacious place with a towering soda
fountain situated amid twelve tables with four chairs each. The
confectionary, boasted an ad in the *Tulsa Star*, was the "headquarters for sweets, candies, nuts, fruits in season, ice cream, cold
drinks, cigars, tobacco, and fresh butter every day."

"Don't get disgusted because the warm weather is here," read
another newspaper bulletin in 1913. "Remember Williams' Confectionary is a good place to keep cool. All the latest drinks sold
daily."

No wonder that young Greenwood suitors tendered more marriage proposals at Williams's Confectionary than anywhere else in
black Tulsa. To celebrate, those betrothed couples often stepped
from the confectionary and pushed their way through the happy
crowds, walking north along Greenwood Avenue to the brightly
lit palace that was the Dreamland Theater, yet another example
of John and Loula Williams's golden touch. From the time of its
opening in 1914, almost every Greenwood family built a fifteen-
cent movie ticket into its budget. The Dreamland's eight hundred
seats were generally filled for silent features starring Mary Pickford and Charlie Chaplin, accompanied by a live band, or for
touring vaudeville acts and musical revues passing through town.
With two shows a night, Loula Williams typically locked more
than a thousand dollars into the theater's safe when the doors
were closed, and on Tuesdays made the trip across the tracks to
deposit the earnings at the white-owned Exchange National Bank.

For her family, those nights were part of a frantic but happy
life. Loula looked after young Bill, and rushed back and forth
between the bustling confectionary and the crowded theater. In
the *Tulsa Star*, Andrew Smitherman hailed her as one of
Oklahoma's most proficient businesswomen. Her husband re-
paired engines and sold gas to the whites and their chauffeurs
who lined up outside his shop every day. On weekends, he and
Bill carried their shotguns to the river bottoms, returning with

bags full of duck or quail or goose, because John Williams might have been even handier with a shotgun than he was with a wrench.

Sophronia Jackson died in February 1914. She had attended a Baptist women's convention in Tennessee just a few months earlier, and returned on the train the picture of good health. But a persistent cough began in January, then a fever, and not even the constant attention of Andrew, her son the physician, could save Sophronia from the fatal case of consumption.

Her family gathered at her bedside in the days before she died—Andrew and his beautiful wife Julia; daughter Minnie Mae and Minnie Mae's husband, the lawyer H. A. Guess; Sophronia's other son, Townsend Jackson, Jr. "In the group," Andrew Smitherman wrote in the *Tulsa Star*, "with a lowered head, a sad, heavy heart, with fervent prayers upon his lips, stood her sweetheart of former days—the father of her children, her faithful husband, who cheered her in her final days with the sunshine of his love and devotion. It was a beautiful picture indeed—yet a sad one. He had made most of life's journey with her at his side. Now she had become weary and must drop off and leave him to continue alone." When she died, Captain Jackson took his wife's body back to Guthrie, where he had purchased a family cemetery plot years before.

Sophronia had been a woman of deep faith who had assured her family near the end that she was glad to be meeting her Maker, that she would wait for them all in the Great Beyond. Captain Jackson was equally certain of their coming reunion in heaven. Yet he was greatly saddened at her passing. His wife had had so little time to enjoy the peace they had finally found in Tulsa, the wonderful life they had envisioned through all those years of struggle.

After Sophronia's death, Greenwood people often saw the elderly widower on his solitary evening strolls. He had settled into the quiet life of a gentleman barber who worked from his small home on Cincinnati Avenue. On a few of those sad evenings, Jackson hiked to the top of Standpipe Hill, named for the hundred-foot water pipe that stored some of Tulsa's drinking water. The hill jutted into Greenwood from the northwest like a large peninsula, four hundred feet higher than any other place in the city, therefore offering a fine view of white Tulsa to the south and the foothills of the Ozark Mountains in the other direction, and, of course, to Greenwood itself, and all the Negro lives that were unfolding just below.

The devil was busy on some of those Greenwood streets. There was no denying that. Prostitutes beckoned from the bawdy houses along First Street and Admiral Drive. Seedy men and women commingled in shacks in the alleys off Greenwood Avenue, drinking themselves into stupors with that cheap, milky-white intoxicant distilled from Choctaw root. The state's heroin traffic was said to originate from a shack in Greenwood, too. Many young men were idle and troublesome. Many Greenwood families continued to live on the outskirts in plank shacks with dirt floors.

The newspapers said that things were even worse in other places, two dozen race riots in 1919 alone—Houston, Chicago, Washington, D.C., Atlanta, even Duluth, Minnesota. Every month it seemed that another city was consumed. Whites worried that Negroes would take their jobs, or that Negro men would deflower their women, or the whites were enraged by uppity coloreds who were no longer content to ride in segregated rail cars. So tensions rose and the smallest things could set off an apocalypse. In Chicago, a Negro boy swimming in Lake Michigan had drifted toward a part of the beach reserved for whites. The boy was stoned and drowned, touching off a wild fight between whites and blacks who had seen it happen. Negroes never won fights like that because of the numbers always arrayed against them, so the fight on the beach led to weeks of mayhem, with dozens killed and scores of black homes burned.

In Washington, D.C., it was a white woman's groundless claim that two Negro men raped her. By the next day, white soldiers, sailors, and marines were after any black person they could find, "hauling them from off streetcars, and out of restaurants, chasing them up alleys, and beating them mercilessly on street corners," as one writer put it. Word got back to Greenwood of the horrors in East St. Louis, where nearly two score Negroes were killed in 1917, some by white police who fired into crowds of defenseless black folks huddled together in terror. A white woman there slashed a Negro woman's throat. White girls roamed the streets beating every black female they could find. Whites shot a Negro toddler, then tossed its body from a burning building. It was said that the East St. Louis mob set a black cripple on fire.

Every year, stories like those were becoming more common. Negro veterans were even strung up in uniform. More and more, whites seemed to insist on torturing blacks before lynching them, as if killing a Negro by itself did not sate their lust for hate. A Memphis mob snatched a Negro murder defendant and hacked off his ears before soaking him with gasoline and setting him to a match. Whites thrust a hot poker into the eyes of another Tennessee Negro, jammed hot irons against his genitals, then hurled his body onto a bonfire. Newspapers ran ads inviting the public to witness the burning of live colored men.

No wonder Townsend Jackson saw the rage building in his people as these stories were discussed. The young men in Greenwood were especially agitated. Hundreds had fought in World War I, and had been treated by the French people with respect and dignity. They had fought and bled defending freedom, or so they were told, only to find that their brothers were still being mutilated here at home. In all his years, Jackson had never heard Negro dissatisfaction more widespread.

Yet Jackson was too old to change his stripes now. His optimism was set in stone, sustained by all the hopeful things he saw about him in Tulsa. From the top of Standpipe Hill, he saw a steeple rising from almost every Greenwood corner. Just down the hill, the belfry atop Mount Zion Baptist Church rose majestically into the gloaming, the most imposing Negro sanctuary in the Southwest. Booker T. Washington High School stood just across the street, the spacious brick building where black students learned Latin, trigonometry and algebra, history, and literature from the finest teachers anywhere. There was a Negro hospital, too, and a Negro library on Archer Street that owned all the finest books.

And if only Sophronia could see the children now. Andrew lived in that beautiful brick home just below Standpipe on Detroit Avenue, next to other doctors and lawyers and principals and teachers, and Greenwood's finest class of businessmen. Daughter Minnie Mae, her husband and children, lived only one street over in a house just as fine. Their neighborhoods were places where Beethoven was played on Victrolas, where music poured into the night through open windows along with the sounds of laughing children and the smells of cooking chicken and potatoes and vegetables. Some of the children in Greenwood learned to play the violin.

If only Greenwood's angry young men could have walked where Captain Townsend D. Jackson had walked, could have seen what he had seen. If only they could have known slavery and its equally trying aftermath. Greenwood wasn't perfect, but it was so much better than life for Negroes in America had ever been, and this time, unlike in Guthrie or Memphis, there was little the white man could possibly do to take that good life away. Jackson was certain of that. The Tulsa Negro had come too far; more than ten thousand black people lived in peace and prosperity on the north side of the tracks. *Dear, dear Sophronia. If only the Lord had not called you so soon. If only you had lived just a little longer to enjoy it*.

CHAPTER 2

LINCOLN'S DEVOTEE

The singular public voice of Richard Lloyd Jones had been silent for years by the time of his death in December 1963. Several years earlier he had turned the operation of his newspaper over to his children, and by 1958, the old man's "Saturday Sermonette" a staple of the *Tulsa Tribune* for decades, had disappeared from the editorial pages altogether. But the previous forty years certainly had been time enough for Jones to erect a figurative monument to himself in his adopted city and state—Richard Lloyd Jones as trustee of the memory of Abraham Lincoln; Jones as intrepid political maverick and power broker; Jones as the self-appointed arbiter of white Tulsa's conscience.

The *Tribune*, which Jones had purchased in 1919, thus chronicled his death as it would the passing of an American president, with bold, front-page headlines and a huge photograph of the paper's late patriarch, a once-handsome man gone jowly late in life, whose luxuriant, curly brown hair had turned straight and white and thin.

The long page-one obituary was predictably reverential. "The career of Mr. Jones was one filled with the sharp, brilliant sparkle of a many-faceted diamond, yet also with a warm, compassionate humanism and dedication to public service," it said. Alf Landon, former governor of Kansas and the Republican Party's presidential nominee in 1936, was among those who eulogized Jones in the *Tribune*'s pages that day. It was Jones himself, Landon was quoted as saying, whose encouragement had inspired Landon's presidential ambitions. "His vigor, his integrity and convictions," Landon said, "and his lofty civic courage are an inspiration to all who knew him." Oklahoma Governor Henry Bellmon bemoaned the loss of a "widely respected journalist and a great humanitarian." Tulsa

Mayor James Maxwell grieved for "a loyal, civic-minded citizen and a great leader." Even U.S. Senator Everett Dirksen of Illinois joined the sad chorus: "I was never so refreshed in spirit as when I could spend a few hours listening to him."

To those with only a cursory knowledge of Jones's life, the tributes would have seemed fitting enough. The son of a Union soldier and renowned Unitarian minister from the Midwest, Richard Lloyd Jones had been a lawyer, an actor, and a cowboy before indulging an abiding love of the written word by working as a magazine writer, then finally as editor and publisher of newspapers in Madison, Wisconsin, and in Tulsa. He had also inherited his father's passion for pontificating and was never bashful about using his publications for that purpose. "I have always made my press my pulpit, and I preach," he said once.

But the tapestry of his life was much richer still. As a young writer for *Collier's* magazine, Jones played a key role in purchasing Abraham Lincoln's Kentucky birthplace and erecting a national memorial there. In old age, his grandchildren heard him speak of the time he flew with Orville Wright. He had covered almost every national political convention for fifty-six years and was acquainted with most of the major political figures of his time, including several presidents. As a boy, family stories went, he had met both U.S. Grant and Jefferson Davis. As an adult, he had made the acquaintance of Mark Twain, had even hired the son of Samuel Clemens to work at *Collier's*. As first cousin and friend of the famed architect Frank Lloyd Wright, he was envious of Wright's greater fame. Yet it was Wright whom Jones commissioned in 1930 to design his startling Tulsa mansion on Birmingham Avenue, with its huge windows, many competing angles, and notoriously leaky roof. "This is what happens when you leave a work of art out in the rain," Jones's wife, Georgia, was once said to lament as water came rushing down onto her floors.

But missing amid the bouquets attending his death were the competing, far less savory realities of the man. Not one word in the newspaper, for instance, mentioned his famous stubbornness, and his hair-trigger temper that caused his editors to cower. There was no written mention of the scandal that engulfed Jones shortly after he moved to Tulsa, when private investigators and local members of the Ku Klux Klan took turns peeping through the keyhole of a downtown Tulsa hotel while Jones carried on a torrid affair with his female assistant at the newspaper.

And in Jones's obituary, there was no mention whatsoever of what was known as the Tulsa Race Riot of 1921. In fact, though it later became regarded as the most terrible event of its kind in the history of the nation, scarcely a word of the tragedy ever saw print in the *Tribune* after the ashes of Greenwood had cooled.

Which, in retrospect, was not surprising. For it was not at all pleasant to recall that at the time of the riot, Jones might have been Tulsa's most vocal racist. He was sympathetic to, if not actually a member of, the Ku Klux Klan, that legendary robed order of Negro-, Jew-, and Catholic-hating vigilantes whose ranks had begun to permeate the power structure of white Tulsa at that time. As such, Jones turned his notorious anger and his poison pen against Greenwood, Tulsa's robust community of blacks, which existed on the north side of the Frisco tracks, just below the sixth-floor window of his newspaper office on Archer Street.

It was one particular editorial diatribe printed on the front page of an early edition of the *Tribune* on May 31, 1921, that would ensure Jones's place in history, more so even than his endeavors to preserve the Lincoln birthplace. For arguably, it was Jones and his editorial—Jones more than any other single person—whose actions precipitated the obliteration of America's most thriving black community.

That would certainly be an ironic epitaph for the young magazine writer who, in 1905, shared a table in Louisville's exclusive Pendennis Club with Colonel Henry Watterson, a well-known Kentucky raconteur and writer. That day early in the new century, when the writer was visiting Louisville on assignment, he told Jones about the neglected condition of Abraham Lincoln's birthplace, then a tumbledown farm near the town of Hodgenville, Kentucky. Watterson suggested to Jones that the right buyer might greatly profit by acquiring it, might even develop the site into a national monument to be revered through the ages.

Jones latched onto the idea like a drowning man to a life preserver. To think of it: buying the birthplace of the Great Emancipator himself! That deed alone might eclipse the many accomplishments of Jones's esteemed father, the Reverend Jenkins Lloyd Jones, and it was an endeavor certain to gain for the younger Jones his father's long-coveted blessing.

It was a blessing Richard Lloyd Jones had apparently sought unsuccessfully for most of his early life. His ancestors had immigrated to rural Wisconsin from Wales in the 1840s, and two decades later, fourteen-year-old Jenkins Lloyd Jones had enlisted as a Union drummer boy in the Civil War. The teenager quickly was promoted to artilleryman and was a decorated veteran of major Civil War campaigns in Tennessee and Georgia. His unique devotion to Lincoln dated from that time. In Chicago, the elder Jones, by then a well-known Unitarian minister, founded a place called the Lincoln House, a center to promulgate all things Lincoln, and often referred to the slain president in his front-page sermons printed weekly in the *Chicago Tribune*.

The Lincoln-loving minister indeed cast a large and daunting shadow for his son. As a boy growing up in Chicago, Richard Lloyd Jones was a talented tennis player, swimmer, skater, and horseman, with above-average intelligence. But he would later concede his early unhappiness and aimlessness. "I was in no wise [sic] proficient in any one line of intellectual endeavor. I was full of uncertainty and indecision," Jones wrote in 1939. In fact, he said, he might have spent his life as a cowboy on a Nevada ranch, where he had worked happily for a year as a young man, but his family "felt in some fashion I should follow a white-collar life."

So the younger Jones returned to Chicago and obtained a law degree, but quickly found the legal profession disagreeable. He then pursued his first love—writing—by reporting for and editing small newspapers in Connecticut. He simultaneously dabbled in the New York stage, where he landed acting roles with his "cultured voice, distinguished bearing and ruggedly handsome face," according to Jones's 1963 obituary.

His acting career apparently ended with the opportunity to write for *Collier's*, then one of the nation's most prestigious and crusading journals. Among Jones's endeavors for the magazine was a campaign that, he later wrote, was partially responsible for getting the torch of the Statue of Liberty, which had been dark for years, relit through an act of Congress. But at *Collier's*, it was with the name of Lincoln that Jones would make his greatest mark.

On August 28, 1905, with the backing of the magazine's owner, Robert Collier, Jones purchased the one-hundred-acre Lincoln farm near Hodgenville at a courthouse auction. Jones and Collier then issued an appeal for public donations with which to establish the birthplace memorial. Within months, they had raised $400,000, mostly in twenty-five-cent contributions. On a cold, damp day in February 1909, the centennial anniversary of Lincoln's birth, Jones stood proudly by as President Theodore Roosevelt laid the cornerstone for the Lincoln farm monument. President Howard Taft dedicated the memorial when it was opened to the public two years later.

"Here, over the log cabin in which Abraham Lincoln was born to free the slave and to preserve this union, a grateful people have dedicated this memorial to unity, peace and brotherhood among these United States," read the words inscribed in the memorial's granite facade.

Because of his early work, Jones was appointed by the government to oversee administration of the monument, and served on its board of trustees with such men as President Taft, Samuel Clemens, William Jennings Bryan, and his father, the Reverend Jenkins Lloyd Jones. For the rest of his life, Richard Lloyd Jones traded freely on Lincoln's name and his own role in commemorating Lincoln's birthplace.

On February 12, 1921, in a speech to a group of Tulsa businessmen, Jones recalled his efforts in connection with the Lincoln farm memorial, in which he said it was "the only example in the history of our country where the nation has marked the place where a great life began." In closing his remarks that day, Jones praised Lincoln as a man with "the wit of a philosopher and the courage of a soldier and the heart of a mother. His life has been the inspiration of more books than any other man, the Christ alone excepted . . . fifty-six thousand volumes written about this great American who saved the nation and freed the slaves."

Later, Jones wrote: "It is time to put Mr. Lincoln to work. He is the symbol of American society. He is the symbol of the battle against the sins within. He is the symbol of all that is good in our country."

Perhaps, in 1921, it never occurred to Jones that many of the slaves that Lincoln freed then were now living in Greenwood, only a few blocks from the *Tribune* offices. At the time, Jones and his paper referred to the Negro community as "Niggertown" or "Little Africa," describing it as a veritable human cesspool that needed to be cleaned up. He had no quarrel with docile blacks, Jones was on record as saying, with Negroes who were polite and hardworking and respectful to whites. However, he wrote, "A bad nigger is about the lowest thing that walks on two feet. Give a bad nigger his booze and his dope and a gun and he thinks he can shoot up the world. And all these four things are to be found in Niggertown, booze, dope, bad niggers and guns."

Likewise, perhaps it never occurred to Jones that in 1871, the U.S. government, which then was dominated by the party of Lincoln, had banned a fraternal order formed after the Civil War called the Ku Klux Klan, declaring the Klan's racist and terroristic practices in the South illegal. In 1915, the Klan had been reborn in Georgia, and on the *Tribune* front page of February 4, 1921, Jones's paper published what amounted to a press release for the new KKK, a story that lauded the secret order's ambitions to add chapters in Oklahoma. The new Klan, the story said, was to be a living, lasting memorial to the original Klan members who had saved the South from "a Negro empire [built] upon the ruins of southern homes and institutions." Among the KKK's principles, the *Tribune* story continued, was "supremacy of the white race in social, political and governmental affairs of the nation."

By then, as Jones surely knew, the Klan was already entrenched in Tulsa, and such a press release for the order was highly unnecessary. Most likely, the *Tribune*'s fawning story was merely the newly arrived publisher's attempt to curry favor with Klan members, whose ranks then included, or would soon come to include, Tulsa's leading politicians, law-enforcement officers, judges, businessmen, even an Oklahoma governor and a U.S. senator.

Among the stories proudly passed down through the decades by Jones's descendants was the one from his years in Madison, in which Jones invited Booker T. Washington to stay as his house guest because the famous Negro had been turned away by white hotels in the Midwestern city. Those descendants proffered that anecdote as proof of Jones's equanimity in matters of race. But that trait, if it ever really existed, was little in evidence in Tulsa.

In 1920, when Jones arrived in the booming Oklahoma town, he was deeply in debt from his purchase of the *Tribune* and facing a bitter newspaper war with a superior rival, the *Tulsa World*. In his adopted town, he spewed racial hatred because in Tulsa of that time, racial hatred sold newspapers. And he would take his allies where he found them, even members of the KKK, whether Abraham Lincoln might approve or not.

In 1907, thirteen years before he moved to Tulsa, Richard Lloyd Jones had spent several weeks in Oklahoma researching a *Collier's* article on the nation's newest state. Oklahoma, he wrote then, "springs to life like Athena, full-grown and full facultied. She begins without diffidence or apology." Tulsa, however, did not figure into that hyperbole. Oklahoma leaders whom Jones interviewed at the time didn't consider the little town along the Arkansas River fit to even visit.

"What's in the northeast part of the state?" Jones inquired of Robert L. Owen, a major Oklahoma politician.

"Nothing much, yet," Owen replied. "Not a town of two thousand up there."

Owen, it turned out, was badly misinformed. Even then, in 1907, Tulsa was in the midst of a remarkable transformation from a tiny village in Indian Territory to one of the world's most robust petroleum capitals.

First incorporated in 1898, Tulsa's population at the time of the 1900 census was still a sleepy thirteen hundred, a place still resembling its roots in the 1830s as a Creek Indian village. The name Tulsa, in fact, derived from the Creek word *tullasi*, or "old town." In the 1830s, *Tullasi* and the vast rolling plains surrounding it had been the western terminus of the *Trail of Tears*, the tragic journey of the Creeks and other southeastern tribes forced from their lands by a federal government acting on behalf of encroaching white settlers.

After the forced exodus, the Indians had Oklahoma largely to themselves for decades. Not until 1882, with the coming of the railroad to that section of Indian Territory, did the first permanent white settlers arrive in Tulsa. Seven years later, the first of the great Oklahoma land runs brought white and black settlers to the area by the tens of thousands, among them a group of Tulsa entrepreneurs determined to capitalize on the human influx in the manner of Guthrie in 1889. Shortly after 1900, those Tulsa boosters succeeded in luring three additional railroad lines through the village. In 1904, local businessmen opened a toll bridge across the Arkansas River, connecting the town to still-speculative oil fields on the other side of the water. Their timing could not have been better.

The oil rush came just a year later. Within months of the first gusher south of town, Tulsa celebrated the opening of the First National Bank, a five-story skyscraper boasting the town's first elevator. A high-rise hotel was completed shortly after that. City leaders convinced the Frisco railroad to run a special train, known as the "Coal Oil Johnny," to haul oil-field drillers and roughnecks on daily commutes to work from their homes in Tulsa. By 1907, the town's population had grown to more than seven thousand, and to more than eighteen thousand by the census of 1910. By 1920, Tulsa was home to more than four hundred oil and gas companies, dozens of oil-field supply firms, tank manufacturers and refineries, numbers that could back up the new city's boast of being the "Oil Capital of the World." More than two hundred attorneys practiced in Tulsa by 1921, one hundred and fifty doctors, and sixty dentists. The population had ballooned to more than seventy-five thousand people. Roughly 10 percent of the city was black.

With the laws of statehood and new residents from across the nation there came at least a few civilizing influences. An imposing, four-story county courthouse was built in 1912 of gray, cut limestone at the corner of Sixth Street and Boulder Avenue. Two years later came the magnificent 3,500-seat Convention Hall on Brady. The equally impressive Central High School came to occupy a full block on Sixth Street between Detroit and Cincinnati Avenues. Dozens of churches crowded their way into the increasingly valuable real estate.

In other ways, white Tulsa was a mirror image of the robust Negro community that thrived just north across the Frisco tracks. Just as blacks filled the streets of Deep Greenwood on the maids' day off, flocking into movies and restaurants and jazz joints, white crowds on the south side filled the heart of downtown Tulsa. Pedestrians dodged sedans and touring cars that clogged the newly paved streets, or the electric trolleys that clanged down north-and-south-running lines through the city. White shoppers flush with oil money crowded into Lerner's Department Store, or in the five-and-dimes, or at soda fountains. People flocked to the movies at the Majestic Theater, or the Orpheum, or the Rialto.

Yet those quainter pastimes were part of a thin veneer masking a much grittier, far more unseemly reality of life, both in the city and across the nation as a whole in the years immediately after

World War I. For sheer nastiness, hatred, and paranoia, few other moments in American history could compete; it was a reign of terror and violence, born from the same rancid breeding ground that had inspired human atrocity since the beginning of man: Human beings were inclined to fear, and thus to hate, those different than themselves.

And never before had the young nation been confronted with such diversity. In the two decades after 1900, European immigrants flocked into the United States at a rate of two thousand a day. But these were not the English-language speakers of Britain, or even of Scotland and Ireland. These immigrants, more often than not, hailed from Germany, Italy, and Poland. They were Russians, Russian Jews and Czechs, people who brought with them different languages, customs, and religions, increasingly polluting the cultural landscape in America that white Protestants had come to revere as their exclusive domain.

"If the Melting Pot is allowed to boil without control," said one leading commentator, Madison Grant, "and we continue to follow our national motto and deliberately blind ourselves to all 'distinctions of race, creed or color,' the type of native American of Colonial descent will become as extinct as the Athenian of the age of Pericles and the Viking of the days of Rollo."

Thus was born America's "nativism" movement, whose progeny would include the modern version of the Ku Klux Klan. Cultural tensions further escalated with America's entry into World War I and the widespread distrust of the "hypenated" Americans. "Any man who carries a hyphen about with him carries a dagger that he is ready to plunge into the vitals of this Republic whenever he gets ready," groused President Woodrow Wilson. Sauerkraut was renamed "liberty cabbage." German music, especially Wagner's, was banned from public concerts. Patriotic organizations sprang up by dozens, promulgating paranoia and intolerance as much as love of country. Jews and Catholics, groups ostensibly owing allegiances to foreign powers, were singled out as well. The verdict of an Indiana jury seemed to symbolize those ubiquitous passions.

A murder defendant had been charged with shooting and killing an immigrant who had yelled, "To hell with the United States." The panel took two minutes to find the shooter not guilty.

War's end did little to diffuse such tensions, for new grounds for hysteria had popped up in the national psyche. Many Americans and their leaders observed the triumph of Lenin and Bolshevism in Russia, terrified that the worker revolution would sweep over the United States as well. The growth of labor unions and the corresponding rash of strikes and strike-related violence fueled the nation's first "Red Scare." Laws guaranteeing civil liberties were either ignored or suspended as so-called radicals were rounded up and persecuted. Politicans often parroted the suggestion of one opinion leader who suggested the S.O.S. method of dealing with Reds—"Ship or shoot. I believe we should place them all on a ship of stone, with sails of lead, and that their first stopping place should be hell."

It was into this already volatile mix that Negroes such as W. E. B. Du Bois thrust their strident voices. Tens of thousands of black soldiers had fought and died for their country in the War and expected their patriotism to be rewarded with better treatment at home. When they returned to America, they found that life for their people had, if anything, gotten worse. Only now, white lynch mobs were likely to be met by Negro veterans bearing rifles and pistols, and the result was racial warfare unlike anything the nation had ever seen.

Civility, if it ever had really existed in the United States, had taken a long and bloody hiatus, and no place lived closer to outright anarchy than the bustling new oil city in the northeastern part of Oklahoma. Law enforcement of the time was nonexistent, ineffectual, or corrupt. As a result, the city became a famous haven for outlaws from across the country. Both north and south of the Frisco railroad tracks, whole streets were given over to speakeasies, drug dens, and brothels. "A vice ring consisting of newspapers and politicians operated a protection racket for illegal enterprises," a University of Tulsa student wrote in his 1950 master's thesis on early Tulsa politics. "Many crusades against open town conditions by newspapers in Tulsa's boom years were said to result when the editors were denied their part of the payoff."

But more than anything else, Tulsa life was distinguished by the same deadly cocktail of paranoia in the guise of World War I patriotism, by religious, ethnic, and racial hatred, and by officially sanctioned lawlessness that made the new city a mecca for vigilantes, even by the lawless standards of that day. And in boomtown Tulsa, whites often had as much to fear from the mob as Negroes did, as a group of labor organizers learned in 1917.

That year, twelve members of the Industrial Workers of the World, a labor union then attempting to organize oil-field roughnecks, were arrested at their Tulsa headquarters and charged with vagrancy. The police raid apparently was precipitated by articles in the virulently antiunion *Tulsa World*, which implicated union members in the bombing of the home of a wealthy Tulsa oilman. No such evidence linking the Wobblies to the bombing was ever uncovered, but in the climate of the time, the *World* and the Tulsa mob, ancestor to the city's KKK, were determined to claim a pound of flesh nonetheless. Unionization of the oil fields, according to a *World* editorial, threatened petroleum production, which in turn might jeopardize the ongoing war effort against Germany. While publicly opposed to organizations such as the Klan, Richard Lloyd Jones's competitor, *World* publisher Eugene Lorton, often proved just as intemperate on other matters. The union question was certainly one of them.

"The first step in the whipping of Germany is to strangle the I.W.W.'s. Kill 'em just as you would kill any other kind of snake," a *World* editorial urged. "It is not time to waste money on trials and continuances like that."

Tulsa Judge Thaddeus Evans, soon to become Tulsa's Republican mayor, seemed to agree. Despite scant evidence, Evans not only found the twelve vagrancy defendants guilty, he had five defense witnesses arrested, tried on the spot, and convicted as well. Each was fined a hundred dollars and committed to the county

jail. But the real punishment was meted out beyond the legal
system, and in a most timely fashion. That same night, as police
transferred the men to jail, about fifty men in black robes and
black masks, a group calling itself the "Knights of Liberty," intercepted the caravan. The seventeen prisoners were taken from the
officers, bound hand and foot, and spirited away to a secluded
ravine lit by the headlights of automobiles drawn in a circle. Each
man was then stripped to the waist, tied to a tree, and whipped
"in the name of the outraged women and children of Belgium,"
in the words of one vigilante. One of the victims pleaded with the
mob. "I have lived here for eighteen years, and have raised a large
family. I am not an I.W.W. I am as patriotic as any man here."
But he, too, felt the lash and the hot tar and feathers on his bloody
back. One union leader was whipped twice, the second assault
leaving the tar embedded in his back.

"The number of blows was regulated by the chief of police
himself, who was easily recognizable [beneath his robe] by six of
us at least," one tortured union member later said. "It was all
prearranged. The police knew where we were going."

When the torture was over, the seventeen men were ordered
into the Osage hills, their dispersion hastened by gunshots. That
same night, placards were posted at prominent public places
around Tulsa that read: "Notice to I.W.W.'s. Don't let the sun set
on you in Tulsa." The next day, the *Tulsa World* referred to the
Knights of Liberty as a "patriotic body."

None of this went unnoticed by the Negroes in Greenwood.
The incident, referred to in one white paper as the "Tulsa Tar
Party," revealed "how disastrous the consequences could be for a
group of Tulsans if the power of an influential newspaper, the city
government, and the local courts and police was brought to bear
against them," historian Scott Ellsworth later wrote. "More than
that, it revealed just how dire the results could be even in such
a situation when the defendants were *white* and when the official
charge lodged against them was no more serious than vagrancy."

An even more instructive example of vigilante violence, an even more chilling window into boomtown Tulsa's soul, came three years later, and again it involved a white. He was an eighteen-year-old named Roy Belton, who was arrested by Tulsa police in 1920 for the murder of a cab driver named Homer Nida. Belton had confessed to shooting Nida, according to newspaper accounts, but had told police that his gun had discharged accidentally. Belton would not have the chance to plead his case before a jury. Late on a Saturday night, shortly after Nida's widow issued a teary plea for revenge in the local press, a mob that quickly grew to a thousand men and women assembled in front of the county courthouse, where Belton was held in a jail cell on the top floor. Mob representatives soon entered the courthouse and insisted that the sheriff, a man named Wooley, turn Belton over.

"Let the law take its course, boys," the sheriff replied. "The electric chair will get him before too long, but you know this is no way to interfere with the law."

The vigilantes responded by disarming the sheriff and forcing him to release Belton, who was spirited down from the jail and placed in his victim's taxi that waited outside the courthouse. In a caravan stretching for more than a mile, Belton was driven by the mob to the place just southwest of Tulsa where Nida had been shot. Tulsa police, who arrived after the fact, helped direct traffic. As a huge crowd of spectators roared its approval, the vigilantes led Belton underneath a large billboard. A rope secured from a nearby farmhouse was thrown around Belton's neck. The mob allowed him to smoke a cigarette before he was lynched.

When Belton was cut down, "Sudden pandemonium broke loose," the *World* reported. "Hundreds rushed over the prostrate form to get bits of clothing. The rope was cut into bits for souvenirs. His trousers and shoes were torn into bits and the mob fairly fought over the gruesome souvenirs. . . . An ambulance finally pushed through the jam of automobiles. The body was carried to the car, late arrivals still grabbing for bits of clothing on the now almost nude form."

Tulsa Police Chief John Gustafson said afterward that while he didn't normally condone mob violence, the lynching "will prove of real benefit to Tulsa and vicinity. It was an abject lesson to hijackers and auto thieves, and I believe it will be taken as such."

Such sentiments were echoed on the editorial pages of the city's dominant newspaper. To the *Tulsa World*, Belton's lynching was a "righteous protest. There was not a vestige of mob spirit in the act of Saturday night," the *World* said. "It was citizenship outraged by government inefficiency and a too tender regard for the professional criminal. We predict that unless conditions are speedily improved, [Belton's lynching] will not be the last by any means."

The only public protest of Belton's murder came from the north side of the railroad tracks. "There is no crime, however atrocious, that justifies mob violence," Andrew Smitherman wrote in the *Tulsa Star*. The black editor later gave voice to the fears roiling in so many Negro souls. "The lynching of Roy Belton," Smitherman wrote, "explodes the theory that a prisoner is safe on the top floor of the Courthouse from mob violence."

Just a few months before Belton's murder, Richard Lloyd Jones had arrived in town as the new editor and publisher of the *Tulsa Tribune*, and where the mind-set of his readership was concerned, Jones proved to be a quick study. After another characteristic spate of Tulsa lawlessness, Jones offered this solution in an editorial.

"Every unemployed man in town should be questioned, and if the answer should be unsatisfactory, should be ordered out of town," Jones wrote on December 23, 1920. "At least one thousand reputable and trustworthy citizens should be sworn in as deputy police and given firearms with the orders to shoot to kill anyone found in the act of holdup or robbery. Bad men are better off dead. Let's get rid of them."

So on the fateful day of May 31, 1921, was Jones's reasoning not obvious? Bad men were better off dead. And where bad men were concerned, who could be worse that a shiftless, Negro shoe-shine boy who had the temerity to assault a teenage girl in a downtown elevator in midday? What act was more worthy of swift retribution?

Richard Lloyd Jones cut a dashing figure in Tulsa, a newcomer who would have warranted notice even without his outrageous *Tribune* editorials, which ranged in tone from sanctimony, when discussing moral matters, to vitriol when the topic was ineffectual law enforcement or local and state politics. He was a handsome man with sharp features, six feet tall and athletic-looking even in his forties. His long, curly brown hair, parted down the middle, puffed flamboyantly into wings on either side of his head as he strode quickly down the street. Jones always wore the nicest suits, and often was seen rushing from his office with an expensive over-coat draped over his shoulders like a cape.

The *Tribune* was housed in a handsome six-story, red-brick building on Archer at the northern edge of downtown Tulsa. Jones's spacious corner office was on the top floor, one floor above the newsroom, two above his advertising department. Bookcases covered the walls of his office, filled with works of history, politics, science, and fiction, reflecting the publisher's voracious reading tastes. An oxbow from a farm in Illinois hung from one wall, what Jones thought a quaint reminder of America's humble rural past. From another wall a portrait of a beardless, brooding Abraham Lincoln stared out at visitors. A conference table occupied one end of the room, while Jones's massive wooden desk commanded the other, beneath windows overlooking the Frisco tracks and the community of Negroes to the north.

But the desk seemed largely decorative, for Jones rarely did his most important work sitting down. Instead, he paced the length of his office every morning, dictating to his secretary that day's editorial, rambling with the inflection of a Shakespearean actor or an overheated evangelist, jutting his jaw angrily, pounding his fist into his hand, working himself into a lather as the words flowed.

In Madison, where Jones had purchased the *Wisconsin State Journal* in 1911, those editorials had earned him the enmity of a legendary Wisconsin politician named Robert La Follette, who had formed a rival newspaper to fire back at the irascible publisher.

It was the prospect of a bloody newspaper war in Wisconsin that inspired Jones to seek a paper elsewhere, and he nearly purchased an Indianapolis daily. But at the last minute, a friend from Wisconsin, a man who had made his fortune in Oklahoma oil, urged Jones to consider Tulsa, where a paper called the *Tulsa Democrat* happened to be for sale. The logic was simple, the temptation obvious. Where there were riches to be made in oil, there were riches to be made in print. Sleepy Indianapolis could offer no such inducement. In November 1919, Jones bought the *Democrat* and moved his wife and three children to the Southwest.

He immediately renamed the paper the *Tribune*, and attempted to wage war with the more conservative *World* with such promotions as newspaper-sponsored beauty pageants. Lurid crime stories and local controversies became staples of the paper's news coverage. On the editorial page, it quickly became obvious that Jones had not been cowed in the least by the repercussions of his editorial outspokenness in Madison.

Tribune readers were treated to large doses of his moral prescriptions. "He knew all that was to be known about Abraham Lincoln and no doubt fancied that he possessed many of the virtues of that most wonderful man," John R. Woodard, one of Tulsa's early lawyers and a well-known Jones opponent of that time, wrote of the new publisher. "Morals and righteousness were his main themes and consuming passions. . . . Others were devoid of honor, save him. Historians, authors and poets were at his command. He raided their storage houses in order to satisfy his vanity. He made use of Holy Scriptures to weave his cloak."

When not pontificating, Jones fired repeated and highly personal broadsides at any local politician with whom he disagreed, particularly at the new Republican mayor and former judge,

Thaddeus Evans, whom Jones accused of being soft on crime. Jones otherwise insisted on injecting himself into local controversies concerning the eventual source of the Tulsa water supply, and he alleged malfeasance in the way the city allocated local street-paving contracts. It was the street-paving issue that nearly ended Jones's stay in Tulsa only two years after it had begun.

In March 1922, street-paving contractors, weary of being bruised by the *Tribune* in print, hired Tulsa private investigators to look into rumors that Jones had become overly familiar with his top assistant at the newspaper, a woman named Amy Comstock. It was commonly known that Jones and Comstock often worked together in Room 500 of the Tulsa Hotel, which the publisher had rented as a private office. The investigators took out the room next door, bribed a maid to conceal a Dictaphone in Jones's quarters, then took turns listening and squinting through the keyhole. Over several days, they listened as Jones dictated his editorials. They listened as he and Comstock considered writing a scathing and anonymous letter to discourage a school-board candidate whom Jones opposed. They listened as Jones and Comstock discussed threats against Jones's life. They listened as Jones attempted to fend off angry creditors by promising to send an interest payment on his overdue bank loan. They listened as Jones and Comstock proclaimed their love for each other.

Indeed, only hours after the surveillance began, investigators observed behavior they had hoped to see. At one point, after what seemed a lovers' spat, the room fell silent, except for squeaking bedsprings.

"Several groans were plainly heard from Miss Comstock," private investigator Sam McCanee later testified in a sworn deposition. "Then as the shaking of the springs which increased gradually in speed, or rapidity, and decreased gradually in speed, some more moaning could be heard."

The paving contractors, upon hearing the report, were undoubtedly elated. The repercussions for Jones, a married man making a local newspaper career as a reforming moralist, were obvious. What's more, there could be no more blatant contradiction of moral tenets as espoused by the Ku Klux Klan, an order that in addition to white supremacy, was also devoted to the honor of women and the sanctity of the home. The detectives were, in fact, concerned that they would not be believed in such a volatile matter, and they convinced several local members of the Klan to take their turns at the keyhole. One of the recruited observers, a Tulsa photoengraver, testified that he had watched through the keyhole as Jones pulled Comstock's skirt over her waist and placed his head between her legs.

"She was like the old maid's cat," the photoengraver said of Comstock's expression then. "She looked a little bit tired, and very much satisfied."

On March 21, 1922, when confronted with evidence of his extramarital liaison, Jones responded defiantly, publishing a front-page editorial attacking unnamed rumors that he said were circulating about him. The rumors were merely an attempt at character assassination caused by his crusade for good government, he argued. If need be, Jones promised to edit his paper with a pistol.

Privately, he also convinced Tulsa Klan leaders that the newspaper offices and his home had been targeted for attack.

"All of this must have been a figment of his own imagination because the contractors and those associated with them had no such ideas or contemplation in mind," Woodard wrote. "Anyway, the Klan threw a force of men around Jones to guard him against all imaginary dangers or physical violence."

When a city attorney later issued warrants against Jones and Comstock, charging them with lewd conduct, Klan members intervened to keep the warrants from being served. A Tulsa KKK leader also urged Woodard to desist in his efforts to expose the publisher, because Jones had been a "friend to the Klan."

Woodard soon learned of another, equally important Jones ally, Robert Brewer, president of the Exchange National Bank in Tulsa. While Jones's conduct with Comstock was unfortunate,

Brewer told Woodard, "The contractors would not be able to run him out of town because the bank could not afford to let him go; that the *Tribune* and Mr. Jones owed the bank a lot of money and that it did not have satisfactory security for the indebtedness."

Eventually, the scandal fizzled. Jones and Comstock, who reportedly fled from the city after learning of the warrants issued against them, returned to Tulsa. The "Saturday Sermonette" appeared as before. Comstock went on to become the *Tribune*'s associate editor and a member of the Oklahoma Hall of Fame for Women.

The sex scandal, however, was telling in several ways. Jones's conduct with his aide revealed once again the strain of contradiction and hypocrisy woven throughout his public life. And it gave some clue to the financial pressures bedeviling the overextended publisher after he arrived in Tulsa. It might be expected that with a man like Jones, those pressures would inevitably lead to editorial expediency and recklessness, if such things would sell newspapers and keep the lenders at bay.

So it was in late May of 1921. The Tulsa populace was already inflamed by a series of local jailbreaks on the day when the *Tribune* police reporter brought back word of the alleged assault by a black shoeshine boy named Dick Rowland on a teenage girl in an elevator of the Drexel Building downtown. The charge was highly suspect from the beginning. Rowland had been arrested, but even investigators considered the accusation dubious.

Which did not stop Richard Lloyd Jones, whose paper, on May 31, 1921, printed an inflammatory account of the elevator incident and of Rowland's arrest. And Jones himself would weigh in on the matter

Precisely what his front-page editorial said might never be known. Jones's editors finally prevailed on him to remove his inflammatory piece after only a few hundred copies had been published. No complete copies of that edition are known to exist today. In the archival copy of that day's paper in the Tulsa Public Library, the editorial has been torn away. Decades later, the

Oklahoma Historical Society issued a reward to anyone who could produce a copy of the infamous editorial, but none turned up.

Yet the headline, if not the exact words of the editorial, was easy to remember. No one who read it in those tense hours preceding America's most tragic episode of racial violence could forget it. They were the words undoubtedly bellowed from the lungs of newsboys who hawked the paper on the street corners of downtown Tulsa on that sunny afternoon of 1921. North of the tracks, the paper was passed from person to person along Greenwood Avenue, the sickening headline staring up at them like a call to arms.

TO LYNCH NEGRO TONIGHT, is what it said.

CHAPTER 3

DIAMOND DICK AND THE KKK

The young Negro storekeeper named Damie Rowland was just scraping by herself when the skinny black boy materialized at her front door like an underfed apparition. He seemed about six years old, but it was hard to tell because life as a street orphan could either add years to a child or take them away, depending. The boy was barefoot, and the adult man's shirt he wore that day in 1905 fell over his thin arms and shoulders like canvas over tent poles. At first, when Damie came to the door, the boy spoke only two words.

"I'm hungry," he said.

So Damie invited him into her tiny home in the small town of Vinita, Oklahoma, fixed him a ham sandwich and poured him a glass of milk, and the boy changed the moment he had some food in his belly. A beautiful smile crossed his features as he yammered on about how fine the sandwich tasted, about how the milk helped his thirst. When he finished eating, the boy followed Damie outside to her rocker under the trees. She was just getting over the flu and needed to rest, so he cheerfully fetched her glasses of water, sat playing at her feet, and talked to her for the next hour as she relaxed in the shade.

He said his name was Jimmie Jones. His only living relatives were two older sisters who lived with him on the streets of Vinita, sleeping under railroad trestles, or beneath trees in the woods when it didn't rain. They begged for food from people like Damie, folks lucky enough to have a house, or they panhandled from strangers on the street. The boy chattered on—didn't so much as pause for a breath. There was something so endearing about him beyond his desperate circumstances that tugged immediately at Damie's heart. He was charming. That was it. Even at six years old, or however old he was, even as an orphan on the street, even barefoot and dressed in a man's shirt, the boy named Jimmie had a personality that made him a joy to have around.

So Damie didn't hesitate that first day when he offered to help with her chores in return for food. She was a divorced young woman, living alone in Vinita while her parents were still in Muskogee. She was lonely, and this little boy was charming.

"Run on and fetch your sisters. I have to ask them first," Damie told him.

He dashed off down the street, returning shortly with two girls who were a few years older.

"How about Jimmie comes and stays with me?" Damie asked them.

"Fine with us," one of them replied. "One less mouth to feed."

So Jimmie stayed with Damie. With what little money she could spare, Damie bought him secondhand shoes and socks, pants and shirts. He worked in her one-room grocery store during the day—sweeping the floor, stocking shelves, and carrying groceries for her customers. At night, he slept on a pallet in her tiny dining room. All day long he talked Damie's ear off and made her customers laugh. "Aunt Damie" was what he called her, though within a few days of their meeting, Damie and the boy both knew she had become his mother in everything but name. Soon Damie loved him just as surely and as deeply as if she had given birth to him herself.

Damie could scarcely feed herself in Vinita, much less she and Jimmie both. Word was spreading that Negroes were getting rich in Tulsa, just forty miles to the south, so she closed up her store and off they went, like so many others. Damie worked odd jobs when they arrived in Greenwood, and it wasn't long before she had scraped up enough money to buy a home on Archer Street. She earned their living by renting out their extra rooms, a prosperous trade in those days because of all the newcomers arriving every day to the north side of the Frisco tracks.

Jimmie never strayed far from Damie's side in those early Tulsa years. He cleaned the rooms after tenants moved on, did other odd jobs, and still made her laugh. But then he began to change, drifting in what Damie soon recognized was a dangerous direction.

Jimmie chose his new name on his first day of elementary school. For some reason, he'd always loved the name Dick, so on that first day when the teacher asked him his name, he answered, "Dick Rowland." From then on, he insisted that Damie call him that, too, because the little boy who had shown up on her doorstep in Vinita was getting quite a mind of his own.

He'd always been smarter than an old owl, and in the first years of school, Dick brought home very good grades. But then he got older, and his arms thickened with muscle, and he grew tall and so very handsome, and the taller he grew, the less interest he showed in his books. Damie heard that the boy's charms were regularly on display in the jazz joints just off Greenwood Avenue. Folks said that Dick Rowland, though just a teenager, was one of the best dancers in Tulsa's Negro quarter. His grades fell as his dancing improved. He loved playing high-school football, but dropped out of school two years in a row as soon as the season was over.

Damie, who had dropped out herself after the fourth grade, pleaded with him then. Greenwood was filled with doctors, lawyers, dentists, businessmen, teachers, and newspaper editors, each of them living examples of the sort of treasures an education might provide. Damie envied those Negro men, and even a few women, in their automobiles and fine clothes; she dreamed of the day when Dick might have a high-school diploma of his own. As smart as he was, maybe he could even attend college and become a doctor. But he would never listen to her.

"Why should I, Aunt Damie?" he'd reply when Damie mentioned returning to school. "Look at this."

And from his pocket would come a roll of bills. Most were ones, but some were fives and tens, which astounded her. She could not believe Dick made that kind of money shining shoes and was sure he was breaking the law to get it. But he was adamant.

"With the oil and all, these white folks go to bed poor and wake up as rich as country butter," Dick told her. "They'll tip you five dollars for a fifteen-cent shine just because the guy before tipped you four. You better believe they will!"

And Dick would peel a five-dollar bill from his roll and hand it to her, casual as could be.

"Treat yourself to something nice, Aunt Damie," he'd say, smiling as he trotted happily out the door of the boardinghouse. "Real nice."

Yet, she worried. Any mother would. Every week he seemed more flamboyant than he was the week before. One year Dick bought himself a diamond ring as a birthday present, so friends started calling him "Diamond Dick," which pleased him greatly. Damie knew that he had learned to love his liquor, and love his music, and that he had fallen in with the wrong crowd. She knew that he had grown to crave the excitement of life on Tulsa's First Street, on the northeast edge of Greenwood, home to the choc joints, the brothels and opium dens. A man had his choice of Negro or white prostitutes on First Street, and Dick seemed to know plenty of both. They were just friends, he said to Damie, laughing when she voiced her concerns. The girls were just his friends.

But Damie knew from the width of Dick's smile and the gleam in his eye that the new white girl was more than a friend. Damie never knew for sure whether Dick and the girl named Sarah Page were anything more than acquaintances. But in the spring of 1921, it was clear that the young man had aspirations that went far beyond friendship. Sarah was seventeen that year and living in a rented place on North Boston. Two years younger than Dick, she'd already been married and divorced. People said she had ditched her husband in Kansas City and come to Tulsa to live with a relative. Tulsa's sheriff served divorce papers on her that spring and was heard to comment that if half of the charges in the divorce petition were true, "she was a notorious character." But in those days, the more notorious a person was, the more Dick seemed to be attracted.

Sarah ran an elevator in the Drexel Building downtown, where Dick's employer at the shoeshine stand had arranged for his bootblacks to use the bathroom on the fourth floor, a dirty little cubicle marked COLOREDS ONLY. Dick didn't complain. That bathroom gave him an excuse to ride Sarah's elevator several times a day.

The boy had taken leave of his senses. Dick read the newspapers, too, didn't he? He heard the same talk as Damie. Every other day brought a story about another race riot somewhere in the country, or the report of another Negro being lynched. How many times had the trouble started with a Negro man smiling at a white woman, who would scream bloody rape, causing a mob of outraged white men to avenge the woman's honor, and another black corpse to dangle from the end of a rope?

It was almost funny when you looked around and saw all the mulatto men and women, tens of thousands of them, everywhere you turned in the Negro neighborhoods across the United States. That was the final proof that white men never hesitated to find their pleasure with Negro women. Before the Civil War, Southern slave owners kept their white women on pedestals, hidden away from the slaves; they made those women icons to white purity and the Southern way of life. But such veneration came with a cost. Women on pedestals tended to be frosty in bed, so the white man had his way with the Negro women and girls. Southern white boys crossed the threshold into manhood with a romp with a woman slave, who refused at the risk of a whipping, or worse. Even the white overseer could help himself whenever the urge arose, and it arose often, and all those mulatto babies were the result.

But then the Union triumphed and the slaves were freed. Mingled with the Southern white man's fury at the destruction of his way of life was this fear: what sort of retribution might the "black buck" now exact on white women? Negro men were now free to do to the white men's beloved wives and daughters what the white men had done to the Negro women. Great vigilance was required to prevent such abominations. After all, how many rapes began with just a smile?

The white man's guilt further added to his rage. He saw his crime in every mulatto, the threat of Negro rape in every black gesture. So black men swung by their necks by the dozens, murdered again and again for sex crimes almost always more imagined than real.

Dick knew those things as well as anyone. But that diamond on his finger, that roll of bills in his pocket, and that love for a white girl in his heart had washed away whatever was left of his better judgment, at least until it was too late, until he had crossed that terrible line and stepped into history.

It was about noon on May 30, 1921, when Dick appeared at Damie's boardinghouse on Archer Street. He almost never came home at that time of day, when the oilmen poured out of the tall buildings downtown for their lunchtime shines. But on that day, Dick raced home with sweat pouring down his handsome face. He couldn't speak for several seconds, gathering his breath from his mile-long sprint from the Drexel Building downtown.

Just as Damie immediately suspected, the Page girl was at the center of Dick's troubles. It had been a busy day for Dick, what with the crowds who had come for the Memorial Day Parade downtown. Dick had taken a different elevator up to deliver a customer's shoes to the third floor of the Drexel Building, climbed the stairs to use the bathroom one floor up, then waited for Sarah's elevator to take him back down. The lift came creaking up, and the door opened. Dick smiled at Sarah, and he hurried onto the elevator. But in his excitement, he caught his foot and fell into Sarah by accident. Damie had to believe that! He wouldn't grope a white girl in downtown Tulsa in the middle of the day. It was just an accident that he fell into Sarah and tromped on her toe, which was already tender from an ingrown nail. He tried to apologize, but the girl had a temper, and the pain of her toe made her so mad that she pounded Dick again and again over the head with her purse, pounded him hard enough to snap its leather handles.

"I reached up to hold her arms back and keep her from pounding my head, and held them there," Dick told Damie. "When the elevator reached the ground floor, Sarah screamed, 'I've been assaulted!' A clerk came running out from Renberg's Clothiers right next to the elevator shaft and started to try to catch me. But I outran him and came here."

Dick looked like he was about to cry. Damie went to hug him.

"I've got to hide until tomorrow," he said.

"What do we do then?" Damie asked.

"I don't know," Dick said.

Damie lowered the blinds of the boardinghouse, but she and Dick both knew that there would be no hiding from what he had done. Whether Dick was innocent or not, it didn't matter. No one would believe him. Sooner or later, there would be hell to pay for touching a white girl, and as it turned out, the hell had arrived sooner. Dick had given the whites an excuse.

The first night passed quietly. All night long they waited for a knock at Damie's front door, but none came, and the spirits of Dick and Damie lifted some. In fact, Dick snuck out the next day to see his friends. But within a few hours, police spotted him on the street, slapped him into handcuffs and hauled him to the city jail on Second Street. Dick was in tears when he called Damie from the jail, pleading with her to get him an attorney.

Damie, her own heart breaking, her body trembling with fear, promised to help him as best she could. She wept as she stepped from the boardinghouse into the sunshine of late spring, crossed the Frisco tracks and walked up Boulder Avenue toward the county courthouse. On every block she thought of the skinny little boy who had appeared on her doorstep in Vinita, of how he'd smiled and jabbered once he'd eaten. Now, though he was guilty of nothing but stupidity, she wondered whether he would live to see his twentieth birthday.

At the courthouse, the sheriff made her feel a little better. His name was William McCullough, a tall, kindly man with a thick handlebar mustache who invited her into his office and made her comfortable. McCullough said the Page girl was nothing but trouble and that Tulsa detectives already were skeptical of what she'd said. In any event, the sheriff promised Damie that Dick would get his day in court.

To that end, the sheriff arranged for Damie to contact a prominent attorney in town, a white man named Washington Hudson. Hudson was the best lawyer in Tulsa, the sheriff said, and knew all the right people. Within a few years, in fact, he became the Democratic floor leader in the Oklahoma State Senate. What McCullough didn't tell her that day, what Damie couldn't have known, was that Hudson would also soon become a leading member of Tulsa's Ku Klux Klan.

Ruth Sigler's father, a wealthy oil and real estate man, had died the previous year, when she was only five. But the rest of the family—her mother, brother, aunt and uncle—insisted on continuing a cherished Sunday custom, driving out to the ranch from their homes in Tulsa to enjoy the country quiet and scenery and sit together for their Sunday meal.

This night in 1920, as on the Sunday nights before, they had started the trip back to town when the dishes were done and the sun had slipped behind the rolling hills to the west. As the world darkened, the lights of Tulsa twinkled ahead of them to the north. Ruth rode in the backseat of the Ford sedan owned by her Uncle Ross, who drove slowly because the road curved up and down through the hills and was riddled with bumps and potholes, and the country was very dark.

But on this night, something unusual caught their eyes on the landscape. Uncle Ross and Aunt Jessie noticed it first, a speck of brightness atop a nearby hill called Shadow Mountain, the highest spot in the countryside surrounding Tulsa. The road to Tulsa took them over the mountain and as they inched their way up, the light grew into flames on a burning cross at least thirty feet high. Dozens of cars encircled the cross, their headlamps burning. A bonfire crackled nearby. The bonfire, the headlamps, the burning cross—all conspired to lend a silvery hue to the white robes and white hoods of fifty anonymous men gathered there. Uncle Ross pulled his Ford into the grass at the side of the road, joining about six other carloads of people who had happened upon the evening ritual of the Ku Klux Klan.

The Klansmen ignored the spectators; their attention was focused elsewhere. When Ruth's eyes adjusted to the brightness of the burning cross and the fire, she saw that the Klansmen had bound a naked Negro to a long pole, hand and foot, and were trotting the poor man around the burning cross. Ruth heard the Negro's moans, and the laughter of the men in white. Something shiny and moist dropped from the Negro's body. That was tar, Uncle Ross said, and the Klansmen, roaring with glee, showered the Negro with handfuls of feathers as they ran him around the cross.

After a few minutes, Uncle started up the Ford and drove away into the night.

"Isn't that awful?" Aunt Jessie said.

"They'll probably just leave him up there alive when they go away," Uncle Ross said, as if to console her.

Ruth kept quiet on the way home. She tried to think of her Lessons for the next day at school, but her mind kept returning to the burning cross and the laughter of the hooded men. What had that Negro done to deserve such treatment? The question, and the terrible scene from their Sunday drive that night in 1920, haunted her for the rest of her life.

One night in 1866, six bored Confederate veterans, young men chafing beneath the occupation of the Union Army, embittered by the South's defeat in the Civil War, met in their hometown of Pulaski, Tennessee, to seek a cure for their malaise.

"Why don't we form a club of some kind?" suggested John Lester, one of the six.

His cohorts thought that a superb idea. Three of them were quickly assigned to establish rules for their fraternal organization, the others the task of coming up with a clever name. After a few days, the best that came to mind was "The Circle," which they all agreed was too prosaic. After further brainstorming, John Kennedy, an educated man of twenty-five who had been wounded three times by the Yankees, proposed this: Why not translate the word "Circle" into its Greek equivalent—*kuklos*.

Kuklos became Kuklux as they talked, which was even better, rather humorous. But still there was a problem. "Call it Kuklux and no one will know what it means," one said.

Kennedy had the solution there, too. Weren't they all Scotch–Irish? Why not add *klan* to the end for clarity, and to give the name even more alliterative spice? The words were scarcely out of Kennedy's mouth when he and his friends realized their boredom was over. None yet knew the purpose of their new order, but that wasn't important, at least not in the beginning. That fantastic name was the thing. Kennedy had stumbled upon a moniker that was mythic, darkly poetic, and ghostly, words that conjured "the sound of bones rattling together," and rattling some bones was precisely what their surly mood craved.

The ghostly specter of the new club called the Ku Klux Klan dictated what the Pulaski six did next. They adorned themselves in sheets and pulled pillowcases over their heads and embarked on a boisterous nighttime ride through town on horseback, a loud frolic that drew considerable notice from the locals, attention that served to multiply the pioneering Klansmen's glee.

Little matter that at first, their club was tantamount to children dressing up in costumes at Halloween. They had that name, one unlike any other in history, a name that insisted upon costumes as elaborate and menacing and spooky as the members could make them. Simple bed sheets quickly evolved into white gowns belted at the waist and decorated with occult symbols such as stars and half-moons. Pillowcases evolved into conical witches' hats, made from cardboard with eyeholes punched out for vision, headwear designed to exaggerate both a Klansman's height and his ghostly menace.

In the beginning, that menace was more feigned than real. The original Klan members just wanted to amuse themselves with a bit of public mischief, colorful antics that were warmly received by the embittered residents of postwar Pulaski, who "enjoyed the nocturnal marches of these harmless bogeymen with the 'gleaming death's heads, skeletons and chains,'" historian Wyn Craig Wade later wrote. "Invasions by these specters provided a rollicking diversion at barbeques and outdoor evening parties."

But the Klan did not long remain a quaint amusement confined to a rural section of Tennessee. The robed mischief rapidly became a popular evening diversion for men in neighboring counties, and then, neighboring Southern states. Scores of men in other places applied to the Pulaski founders for permission to establish KKK dens of their own. As Klan membership exploded, its members also quickly grew bored with their more innocent pranks, were less content with the amusement derived from the hazing of their own initiates. So the robed order turned its attentions toward the bedevilment of freed Southern Negroes.

"The impression sought to be made upon [the freedmen]," an original Klansman said, "was that these white-robed night prowlers were the ghosts of Confederate dead, who had arisen from their graves in order to wreak vengeance on an undesirable class."

The pranks against blacks became more and more elaborate, and as they did, they were enthusiastically reported by Southern newspapers, which caused Klan membership to swell even further—thousands of Confederate soldiers enlisting in a jolly order promoting the same camaraderie as in the military service.

Given the bitterness of the Klan members, the oppressiveness of radical Reconstruction, and the defeated South's humiliating lack of legal recourse, it was inevitable that the Klan's mischief would evolve into something much more sinister. The Pulaski six had struck upon more than a catchy name. Within just a few years, the Ku Klux Klan became a terrifying and ruthlessly effective tool for expressing wounded Southern pride, for punishing Northern carpetbaggers, and for reminding the freed Negro of his place.

Stories of the tortures and murders of blacks and their white Southern sympathizers became ever more common across the South, and increasingly horrendous. By 1870, North Carolina Governor William Holden reported that the Klan had maimed or murdered state legislators, sheriffs, schoolteachers, and countless black voters.

"Some of these victims were shot," Holden said. "Some were whipped, some of them were hanged, some of them were drowned, some of them were tortured, some had their mouths lacerated with gags; one of them had his ears cropped; and others, of both sexes, were subjected to indignities which were disgraceful not merely to civilization but to humanity itself."

Within four years, what had begun as a loose order of bored pranksters had become a paramilitary force numbering in the tens of thousands, one that had engendered attention and outrage at the highest levels of the federal government in the North. In Washington, D.C., congressional hearings on the Klan elicited testimony of mind-numbing atrocities, and caused congressional investigators to conclude that the aims of the Klan coincided with those of the conquered Confederacy itself.

In April 1871, President Grant signed a bill designed to end the reign of terror. The law forbade two or more persons from conspiring together or traveling "in disguise upon the public highway or upon the premises of another" with the intent to deprive anyone of his constitutional rights. The law also empowered the President to use military force and suspend habeas corpus when that conduct was widespread and particularly destructive. Grant did just that later that same year, suspending habeas corpus and sending in federal troops to put down the Klan in South Carolina, where it had been at its most aggressive and ruthless.

With that show of federal resolve and military muscle, the secret order withered as quickly as it had flourished and the night rides of the white-robed vigilantes retreated into Southern lore. But with the Klan's passing, Southerners could take solace in the fact that in the following decades, organizations such as the KKK were not really necessary. By the end of the 1870s, the North had effectively washed its hands of the South, abandoning its attempts to secure and protect the rights of the freedmen. Jim Crow reigned. Hoods became unnecessary for those participating in public murders, lynchings that were often a cause for school holidays and community festivals, whose goings-on were reported in newspapers across the South like baseball box scores were.

Then, in 1915, the Klan reemerged from the realm of myth and was rehabilitated in a means so compelling that the memory of the original robed order was embraced and celebrated by North and South alike.

Incomprehensible as it would seem eighty-five years later, the first Hollywood blockbuster was the story of a white-robed Southern army triumphing over crazed and libidinous Negroes; blacks were portrayed in that groundbreaking film in the vilest of racist stereotypes. The name of the movie was *Birth of a Nation*, directed by legendary filmmaker D. W. Griffith.

Griffith was an ambitious and uniquely talented young Southerner who in a best-selling novel called *The Clansman*, had discovered the perfect vehicle to further his artistic dreams. *The Clansman*, a melodramatic parable of the Civil War, Reconstruction, and the South's redemption by the KKK, had been written by another native Southerner, Thomas Dixon, an acid-tongued

Baptist preacher who in the late nineteenth century, attracted large crowds to his Manhattan pulpit by preaching against "creeping Negroidism." The racist evangelist eventually turned to writing as a means to reach a larger audience, succeeding beyond his wildest imaginings.

That *The Clansman* became a national best-seller offered a chilling glimpse into the state of American racism, both Northern and Southern, early in the twentieth century. For as historian Wyn Craig Wade later related, Dixon's novel featured "painful descriptions of black mobs with 'onion-laden breath, mixed with perspiring African odour.' Its author is obsessed with the theme of rape—the literal rape of whites by blacks as well as the symbolic rape of the South by the North in its program of 'Negro rule' during Reconstruction."

"For a thick-lipped, flat-nosed, spindle-shanked Negro, exuding his nauseating animal odour, to shout in derision over the hearth and homes of white men and women is an atrocity too monstrous for belief," Dixon wrote in *The Clansman*. "Our people are yet dazed by its horror."

Even more startling, at least in retrospect, was the nationwide acclaim accorded the motion picture adapted from Dixon's book, a film whose racial depictions were every bit as odious. *Birth of a Nation* opened with scenes from the lives of two families, one Southern, one Northern, in the years just prior to the Civil War. The movie continued with graphic but brilliant depictions of Civil War combat itself, followed by the assassination of Abraham Lincoln. Following intermission, the silent film, accompanied by a rousing orchestral score, focused on the alleged indignities perpetrated upon the South during Radical Reconstruction.

"Black militiamen take over South Carolina's streets in a reign of terror," Wade wrote in his synopsis of the film. "Flashes are shown of helpless white virgins being whisked indoors by lusty black bucks. At a carpetbaggers' rally, wildly animated blacks carry placards proclaiming EQUAL RIGHTS, EQUAL POLITICS,

EQUAL MARRIAGE. At the subsequent election, whites are disenfranchised while grossly stupid blacks vote—some of them more than once. . . . In agony of soul over the degradation and ruin of his people, young Ben Cameron conceives of the idea of the Ku Klux Klan. Disguised in white sheets, the new vigilantes take advantage of the superstitiousness of blacks and begin frightening them into law and order."

The film's dramatic crescendo predictably depicts the heroic efforts of the Klan to avenge the murder of a young white girl who is the little sister of the Klan's founder. The perpetrator is a crazed black renegade named Gus. In his deadly pursuit of the girl, Gus "runs low to the ground with his shoulders thrown back like an ape. He froths at the mouth and his profusely dripping sputum suggests the ejaculation of semen. The segments of Little Sister in flight and Gus in pursuit become shorter and shorter, creating unbearable suspense . . . Gus chases the now hysterical girl to the edge of a cliff." Rather than succumb to the Negro beast, Little Sister tumbles over the cliff to her death. In the end, the Klansmen not only avenge Little Sister's murder by lynching Gus, but also ride in triumph against blacks generally "in defense of their Aryan birthright."

No wonder that as the movie's premiere neared, black groups such as the NAACP fought desperately in the courts to prevent it from being shown. Oswald Garrison Villard, a founder of the NAACP and owner of the *New York Post*, decried the film as "a direct incitement to crime. It is a deliberate effort to arouse racial prejudices and to injure a large class of our citizens." It soon became clear, however, that attempts to block the movie's distribution were futile. It turned out that *Birth of a Nation* had been secretly previewed and endorsed by both President Woodrow Wilson and Edward D. White, chief justice of the U.S. Supreme Court. "It is like writing history with lightning and my only regret is that it is all so terribly true," Wilson said. Northern critics almost unanimously celebrated Griffith's film as a watershed moment in American movie-making. Audiences packed theaters from coast to coast. The movie ran for forty-seven weeks in New York City alone.

"It makes me want to go out and kill the first Negro I see," one Northerner said on his way from a theater.

"Others questioned whether their ancestors had fought on the wrong side during the Civil War," Wade, the historian, wrote. "A 'Ku-Klux fever,' similar to that of Reconstruction, was revived in the North, and manufacturers responded with the production of Ku-Klux hats and Ku-Klux kitchen aprons. New York society matrons held Ku-Klux balls. And on Halloween, students at the University of Chicago threw a party where two thousand young people cavorted in improvised Klan costumes."

In the South, Griffith's movie was revered as "a sacred epic." Audiences wept and cheered. In one Southern theater, a man shot up the screen trying to protect Little Sister from the beastly Gus. With his film, Griffith seemed to unite white Americans on both sides of the Mason–Dixon line in their racial fears and hatreds. *Birth of a Nation* also ensured that the white-robed order would ride again.

It was also in 1915 that a man named William Joseph Simmons, while recuperating from a serious automobile accident in Atlanta, began to conceive of the twentieth-century successor to the Klan of Reconstruction, the murderous order so celebrated in Griffith's art. By then, Simmons, an alcoholic and a failed Methodist minister, had turned to promoting fraternal organizations as a means to make a living. But he never forgot the drunken vision he once had of ghost-riders in the sky, a vision that resonated even more with his reading of Dixon's novel. As the novel became a movie and quickly a cultural sensation, Simmons came to regard his besotted vision as prophetic.

The same week as the Atlanta premiere of *Birth of a Nation*, Simmons convinced about a dozen acquaintances from other fraternal organizations to join him at the top of Atlanta's Stone

Mountain for an ostentatious ritual. The rite consisted of an altar made of piled stones, a Bible, and old American flag, and a burning cross around which solemn oaths were administered.

"Bathed in the sacred glow of the fiery cross," Simmons himself later wrote, "the Invisible Empire was called from its slumber of half a century to take up a new task and fulfill a new mission for humanity's good."

While careful to publicly insist that its intentions were strictly law-abiding, Simmons's new organization made no secret of its reverence for its violent forebears of the last century, and of its repugnance for anyone who was not a white, native-born Protestant.

"Only native-born American citizens who believe in the tenets of the Christian religion and owe no allegiance of any degree or nature to any foreign government, nation, political institution, sect, people or person are eligible," early Klan literature stated. "We avow the distinction between races of man has been decreed by the Creator, and we shall ever be true to the faithful maintenance of White Supremacy and will strenuously oppose any compromise thereof in any and all things."

Thanks to a brilliant marketing scheme that piled millions of dollars into its national bank account, and to a virulent antiblack, anti-immigrant, anti-Bolshevik paranoia then sweeping the country, KKK membership eventually grew to more than a million in klaverns, or chapters, across the country. And despite the public disavowals of violence from the leadership, local members were happy to freelance, to extend the terroristic and bloody script of *Birth of a Nation*. Stories of Klan floggings, mutilations, and murders of blacks and many whites friendly to them increasingly appeared in the national press.

As in the last century, congressional hearings were convened to investigate the allegations. But unlike 1871, the government would take no action to curb the secret fraternal order. In long and dramatic testimony before a congressional committee, Simmons himself convincingly denied that the Klan was behind any alleged mayhem. While the Klan was avowedly white supremacist in principle, it also stood for the sanctity of family, the honor of women, and law and order. The KKK, Simmons said finally, was devoted to "race pride," and not to "race hatred." His appearance was so convincing that a short time after his testimony, he and four of his Klan brethren were invited to the White House, where they administered their secret Klan oath to President Warren G. Harding himself.

Young Philip Rhees lived with his family at 720 South Elgin Avenue in Tulsa, just a few blocks from the Tulsa County Courthouse at Sixth Street and Boulder. On two or three occasions in 1919 or 1920, Philip's father took him by one hand, and his older brother by the other, and walked them to the courthouse to witness a new and peculiarly exciting form of entertainment.

It was a spectacular sight indeed for a boy of Philip's age, then no more than six or seven years old. All cars were gone from the streets and hundreds of people adorned in white robes, scary white masks with eyeholes covering their heads, silently marched up and down in an imposing and ghostly sea of white. By the size of some of them, a few of the robed marchers were children no older than Philip himself.

"That's old so-and-so out there," Philip's dad remarked one night as the Klansmen passed.

"How do you know?" Philip's brother asked.

"I can tell by his feet," his father replied, chuckling.

At that time in Tulsa, however, no one would have been surprised to find familiar faces beneath the masks in the Klan marches that sometimes continued for hours. Klan membership in boomtown Tulsa eventually numbered in the thousands, transcending every category of profession and income. Doctors marched next to oil-field roughnecks, judges next to carpenters, bankers next to store clerks, ministers next to farmers—all part of a spectacularly democratic assemblage whose members shared only their skin color and a Protestant religious background.

The first Tulsans swore the Klan oath as early as 1918, some for what they considered the most honorable of reasons. To the law-abiding citizen, the city seemed a cesspool of bootlegging, gambling, drugs, prostitution, robbery, and murder. Insurance companies no longer covered the inventory of many Tulsa businesses because of thefts and burglaries, and had canceled auto-insurance policies because so many vehicles were being stolen. Robberies were a nightly occurrence in the most affluent Tulsa neighborhoods. Weary of a police department that was both inept and corrupt, reputable citizens often looked to the KKK, the organization then celebrated in literature and film, as a means of restoring order, and by 1921, outlaws in Tulsa, both white and Negro, had as much to fear from floggings by white-robed vigilantes as they did arrest by uniformed officers.

But hundreds of others were drawn to the Klan for the same reasons that disaffected Confederate soldiers had embraced the order during the Reconstruction decades before: as a means of vigilante violence that expressed hatreds of all descriptions in the most forceful of terms. And in the Tulsa of that time, those hatreds simmered as intensely as anywhere in America.

White veterans of World War I returned to Tulsa armed with caches of smuggled weapons and wartime nightmares, only to find their jobs had evaporated with falling oil prices. The end of the War had gutted the demand for oil, plunging towns like Tulsa into a deep, if temporary, recession. So idleness, combined with bootleg whiskey, fanned the veterans' collective rage.

But in Tulsa, nothing inflamed them more than what they saw north across the railroad tracks in Greenwood—the sturdy, brown-brick businesses along Greenwood Avenue, the fancy homes, the cars, and the gold pieces flashed around by bootblacks. In the hierarchy of Negro sins, "uppityness" was second only to defiling white women.

So the grumbling intensified in the crude Tulsa speakeasies where the white veterans and oil-field roughnecks and cab drivers and construction workers bought their Prohibition liquor.

Drunken white ruffians groused about black men riding in limos while white men walked. They grumbled about the vulgar new music, jazz and blues, that wafted toward them from Greenwood at night. They grumbled that the Negro's choc beer was cheaper than their own bathtub gin. They grumbled about the Negro veterans who showed up in uniform on Memorial Day, insisting on their place in the downtown parades.

At the same time, many who made up Tulsa's white gentry— politicians, professionals, even the ministers—endorsed the racist vitriol of men like *Tulsa Tribune* publisher Richard Lloyd Jones. Unlike their blue-collar brethren, those men were more apt to have read *The Clansman* or gone to see *Birth of a Nation*, to have thus found their own hatreds so convincingly affirmed in such sophisticated ways. To them, the best Negroes were subservient and childlike beings, dependent on the white man as a toddler was to a parent. Such toddlers were capable of cooking the whites' dinners, or washing their floors, doing their laundry, even suckling their children. The worst of them, however, were the beasts portrayed in literature and film, the "lowest things walking on two feet," as Richard Lloyd Jones wrote, depraved, lusty animals who coveted white women. And now, in Greenwood, the Negroes had clearly overstepped themselves. Black instigators like Smitherman and Stradford were advocating that Negroes bite the very hand that had fed them since the end of the Civil War. Greenwood was an affront to the superior race.

So in Tulsa each month, dozens of new KKK initiates would swear on the Bible, promise to study the Kloran, learn the secret handshake, prick their fingers and sign the Klan oath in blood, pay their dues, and receive the familiar white regalia. Klan members organized picnics, took up collections in church, helped white widows, and distributed Klan literature. It was widely assumed in Tulsa that Klansmen, without their robes, were at the heart of the Roy Belton lynch mob in 1920. Burning crosses sprouted on nearby hilltops, and young Ruth Avery watched as a whimpering Negro man was tarred and feathered and paraded around in the ghastly firelight by laughing men in white robes.

In the decades to come, the Klan's role in the obliteration of Greenwood would never be officially documented. Some historians argued that Tulsa's singular appetite for the Klan was incidental to the attack, symptomatic only of a community capable of perpetrating such an atrocity. But it was beyond debate that the KKK fanned racial fears and hatreds more effectively than any other organization of its day. Its very survival was based on them. The robed order, with the assistance of the popular culture of that time, was relentless in promulgating and encouraging the white man's worst notions about the American Negro.

But it is just as likely that the Klan was more than just a symptom, that the Klan played a direct and crucial role in Tulsa's historic tragedy. More than a half-century later, on a hot summer day in 1972, a Klansman of that time, Andre Wilkes, agreed to sit for an interview with Ruth Sigler Avery, the same woman who as a little girl had witnessed the terrible Klan ritual that night in the country. Wilkes was an old man by then and had long ago forsworn his Klan membership. But he said that a half-century before, in 1918, he had been one of the first in Tulsa to promise his lifelong allegiance to the KKK. He added that within a few years, he and virtually every other member of the Majestic Theater orchestra had white robes hanging in their closets.

Wilkes spoke of the blood oaths, the marches, the special squads that undertook the whippings, or worse. Though he denied participating himself, he said he had no doubt that the Klan in Tulsa had encouraged mayhem and engaged in murder. He had heard the following advice, passed along to Tulsa Klan leaders from the national officers of the order.

"The best way to increase membership," Tulsa's Klan leaders were reportedly told, "is to have a good riot."

CHAPTER 4

THE SHERIFF'S PROMISE

Among the stories in the May 31, 1921, edition of the *Tulsa World* was the report of a local girl's apparent elopement with "a young man with whom she had been keeping company against her mother's wishes." Police were said to be investigating. A second article listed a popular Iowa congressman among seven victims of a Midwestern plane crash. A third briefly detailed the fruit menace ravaging the Kansas apple crop.

Nearly lost amid those accounts was a one-paragraph article from Charleston, South Carolina, one that was probably more reflective of that time in America. The day before, the story said, more than a score of rope-bearing U.S. Marines attempted to force their way into Charleston's county jail, seeking a Negro prisoner named Wilson Green. Green had been charged with killing a white marine who was escorting two white women to their homes. The marine's outraged comrades were apparently not content to let the accused killer's fate be handled by the justice system.

"City police held the marines off until a squad from the marine barracks at the navy yard arrived and dispersed the would-be lynchers," the story said. "Officers are investigating."

That day's edition of the *World*, meanwhile, ignored another potentially explosive story unfolding much closer to home. On May 31, not one word in Eugene Lorton's paper mentioned Dick Rowland's arrest the day before, or Sarah Page's accusation of assault in the Drexel Building elevator. The absence was probably explained by the skepticism of the Tulsa police. When questioned by detectives, Page's account of the elevator incident in fact varied little from Rowland's. The girl said he had grabbed her arm, but whether it was to brace his fall or an act of assault was not clear.

It could very well have been an accident, as Rowland had claimed. That the case against Rowland would be prosecuted was uncertain, and at that point, his incarceration was as much for his own protection as anything else.

But in the offices of the *World*'s competition, *Tribune* publisher Richard Lloyd Jones had independently reached a different conclusion about the matter, and thereby ensured that his paper's coverage of Rowland's arrest would be much less timid. That week, the *Tulsa Tribune*'s front page had been dominated by large photographs of smiling young beauties vying for the title of Miss Tulsa, a beauty pageant sponsored by the newspaper. The publisher considered Rowland's arrest an outrage, to be sure. But the travesty was also an opportunity, offering Jones another means of boosting the paper's circulation in the ongoing war with the *World*.

Thus the eye-catching headline that ran prominently on the front page, crowding against the photos of Tulsa's aspiring beauty queens: NAB NEGRO FOR ATTACKING GIRL IN ELEVATOR.

In the story beneath it, the *Tribune* breathlessly recounted Dick Rowland's arrest, identifying him as "Diamond Dick," a Negro delivery boy. Sarah Page, the paper said, "noticed the Negro a few minutes before the attempted assault looking up and down the hallway of the third floor of the Drexel Building as if to see if there was anyone in sight. . . . A few minutes later he entered the elevator, she claimed, and attacked her, scratching her hands and face and tearing her clothes. Her screams brought a clerk from Renberg's store to her assistance and the Negro fled."

The story concluded by describing Page as "an orphan who works as an elevator operator to pay her way through business college."

In a city immersed as it was in hatred, that slanted account alone might have been sufficient to precipitate the catastrophe that followed. But Jones and his paper did not stop there. Despite the pleadings of editorial underlings at the *Tribune*, who urged restraint in such a volatile matter, the publisher was adamant about thrusting his own opinion into the mix.

It can be assumed that Jones created his most fateful editorial in the same manner as the others, pacing his sixth-floor office, jaw jutting forward, pounding his hand in his palm, bellowing as if for theatergoers in the last row. This was no time for circumspection. Diamond Dick Rowland was certain to be one of those "bad Negroes," one of the "lowest things walking on two legs," a beast reminiscent of the character Gus in *Birth of a Nation*. When finished, Jones's editorial diatribe ran beneath the famous headline that seemed to foretell Rowland's lynching.

The first street edition rolled off the *Tribune* presses and into the arms of the paperboys at about three o'clock on that warm, sunny Tuesday afternoon. At each downtown street corner, the *Tribune* paperboys, competing with those who sold the *World*, hawked their wares to passing roustabouts, taxi drivers, and businessmen, bellowing the most jarring headline of the day: EXTRA! EXTRA! TO LYNCH NEGRO TONIGHT! READ ALL ABOUT IT!

The few hundred copies of that edition were snapped up in minutes and passed hand to hand across Tulsa. Starting the day before, rumors of Rowland's arrest had circulated widely. But that Tuesday, the spectacular *Tribune* coverage was the first that many had heard of it. Some citizens tossed the paper away in disgust, appalled by such a transparent example of yellow journalism. But many others took the headlines as a call to arms. This time, it would not be necessary to conduct secret, hooded rituals on hilltops in the country. This time, it would not be necessary to pull their white robes from the closet. This time, the lawlessness was blessed with the highest measure of legitimacy—vigilantism endorsed, even instigated, by the *Tulsa Tribune* and its owner, the man with such a public affinity for Abraham Lincoln; Richard Lloyd Jones himself.

Thus the dark pulse of the oil town began to race. Not since the lynching of Roy Belton had the city been swept up in such excitement, its fervor exacerbated by the fact that this time, it was not a young white murderer, but a Negro who would swing for his crime. Only minutes after the *Tribune* hit the streets, the first members of the Tulsa mob headed for the county courthouse, where Dick Rowland was then being held. The mob grew further as men and women got off work and rushed from their downtown offices to the courthouse.

The lynching talk spread to the upper floors of the *Tribune* Building just as quickly. Editors immediately renewed their pleas with the publisher, and Richard Lloyd Jones finally relented. Copy boys were sent scurrying into the street to attempt to retrieve the offending papers, but by then, most of them had vanished into history. Only a handful were recovered. Jones's editorial was pulled from subsequent editions and torn out of any papers that could be located, but to little avail; it was too late. The paper had cast a match to the dry kindling of race in Tulsa. The machinery of catastrophe had been set in gear, an engine fueled by hatred so intense that no human power could prevail against it.

Shortly after the *Tribune* hit the streets, sheriff's deputies hustled Dick Rowland through a basement entrance into the county courthouse for a short elevator ride to the sheriff's office on the first floor, where the nervous prisoner dutifully signed the documents booking him into jail. Then came the longer trip up, past the four courtrooms on the second floor, past the jury room and the law library on the third, to the jail on the fourth floor. Other than the elevator, only one other entrance opened into the jail, a reinforced steel door with steel bars at the top of a steep flight of steps wide enough to accommodate only one person at a time.

Prisoners found the fourth floor a particularly ominous environment. A crude gallows loomed down a short corridor from the small cell block. Occasionally, when the mood for mischief got ahold of them, deputies sprang the trapdoor in the middle of the night, the metal clanging loud enough to wake the prisoners and remind them of the potentially fatal consequences of misbehavior.

But that day as he surveyed his cell, Dick Rowland's worries were undoubtedly more focused on the world outside. His cell was the place where Roy Belton had awaited the lynch mob only seven months earlier, and that afternoon, based on what he could hear from the streets below, Rowland could have had no doubt that the same fate was in store for him.

The courthouse, a fortresslike building that occupied most of a city block, sat upon a high embankment at the corner of Sixth Street and Boulder Avenue. The three double doors of its main entrance faced west. Steep sandstone steps led to the doors, which were flanked on either side by broad limestone terraces. Most days, a handful of old-timers lingered there, smoking cigarettes and dangling their boots from the edge as they watched cars, trucks, and pedestrians pass on the busy street below.

But on several other occasions, crowds of Tulsans gathered as one, jostling elbow to elbow on the terraces, waiting for tidbits of juicy courtroom testimony, or for the verdict of a spectacular trial, or, in the case of Roy Belton, for a deserving criminal to be handed over to the mob. On the afternoon of May 31, beginning about four o'clock, Rowland heard the buzzing of the crowds that formed on the terrace below, a noise that grew louder by the hour. Members of the crowd began to taunt him. It was just a matter of time before the steel door to the jail would swing open and Rowland would be handed over to the vigilantes—the latest guest of honor in what had become known locally as "a necktie affair."

Sheriff William McCullough's stomach tightened when a deputy brought him a copy of that day's *Tribune*. He was an officer with a profound distaste for vigilante violence, particularly hanging, and had been appalled when his predecessor as sheriff had so meekly surrendered Roy Belton to the mob only a few months before. Hanging a man was ugly enough when it was done with the force of law behind it, McCullough knew, the sort of thing that tended to linger in a man's thoughts and dreams. The sheriff had learned that lesson himself exactly a decade before.

He always marveled at what a pretty morning it had been, cloudless and warm for so early in the spring. The sun had just crested the eastern horizon on March 1, 1911, when McCullough led his heavily shackled prisoner from jail, shuffling through a taunting crowd toward the crude gallows that deputies had built in a nearby vacant lot the day before. The court had said that the tall, skinny Negro boy had killed a deputy in nearby Dawson, and McCullough supposed that was true. But he also knew it was common enough for white law officers to abuse Negroes for the sport of it, and he couldn't help wondering whether the white officer himself might have deserved killing somehow. . . .

For the Negro boy didn't seem the murderous type. He had requested oysters for his final meal, so McCullough had ordered a heaping plate of fried oysters from a restaurant across the street. When he delivered the food, he found the boy sitting on the floor of his cell, his back to the cold wall, an old Bible open on his lap. The Negro thumbed through the dog-eared pages and smiled up at McCullough when he entered the cell.

"This is a good book, isn't it?" the prisoner said, smiling.

"Yes," McCullough replied. "It's a pretty good book."

The boy's face turned serious. "Don't you think it's bad to take my life?" he asked.

"Yes, but it's a job that I have to do," McCullough replied.

The sheriff saw moisture gather at the corners of the young prisoner's large eyes. McCullough's stomach tumbled and he felt a burning in his own cheeks. He'd been tempted to ask the boy why he had killed the deputy, but didn't.

"Thank you for the oysters," the boy said after a minute.

"You're welcome," McCullough replied.

"You seem like a nice fella. Not like the rest of them."

"That's kind of you to say."

"I wish someone else would do my hanging, to spare you from having to do it," the Negro said.

"Thank you again," the sheriff replied. "But it's my duty."

"I suppose it is," the Negro replied.

"You might want to eat those oysters before they're all cold," McCullough said.

"Yes, sir. Thank you again. And good night."

McCullough had tried to sleep that night on a cot in his office, but couldn't. He'd looked in on the boy several times as the hours passed. The half-eaten plate of oysters sat next to the prisoner on the floor of the cell as he read the Bible in the dim light cast from one naked bulb outside. His lips moved silently as he read.

The sheriff had heard the crowd milling outside before daybreak. The black night had turned to the weak gray light of dawn when McCullough entered the Negro's cell and said it was time to go. The boy closed his Bible and asked the sheriff to make sure his aunt got it when he was gone. McCullough promised he would pass the book along.

The boy's leg shackles jingled as McCullough led him from the cell. Tears fell down the prisoner's cheeks as he and the sheriff walked down a short hall to the front door. Outside, the loud, angry crowd parted as McCullough, the prisoner, and a few deputies with rifles inched their way toward the scaffold. The sheriff kept one hand lightly on the prisoner's shoulder and the other held his pearl-handled .45 so no one in the crowd would see how badly his hands were trembling.

The Negro climbed the four steps of the gallows one halting step at a time and stepped slowly to the place where the noose hung waiting for him. A deputy handed McCullough a black hood and the sheriff slipped it over the boy's head.

"Sheriff, if you would take this up for just a second, there are a few words I'd like to say," the Negro said.

"Okay," McCullough replied. "But just for a second."

The sheriff removed the hood and the crowd fell silent. The prisoner cleared his throat and spoke in a loud voice.

"Now I want to say that all people should tell the truth when they come to the courthouse," the condemned man said. "And I hope God Almighty blesses each and every one of you."

Then the Negro looked toward the sheriff.

"Now I'm ready," he said.

McCullough slipped the hood back over the boy's head. He dropped the noose around the Negro's neck and tightened it. For a few terrible seconds, McCullough thought he might vomit up there on the scaffold, in front of all those people. Then he gently nudged the prisoner off the edge of the gallows, and the rope snapped taut.

McCullough saw the boy's face in his dreams for the rest of his life. His stomach rolled every time he smelled fried oysters. The sheriff was voted in and out of office three times over the next decade, because some Tulsa voters didn't particularly care for his upright brand of law enforcement. But he had been voted back in as sheriff in the fall of 1920, and every day when he went to work, he remembered the face of that Negro boy. So he meant every word to Damie Rowland that day in the spring of 1921. He knew what it was like for a man to hang. No lynch mob would undertake the task. Dick Rowland would live to have his day in court.

On that Tuesday afternoon, McCullough ordered Rowland transferred from the municipal jail to the county lockup, a facility where officers were better situated to protect prisoners. As the day wore on, the sheriff still hoped the Rowland matter would resolve itself quietly, that Rowland and the Page girl would patch up what seemed to McCullough to be little more than a lovers' tiff. But then the deputy handed him the newspaper, and he got his first glance at the *Tribune*'s front page. Almost simultaneously came the telephone call from the Tulsa police commissioner, J. M. Adkison, who had seen the same article and knew the mayhem it was bound to incite. By then, crowds had begun to materialize on the terraces and stood in excited clusters in the streets surrounding the courthouse. Adkison suggested it might be best to hustle Rowland out of town right then. McCullough decided to wait, a decision he would soon come to regret.

The mob outside the courthouse grew. The chants intensified. "Give us the nigger! Give us the nigger!" As the sun set on the radiant spring day, McCullough's mind went back to that other Negro boy, about Dick Rowland's age, who had been reading that Bible in his cell before McCullough had led him off to be hung. But by then, the sheriff began to realize that his promise to Damie Rowland would not be easy to keep.

The lynching talk spread just as quickly on the north side of the Frisco tracks. Within minutes of the *Tribune*'s publication, E. W. Woods, the principal at Booker T. Washington High School, received an anonymous telephone call from what sounded like a white man, warning of the movement to lynch Dick Rowland. Woods immediately excused his students, who hurried home to their parents with the terrible news.

On Greenwood Avenue, small crowds huddled together, aghast while looking over each other's shoulders at the front page of the white newspaper, which porters and shoeshine boys had rushed north across the Frisco tracks as soon as it hit the streets. Most in Greenwood were at least faintly familiar with the young man mentioned there, the young man whose life now seemed threatened. Dick Rowland was Damie's adopted son, the flashy troublemaker who loitered around the choc joints and whorehouses. Incorrigible as he was, Dick Rowland certainly didn't deserve what the paper had promised would be his fate.

Among those in the excited crowds on Greenwood Avenue, young Robert Fairchild knew Rowland better than most. To him, Rowland was a friend of sorts, a colleague. Fairchild was only sixteen that year, still a student at Booker T. Washington High. But almost every day after school, he had hurried to the eight-chair shining parlor at the corner of Second Street and Main, working side by side with Rowland for tips that put fat rolls of cash in each boy's pockets.

Boys in the parlor envied Rowland his good looks, his style on the dance floor, and his uninhibited way with the ladies. Rowland drank too much, which Fairchild didn't care for, but he had always kept them laughing as they sweated over the white man's boots. When he saw the *Tribune* for himself, Fairchild's heart raced as he pondered his friend's peril.

What hogwash! Fairchild thought. He had been in school the day before, when Rowland was supposed to have assaulted Sarah Page on the Drexel elevator. But Fairchild didn't believe the charge for a second. Rowland flirted with that girl like he flirted with any other. He was a harmless, happy sort, and in no way stupid enough to attack a white girl that way. Yet there it was in newspaper black and white: his friend in a real mess, the whites ready to string him up by the neck, probably some of the same white folks whose shoes they shined every week.

Or maybe, Fairchild thought, the whites wouldn't get the chance. Maybe the Negroes in Greenwood would back up their tough talk and make a stand. As he read the *Tribune* headline, Fairchild recalled the nights he'd spent in the smoky Greenwood pool halls, entertained by the hustlers who strutted about the tables there. Many had just come home from the War, bringing heavenly stories of French women and hellish tales of combat. Those young Negroes were not at all in the mood to give whites any quarter. Over and over in the pool halls, Fairchild heard them repeat the tale of the Negro woman from Waggoner, the little town just down the road. The woman was a whore who sliced up a white man when he wouldn't pay for her services. One night in 1914, the boys in the halls said, a hundred whites stormed the county jail, dragged the prostitute down the street by her neck, and lynched her in the middle of the town.

But just let the whites try something like that in Tulsa. That's what the hustlers said.

"They'd better not even try to lynch a Negro here, because if they do, we're going to be right in the middle of it," the pool sharks boasted. "If they try that over here, we're going to fix them."

By the looks of things on Greenwood Avenue, the men meant what they said. Within an hour, word of Dick Rowland's predicament had inflamed Greenwood. Men rushed home to grab their pistols and shotguns. Fairchild watched as they rode up and down the streets of the black quarter, crowded onto the floorboards of the touring cars, yelling defiantly and firing their weapons into the air.

As tensions mounted on both sides of the Frisco tracks, Tulsans both white and black attempted to maintain the façade of civility and normalcy by clinging to the rituals that marked the end of the school year. On the south side, Catholic mothers dressed their daughters in white and ran brushes through their hair in preparation for the graduation pageant of the Holy Family Catholic School, to be held that evening at Tulsa's Convention Hall.

The sunny Tuesday was also a highlight of the school calendar for older students at Tulsa's Central High School. Hundreds of white teenagers and their parents drove their cars or rode in trolleys to Sand Springs Park, just outside of town, for what was called the Junior–Senior Pow Wow. The warm afternoon allowed the young revelers to bathe in the area's only swimming hole. There were also amusement rides and games, and mountains of sandwiches prepared by the Central High mothers.

Greenwood also made ready for graduation. Bill Williams, the son of the famous Greenwood entrepreneurs John and Loula, was sixteen that afternoon, so he joined his junior-year classmates in the luxurious ballroom of the Stradford Hotel, placing flowers on the tables and hanging colored paper from the ceiling for Booker T. Washington High School's junior/senior prom, scheduled for the following night, June 1. It was close to supper when he left the Stradford for the short walk south down Greenwood Avenue to his home, on the second floor of the Williams Building.

By then, cars full of yelling young men raced up and down the street, and hundreds of people talked excitedly in small groups. To Bill Williams, the activity made it seem like a Thursday night, like the maids' night off, and he could not imagine what was behind the strange uproar. He found out when he climbed the steps to his family's apartment and his mother handed him a copy of the *Tulsa Tribune* with a look of concern on her face. His father, the ace mechanic and crack-shot hunter, was busy cleaning his guns.

A few blocks east, on Kenosha Avenue, a teenage girl named Veneice Dunn watched the cars race across her neighborhood toward Greenwood Avenue, her neighbors speeding off to try to learn what was causing all the excitement. The news they brought back was not good. Some Negroes planned to head downtown to save a black boy from being lynched, and God only knew what that might lead to. For years, the papers had been full of bloody race riots in other places, and now that same prospect seemed imminent right here in Tulsa. Some Greenwood families packed belongings and headed for the country that very afternoon.

Veneice Dunn prayed that somehow it would all just die down, that life would return to normal. She worried for her safety, of course, and for that of her parents and five younger siblings. But she had another reason for concern. She had dreamed for years of the following night, when she would finally put on the borrowed jewelry, and don that new blue dress, and fix her hair like it had never been fixed before, and step into the Stradford Ballroom, arm in arm with that nice young man named Sylvester Gradington, her date for the prom.

Until that spring, her daddy, the bus mechanic Fritz Dunn, had always been so strict. He had grown up in a family of seven boys, therefore claimed to have an understanding of a male teenager's intent where young ladies were concerned, and thus was determined to spare Veneice and her four younger sisters from that particular form of adolescent wickedness. No dating allowed.

Veneice both respected and adored her father, and could never bring herself to argue with him. Fritz Dunn worked long hours repairing city buses, which paid for their beautiful home on Kenosha, with three bedrooms, a living room, dining room, breakfast room, and bath. Veneice and her family knew how blessed they were, their lives full of the finest things because of their father, so a girl could hardly complain about his overprotectiveness.

But now Veneice was a junior at Booker T. Washington High School and for the first time, eligible to attend the prom. Year after year, she had watched the older girls in their fine evening dresses and fake pearls and special hairstyles drive off down the street with their handsome dates, and now that she was old enough, she desperately wanted to go herself. Even Fritz Dunn came around to understand how important a night like that was to a young lady. He was assured that the hotel gala would be well-chaperoned and that her date was of reputable character. Still, Veneice had been both elated and a bit surprised when her father finally gave his blessing.

A seamstress friend of her mother's, Mrs. Broadus, quickly sewed Veneice a beautiful new dress from silky blue material, and Veneice nearly fainted from happiness when she first tried it on. In that dress, she would have the time of her life. She would be Cinderella. For once, she would be beyond the protective eyes of her parents, would step out to have fun on her own. Everything was ready, the prom only one night away. On the afternoon of May 31, the blue dress was carefully folded and lying on her bed, a tantalizing forecast of the night to come.

But the furor in Tulsa only intensified. Later in the afternoon, a white friend of her father's, a man named McMullen, drove up to the family's home on Kenosha to warn Fritz Dunn of the deteriorating situation downtown. The anger of the white mob clearly threatened not just Dick Rowland, but the whole com-

munity of Greenwood, especially if the blacks attempted to inter-
vene. Kenosha was only a few blocks from the white side of the
tracks, so McMullen suggested that Fritz Dunn and his family
might be better off staying with him in the country until things
in Tulsa calmed down. Veneice's father reluctantly agreed. He
told his wife and children to grab a few articles of clothing, and
they set out north to McMullen's home in the country. As they
drove, Veneice prayed that their exile would be brief. She had
left her dress folded on the bed.

But her worst fears were realized the next morning. Veneice
and her family watched in horror from the McMullens' living
room as black smoke spread across the sky over Greenwood.
Somewhere beneath the cloud, their home was ransacked. Beneath that cloud, someone in the white mob discovered the girl's
blue dress neatly folded for the prom and stole it away with the
rest of the Dunn family's valuables. Then Fritz Dunn's home, like
most of those surrounding it in Greenwood, was put to the torch.

For decades thereafter, whenever she ventured into white
Tulsa, Veneice could not stop looking for her beloved blue dress
that she never got to wear. She was a gentle person by nature,
but if that dress ever appeared on another woman's body, Veneice
knew she would go right over and rip it off.

Throughout her young life, Wilhelmina Guess had been nour-
ished in the womb of an extended family. Her kindly grandfather
Captain Townsend Jackson, and her uncle, Townsend Jackson, Jr.,
both lived nearby in Greenwood. Wilhelmina always marveled
at the beauty and refinement of her aunt, Julia Jackson, who
taught art at Booker T. Washington. But Wilhelmina's favorite
relative by far was Julia's husband, Dr. Andrew Jackson. Uncle
Andrew was tall and handsome, gentle, and always kind. But more
than anything, Wilhemina loved him best because he had saved
her life.

She was only eight years old that day in 1915 when she left for
school complaining of a headache to her mother, Minnie Mae

Guess. Wilhelmina returned that afternoon with a sore throat. By supper, her teeth chattered and her bedclothes were damp from fever. Wilhelmina saw the concern on the face of her mother and the worry of her father, the famous lawyer H. A. Guess, as they stood over her bed.

"You better run and fetch Andrew," Minnie Mae said of her brother, and H. A. Guess quickly disappeared.

Wilhelmina had never seen her Uncle Andrew like she saw him that night. Maybe it was the fever. He appeared in the candlelight of her bedroom like a tall, beautiful angel, with smooth brown skin and a perfect mustache on a thin, perfect face. He didn't speak to her at first, just sat at the edge of her bed, smiled calmly down at her, and touched her blazing forehead with the back of his cool hand.

"Can you open up, sweetheart?" Uncle Andrew asked.

He held a candle near her mouth and looked in at her tongue, then smiled again while Wilhelmina's mother and father watched from the shadows. The young doctor reached into his black medical bag on the floor, pulled out a small brown bottle and poured a bit of milky liquid into a glass.

"This will pucker your mouth, but it will make you feel better soon," Uncle Andrew said.

The medicine made her gag, but Wilhelmina forced it down because the angel at her bed told her to.

"Now try to rest," he said, and her parents followed him out of the room.

After that, Uncle Andrew returned to Wilhelmina's house on Elgin every few hours for many days. Her tongue grew so swollen that she could no longer speak, and a brilliant red rash as gritty as sandpaper covered her body, everywhere except her face. Wilhelmina saw the terror in the eyes of both her mother and father, and she never felt safe until she saw the thin form of Uncle Andrew, his medical bag at his side, again standing at her bedroom door. He sat on her bed and smiled down at her; his cool hands

caressed her burning cheeks. He coaxed her into taking the medicine that he said would make her better.

Not until many years later, after the horrible tragedy in Tulsa,
did Wilhelmina's mother tell her the whole story. The girl had
contracted scarlet fever, which killed many children in those days,
or severely damaged their hearts. Wilhelmina's fever lasted for
days, and there were times when her family was certain she would
die, too.

"I won't let that happen," Uncle Andrew had said.

Just the year before, Uncle Andrew had sat at the bedside of
his mother, who was dying from tuberculosis. He watched help-
lessly as the beloved Sophronia had faded, all his training to no
avail. That time, there was nothing he could do.

"I'm not going to lose this little girl, too," Uncle Andrew said
to his sister in his quiet voice.

The fever eventually broke, and Wilhelmina's tongue shrank
back to normal. The rash also retreated. The angel in her bedroom had saved her. Who wouldn't adore a man after that?

It was strange how wistfully Wilhelmina remembered those
days in the years to come. She had nearly died, but she also got
to see her Uncle Andrew several times a day, to see his smile
and feel his cool fingers on her cheeks, to have his full attention.
She loved him so much that being so sick almost seemed a fair
trade-off.

But when she recovered, his attentions turned elsewhere. He
drove his new Ford motorcar from one end of Greenwood to the
other, caring for folks who were as desperately in need of his
services as Wilhelmina had been. Then, for several years, Uncle
Andrew left Tulsa altogether, and she was forced to eavesdrop on
the conversations of her parents to keep up with the young doctor's whereabouts. One year he had gone off to study special rem-
edies for tuberculosis, the terrible disease that had killed
Grandmother Sophronia. The next Wilhelmina heard, Uncle Andrew had opened a clinic in the town of Claremore, experiment-

ing with radium baths as a cure for chronic diseases. Then he was off to Memphis for special training in surgery.

Uncle Andrew was clearly becoming an important man, known to other physicians across the country. Even the famous doctors from Minnesota, the Mayo brothers, had praised Uncle Andrew as one of the finest Negro surgeons in the nation. Surely a man like that had more exotic places to live in than Tulsa, Oklahoma. With each new detail of his success, Wilhelmina's heart ached for Uncle Andrew even more, as she realized that he would never live in Greenwood again.

But she was wrong. Uncle Andrew came home for good in 1919. He and Julia built a beautiful new home up the hill on Detroit Avenue, just a few blocks from where Wilhelmina and her family lived on Elgin. His photograph was in the *Tulsa Star*, with the caption reading: CHRONIC DISEASES AND SURGERY FOR WOMEN, MY SPECIALTY FOR FIFTEEN YEARS. The advertisement said that there was no ailment Dr. Jackson could not remedy, and Wilhelmina thought herself living proof of that. "Get well under my special treatment," the ad in the *Star* said. "Take my special examination and hear the truth about your condition."

He was still so busy. It was said that even white people came to be treated by her uncle. Wilhelmina continued to dream of her bout with scarlet fever, when Uncle Andrew had appeared in her bedroom several times a day. She remembered the glow of his undivided love and attention. But now at least she saw him on Sundays when the family gathered for dinner. And she saw him driving to and from his house calls, dressed in his fine dark suits, a straw hat on his head. Lately, Uncle Andrew had adopted a three-legged stray pup named Teddy, and the mongrel had taken to sitting on the front seat of the car, next to the doctor as he made his rounds. Uncle Andrew smiled and waved at Wilhelmina whenever he passed, and her heart fluttered every time.

Which is what happened on the sunny afternoon of May 31, 1921. Wilhelmina and her sister had yet to learn of the trouble brewing downtown. They had gone to play on Easton Avenue, near the high school, when Uncle Andrew motored slowly by in his Ford, probably on his way to visit his wife between appointments. He tipped his hat to his nieces and smiled, Teddy's shaggy head poking out the window. Wilhelmina's heart fluttered again that final time she ever saw Dr. Andrew Jackson alive.

CHAPTER 5

DOWN THE ROAD TO APOCALYPSE

Everyone in Greenwood knew that inside O. B. Mann's saddlebag there was a pillowcase and that inside the pillowcase there was a thousand dollars in cash if there was a dime. But Mann just dared someone to make a move for the money as he and his beautiful brown horse clopped deliberately down Greenwood Avenue, cars stopping to let him pass on his trip to the white bank across the tracks. Mann undertook the showy errand two or three times a week, depositing the earnings from Mann Brothers Grocery Store on Lansing. He would remove his white apron and load the cash from the safe into the pillowcase, then climb up onto his big horse and saunter to the bank like a peacock, delighting in the envious glances toward his precious saddlebag, toward which no one in his right mind would dare lift a finger.

For O. B. Mann was six-feet-four and built like one of those brick buildings along Greenwood Avenue. A huge, handsome head sat atop a neck that was the girth of an average man's waist. Mann could probably kill with one withering glance from his large green eyes. He was the youngest of nine children, seven of them boys, but even his older siblings were afraid of him, especially after that day he chased down the fellow who tried to rob the family store and nearly killed the would-be thief with his bare hands, until half a dozen men finally pulled him off.

Mann's grandfather had been a seven-foot slave owner from Texas, a man named Porter. When Porter's wife died, the white giant selected his most handsome female slave and commenced breeding a large mulatto family, which included O. B.'s mother. After the war, she married a Negro fellow named Pleasant Mann, whose grocery store in Tulsa had a meat locker, and a canned-goods section, and a place for fresh vegetables, and live chickens out front that were killed and plucked at a customer's request. When Pleasant Mann died, his widow turned the store over to O. B. and his brother McKinley, though the two of them were scarcely boys at the time.

But O. B. Mann always seemed older than the candles on his birthday cake. He towered over everyone from the time he was twelve, and his disposition could turn flinty in a heartbeat. No one in Greenwood cut a more imposing figure than the strapping young grocer. No one was given a wider berth.

That was true before the War. O. B. Mann's local legend was further enhanced by stories of his battlefield exploits on the front lines in France. On a night in May 1918, he and two dozen other Greenwood inductees said good-bye to their friends and loved ones at Cleaver–Cherry Hall, dancing as they had never danced before, stuffing themselves with cake and ice cream and the best wishes of their community. Then they left for the Army camp in Kansas and were shipped overseas, where they helped put down the Kaiser, serving with as much courage and distinction as any white soldier, and naively thinking their sacrifice would serve to improve their lives when they returned home.

But those black soldiers found only disappointment. If anything, the plight of Negroes in America had worsened after the War. It was then, after returning to Tulsa, that the chip on O. B. Mann's shoulder became a boulder. His grocery store flourished in the years after he came home, but the money did nothing to tamp down the persistent rage that consumed him, a fury that grew every time he heard of another Negro veteran strung up by whites someplace in America; a fury that grew every time he walked by a store in downtown Tulsa where a sign out front said people of his color were not welcome; a fury that grew every time he and his fellow black soldiers were shunned as they tried to join in the Memorial Day parades beneath Tulsa's white-owned sky-scrapers, and thus were forced to march by themselves as the whites jeered. Just the day before, on May 30, Memorial Day of

1921, Mann and his fellow soldiers put on their old uniforms, marched down Tulsa's rain-slickened Main Avenue, and listened to the taunts of all the white folks with red poppies pinned to their lapels.

Maybe the Germans had been right. In 1918, Mann had shivered in the French muck of the trenches in the Argonne Forest with the rest of the Negroes of the U.S. Army's Ninety-Second Division. He saw firsthand what a bullet or mortar round did to a soldier if it caught him just right. But where the Negroes were concerned, bullets and bombs and poison gas weren't the only weapons used by the Germans. Their planes swooped low and dropped leaflets of paper that landed at the feet of the black soldiers, paper that was almost as defeating as the enemy ordinance.

"Hello, boys," one of the leaflets began. "What are you doing over here? Fighting the Germans? Why? What is Democracy? Personal freedom; all citizens enjoying the same rights socially and before law. Do you enjoy the same rights as the white people do in America, the land of freedom and Democracy, or are you not treated over there as second-class citizens?"

The questions kept coming.

"Can you get into a restaurant where white people dine? Can you get a seat in a theater where white people sit? Can you get a berth in a railroad car, or can you even ride in the South in the same streetcar with the white people?

"And how about the law? Is lynching, and the most horrible crimes connected therewith, a lawful proceeding in a Democratic country?" the propaganda asked. "You have been made the tool of the egoistic and rapacious rich in America, and there is nothing in [this] whole game for you but broken bones, horrible wounds, spoiled health and death. No satisfaction whatever will you get out of this unjust war. You have never seen Germany, so you are fools if you allow people to make you hate us. Come over and see for yourself. Don't let them use you as cannon fodder.

"To carry a gun in this service is not an honor, but a shame.

Throw it away and come over to the German lines. You will find friends who will help you."

How those words had echoed in the hearts and minds of Mann and his Negro comrades. Amid the smoke and blood and horrible death, the German propaganda tempted many of them, but few gave in, few deserted, because the Negro soldiers thought their sacrifices for the cause of democracy would finally be recognized at home. Life for them and their families would finally be different. Black soldiers, in fact, would insist on that. The great W. E. B. Du Bois spoke for Mann and most returning Negro veterans when he wrote: "Under similar circumstances, we would fight again. But by the God of heaven, we are cowards and jackasses if now that the war is over, we do not marshal every ounce of our brain and brawn to fight a sterner, longer, more unbending battle against the forces of hell in our own land."

Now, on the afternoon and evening of May 31, 1921, the battle to which Du Bois referred was at hand. Mann was sure of it. This time, the whites had finally done it, just as Mann had known they eventually would. It had only been a matter of time before Tulsa whites crossed the line into treachery, as whites had done in so many other places in America, and forced this new generation of Negroes to demonstrate their resolve, just as they had demonstrated it against the Germans across the Atlantic.

Customers at the Mann Brothers Grocery Store brought the first word of Dick Rowland's predicament. So that afternoon, Mann removed his store apron and jumped onto his horse and galloped to Deep Greenwood, where the excited crowds had gathered. He grabbed a copy of the *Tribune*, his blood quickening as he read the front page for himself. People on the street said that the Ku Klux Klan was planning to take its cue from the white newspaper, plotting an assault on the jail to get that Negro boy.

Mann pushed his way through the largest crowd, the one outside the *Tulsa Star*, where Greenwood's elders had gathered in the crisis. They were fine men for the most part: Andrew Smitherman; the businessmen John Stradford, John Williams, and

O. W. Gurley; the lawyer named Spears, and the Negro deputy Barney Cleaver. But none of them had seen what O. B. Mann had seen in Europe. None of them had watched those insulting German leaflets drop at his feet while Negro soldiers all around were being cut down by bullets and choking from the gas. That night in the office of the *Star*, the Greenwood elders were preaching calm, patience, until they could determine the scope of the threat to Rowland. But the patience of O. B. Mann had expired long ago. With each minute of inaction, Mann's rage multiplied.

Mann angrily left the *Star* and strode north through the crowds for a short distance to the Dreamland Theater. There he pushed open the front doors without purchasing a ticket. Movie-watchers were distracted from the screen by the outline of his thick, tall body moving quickly down the aisle through the darkness. He climbed onto the stage, where his frame was caught in the projection lights, a massive human shadow outlined on the screen behind him. A few muttered complaints drifted up toward him, but only a few, because the audience soon recognized who was behind the intrusion.

"Turn up these lights!" O. B. Mann yelled. "The movie's over, 'cause I got news! The whites are getting ready to hang a Negro boy downtown, and I say Tulsa niggers ain't about to let that happen. We're going to go down to stop it, and if you want to join us, come on!"

With that, Mann leaped from the stage and raced up the aisle toward the doors. The Dreamland Theater, full that night as always, emptied within five minutes, the audience pouring out into the mounting chaos of the street.

It was a Greenwood physician, Dr. Gentry, who called with the news in late afternoon, and O. W. Gurley's stomach sank the moment he heard it. Gurley, the Greenwood pioneer, knew that if Tulsa whites dared to try to lynch that Negro boy, they had a heck of a fight waiting for them. Too many militant race men like

Smitherman and Stradford had been spouting off for too long not to back up their words now. On top of that, Negro soldiers like that big fellow O. B. Mann had come home from the War with exaggerated ideas about equality, thinking they could whip the world. No. If the whites thought they could lynch Dick Rowland and not pay for it with their own blood, they had another think coming. And that meant only one thing to O. W. Gurley: a race war, a conflagration that could wipe out in an hour the riches Gurley had spent the last fifteen years in Greenwood trying to accumulate. Was any racial justice worth that?

Gurley looked out the front window of his hotel and saw Greenwood Avenue already pulsing. The largest crowd was gathered outside the office of the *Tulsa Star*, the two-story, red-brick building almost directly across the street from his hotel. Gurley threw a jacket over his bow tie and starched white shirt and rushed into the street himself, where he ran into the Negro deputy, Barney Cleaver. Cleaver said he had just come from the courthouse, where the sheriff assured him that no harm would come to Rowland, no matter what the paper had said. There would be no lynching in Tulsa that night, Cleaver promised. "You'd never know it by the looks of this street," Gurley replied, hurrying past the deputy and through the crowds to the *Star's* front door.

Men nodded at Gurley as he entered. Predictably, Smitherman and Stradford were doing most of the talking. Let's not take leave of our senses, they were saying. Calm heads are required. But if the whites so much as touch a fingernail on that Negro boy in jail, well . . .

"The day a member of our group is mobbed in Tulsa, the streets will be bathed in blood," Stradford roared at one point. He promised to be the first to avenge Rowland's lynching, if it happened. "If I can't get anyone to go with me, I will go single-handed and empty my automatic into the mob and then resign myself to my fate."

Men around the room nodded. A few shouted "Amen!" Stradford clearly would have plenty of company if such intervention was necessary. In fact, looking around the room, it seemed like many of the men actually spoiled for a fight, a chance to give vent to their rage, fueled in many cases by bellies full of moonshine. They were itching for a reason to strike back at the white oppressor. It was then, as those dangerous passions mounted, that Gurley finally spoke up. He, too, urged calm. "We need more information," he argued, volunteering to drive downtown himself and speak to the sheriff, then to report back firsthand on the state of things there.

After heated discussion, the others eventually agreed, and Gurley set off in his car with a Negro man named Webb for company. They crossed the Frisco tracks on Cincinnati Avenue, driving south to Sixth Street, turning right toward Boulder. The hulking limestone courthouse came into view two blocks away, and Gurley's heart began to thunder the moment it did. The scene was worse than he could have imagined. Hundreds of whites had gathered outside the south and west entrances of the courthouse, and even from two blocks away, he could hear their angry shouts.

He parked his car, and he and Webb tried to skirt the mob as best they could, hurrying up the courthouse steps. They found Sheriff McCullough pacing on the first floor inside. The tall lawman was clearly worried, but he repeated what Cleaver had said earlier.

"There won't be any lynching if you can keep your people away," McCullough told Gurley.

"How can we be sure of that?" Gurley asked.

"Well, maybe you can't be sure," McCullough said. "But anybody who gets that boy up in the jail will have to kill me first. If I need more help, I'll give you boys down there a call, but just sit tight until then."

McCullough had the reputation as a man of his word. Gurley agreed that the worst thing at the moment would be armed, angry Negroes arriving at the courthouse to stir things up even more.

The Greenwood entrepreneur promised the sheriff he would try to calm things with his people. He and McCullough shook hands and bid each other good luck and good night.

But back in Greenwood, the Negro fury had escalated beyond anything one man could hope to diffuse. Greenwood's leaders had dispatched messengers to every corner of the Negro quarter, putting out the call for men and arms, and volunteers arrived every minute, singly and in groups, carrying rifles, pistols, shotguns, garden hoes, rakes, and axes. Young men came with the old, rich men with the poor. As he turned onto Greenwood Avenue, Gurley was forced to dodge a succession of speeding touring cars, with Negro men packed inside or hanging from running boards, yelling and firing their weapons into the night.

The *Star* office was no less volatile. Gurley began by repeating what the sheriff had said.

"You're a liar!" a man named Anderson screamed. Anderson's Winchester rifle was leveled toward Gurley, suddenly aimed straight between his eyes. "The mob took a white man from that same jail and lynched him just a few months ago. So what makes you think the sheriff will lift a finger for a Negro boy!"

As he looked down the barrel of the gun, Gurley was certain he would be the first to die that night, killed by one of his own. Then the lawyer named Spears intervened, grabbing away Anderson's rifle and shoving him toward a corner to cool his heels. Yet who could argue the point? Roy Belton's ghost lingered about the room like the thick blue smoke from the agitated Negroes' cigars and cigarettes. If Tulsa's sheriff couldn't protect a white man from the mob, how could he promise to protect a black? The answer was obvious: He couldn't.

Looking down the barrel of a rifle, on top of all the other tensions of the night, had made Gurley queasy. He saw no purpose in arguing any longer and walked out the front door of the *Star*, disconsolately stepping through the crowd to his hotel, knowing intuitively that his business empire was on the verge of being laid to ruin.

The white crowds outside the courthouse grew steadily as the brilliant afternoon turned into an equally gorgeous evening. The gathering seemed almost festive as men taunted Rowland in the jail above, some of their words prompting loud laughter. Children dashed happily among the ankles of the assembled adults as if a church picnic had spontaneously erupted on the asphalt of downtown Tulsa. The crowds clogged the street, reducing motor traffic immediately around the courthouse to a standstill.

Every few minutes, Sheriff McCullough checked on the crowd through the windows of his first-floor office, and each time he looked, the mass of people had grown larger. Most of them, especially the women and children, were probably just curious or had come to the courthouse simply to be entertained. But McCullough recognized a few outside as members of the Belton mob. At least some of those folks carried pistols in the pockets of their overalls, or in the jacket pockets of their Palm Beach suits. As time passed, McCullough increasingly wished he had snuck the Negro boy out of town while he still had the chance. Now the mob surrounded the courthouse. There was no possible way out. His only course of action was to hunker down, wait, and hope.

Over and over, McCullough rehearsed in his mind what he would say, what he would do, if one or more of those men from the mob approached the courthouse seeking his prisoner. How would they react when he refused? Would they dare shoot a lawman? He checked the clock every few minutes. If somehow he could just make it through the evening, to the wee hours when all but the worst in the mob would grow bored and weary and head home, where they belonged. But every minute seemed an hour. Every minute the crowd grew, eventually spilling onto the front yards of the nearby homes. The laughter and yelling and taunts became louder.

The news from Greenwood was equally grim. Barney Cleaver arrived at the courthouse about seven o'clock with word that hundreds of armed Negroes had gathered on Greenwood Avenue and were poised to come charging to Rowland's defense.

McCullough briefly considered that very possibility. He assumed that the Tulsa police would be of little help at the courthouse. It was said that the chief detective was a high-ranking Klansman, and Police Chief Gustafson, if not a Klansman himself, had let his ambivalence about mob violence be known when Belton was lynched the fall before. Maybe a few squads of armed Negroes might actually help protect Rowland, McCullough thought. But he rejected the idea as quickly as he considered it, recognizing the explosive potential of a courthouse confrontation between angry whites and angry blacks.

McCullough instead dialed up one of the few local men he trusted, his friend Ira Short, who had just been elected to the County Commission. Short immediately agreed to assist in any way he could and, in fact, he had just arrived at the courthouse when three men separated themselves from the crowd, confidently climbed the courthouse steps and brazenly walked through the west doors. They were strangers to McCullough, well-dressed men who had been seen in various places downtown earlier in the afternoon, but not before. Obviously, they had just arrived in Tulsa. It was a safe bet that the three were Klan organizers who had picked a particularly fortuitous time for a recruiting mission, a moment when the racial tensions of Tulsa were ready to explode. Whoever they were, McCullough cut them off before the first one could finish a sentence.

"If anybody tries to harm my prisoner, someone is going to get killed," the sheriff said, his hand resting on his holstered revolver.

The men sensed immediately that McCullough was not bluffing. They smiled politely and nodded toward him then left the way they had come without saying a word, at least not while they were still inside the courthouse. Outside, however, as the crowd gathered around them in the street to learn what had happened, the strangers rediscovered their voices. *The honor and purity of white women everywhere is at issue right here in Tulsa! A young orphan girl has been horribly violated! Can Tulsa stand by for that? Does her pain not deserve avenging? What Tulsa court is sufficient to deal with a Negro beast such as the one who sits behind bars in the jail right up there, just across the street?* The crowd cheered, its voices rising in unison to endorse the orators.

McCullough's own words to the crowd a few minutes later were no match. The sheriff seemed pathetic as he stood on the courthouse steps, yelling to be heard over the jeers, insisting that there would be no lynching, pleading with good Tulsans to ignore the strangers and disperse before things got out of hand, to go home to their families before it was too late and everyone was real sorry.

A handful heeded the sheriff's entreaties and headed to their cars, or walked off down the street to their homes, but as they left, dozens of others arrived to swell the crowd even more.

McCullough finally gave up, sadly shaking his head, and stepped back inside the courthouse. He rode the elevator to the fourth floor and ordered it disabled there. He gathered his six white deputies and made sure that each was heavily armed. He left orders that anyone fool enough to climb the narrow staircase, the only other route to Rowland's cell, should be shot on sight. If the mob outside truly wanted Dick Rowland, a good number of them would die trying to get him. Then McCullough disappeared down the stairs to continue to wrestle with a world rapidly spinning out of control.

A hush came over the crowd as the short convoy of cars approached the courthouse from the west, driving down Sixth Street. It was just after nine o'clock. Only a few in the mob noticed it at first, and they pointed in that direction; then all five hundred or so who had gathered at Sixth and Boulder looked down the street toward the approaching vehicles. In seconds, an anxious silence had replaced the festive atmosphere. As the convoy drew closer, the whites saw that each of the three cars was filled with heavily armed Negroes.

The black leaders of Greenwood had decided in the end that they could not leave Rowland's fate to chance. The time to act was before the mob had a chance to storm the courthouse, not when Rowland was swinging from the same sign where Roy Belton had met his death. The crowd in Deep Greenwood had cheered as the men crowded into the cars for the short drive south.

Stradford and Smitherman, both armed with pistols, led the group. The businessman John Williams drove one car, his shotgun riding at his side. Jake Mays drove his crowded taxi. O. B. Mann was there with several of the toughest Negro veterans.

The sight of the Negro entourage terrified several whites, who dashed into the night. The white mob in the street silently parted to let the Negro vehicles through as they turned right from Sixth onto Boulder in front of the courthouse, the caravan coming to a stop in front of the west entrance. The vehicles' somber occupants deliberately stepped down from the running boards or out of the seats, brandishing their weapons, returning the glares of the whites.

"Get those niggers out of here!" one man called.

But most held their tongue. The whites had a huge advantage in sheer numbers, but the Negroes clearly held the edge in firepower. Many whites sidled away to the south side of the courthouse, away from the Negro weapons.

Inside the courthouse, McCullough heard the crowd go quiet. His heart sank when he saw the blacks approach.

"Lord, would you look at this," he said. "Barney, I think we better get out there."

McCullough and his Negro deputy hurried down the courthouse steps to meet the Greenwood men, who immediately made their resolve known. In the meeting at the bottom of the steps, the Negroes insisted they would stay until satisfied that Rowland was safe, and there was no way any reasonable man could be sure of that as long as this lynch mob surrounded the courthouse. If the sheriff could not protect his prisoner, Dick Rowland's own people would take care of the job for him, the Negroes promised.

At McCullough's instruction, Cleaver did most of the talking. No matter how bad it looked, Cleaver said, a group of deputies waited at the top of the courthouse stairs for anyone to make trouble. Short of setting fire to the courthouse, there was no way a mob of a million men could get its hands on Dick Rowland, the deputy assured his Greenwood neighbors.

"Boys, you are not doing right," Cleaver concluded. "There isn't anybody going to get that boy tonight. He is perfectly safe here. You shouldn't have done this thing, for it only stirs race trouble. Now go on home and behave yourselves."

Cleaver somehow succeeded in convincing them. The Negroes promised to return if events warranted. Then they piled back into their cars, glaring again at the whites surrounding them, and slowly rumbled north on Boulder for the short drive back across the Frisco tracks.

McCullough had no such success with the whites. Noting the peaceful departure of the Negroes, he renewed his pleas for the whites to disperse, but the hooting and jeering only intensified. The white mob was on the verge of hysteria. The Negroes' brazen and infuriating show of force fed the white racists' most visceral fears, hatreds dating to slave times, when slave uprisings were a Southern white's greatest dread. A nigger beast had attacked a white girl in Tulsa, a crime now compounded by carloads of blacks even more belligerent because they had guns and most of the whites did not.

Well, that was about to change.

"The armory!" a man yelled, and within seconds, hundreds began running east on Sixth Street. The first to arrive after the mile-long sprint pounded at the bolted doors of the National Guard Armory. Others tried to break in by detaching the iron grating from around the windows. Hearing the commotion, National

Guard Major James A. Bell rushed from his home across the alley and found himself confronting an angry crowd of four hundred.

"What do you want here?" Bell asked.

"Rifles and ammunition," a leader of the mob replied.

"You won't get any of those things here," Bell said.

"We don't know about that," someone else shouted defiantly. "We guess we can."

"I'll tell you again," Bell said. "Not one bullet leaves this armory without orders from the governor. In the name of the law, I order you to disperse at once."

The mob ignored him and instead, pressed forward, so Bell drew his revolver.

"I've got men in the armory armed with rifles with ball ammunition, and they will promptly shoot any unauthorized person who goes through the front door," Bell said.

With that, the mob was finally convinced. After some defiant shouting, it gradually retreated, scores of men hurrying back down Sixth Street toward the courthouse, not wanting to miss any of the action there. Where weapons were concerned, many of the other whites had better luck. They had scattered to their homes and businesses across Tulsa, grabbing pistols from their drawers, or rifles and shotguns down from their walls. By ten o'clock that night, the white crowd had grown to an electrified mob of more than two thousand. Hundreds of whites now bravely brandished weapons in one hand and bottles of whiskey in the other. "See how brave the niggers will be the next time they dare show up," emboldened mob members said to each other.

Tensions continued to escalate by the minute. Carloads of Negroes teased the whites by speeding near the courthouse, then veering back toward Greenwood when the white mob braced for their approach and filling the night air with oaths.

At the Majestic Theater, two blocks from the courthouse at 406 Main Avenue, a crowd of nine hundred enjoyed a movie called *Snowblind,* a silent feature accompanied as always by the Majestic's fine orchestra. Just after nine o'clock a man burst through a door into the theater yelling, "Nigger fight! Nigger fight!" Several women screamed. A few fainted. Angry voices were heard above general murmuring, and within seconds, the Majestic audience had emptied into the street, a good number heading straight for their cars or to catch a trolley, wanting no part of the trouble. But most rushed in the direction of the courthouse, their hearts racing with perverse anticipation.

At almost the same moment, the students of the Holy Family Catholic School were lined up across the stage of Tulsa's Convention Hall, youngest student to oldest. A thousand proud friends and relatives were seated in the audience in front of them, listening as each student stepped forward to recite his or her single line that was assigned to them in the program. Young Ruth Sigler, dressed in white like all the girls of the Catholic school, had just delivered hers.

"The nicest dolly there is in all this town," the first-grader said proudly, displaying her doll to the audience.

She stepped back into line between Margaret Fitzgerald and her best friend, Virginia Lind. But at almost that moment, the children were startled by the lights of the Convention Hall that suddenly came on. Father John Heiring, the Holy Family pastor, rushed onto the stage.

"I'm sorry, but everyone must take their children and return home immediately," the priest said to his startled audience. "A vicious race riot has erupted. Your lives are in great danger. When I am through with this announcement, please go straight home. Parents, keep hold of your children's hands at all times. Do not drive with your lights on. When at home, pull down all of your window shades to keep anyone from seeing you. Use only candlelight. Do not leave your homes until advised by the newspapers that it is safe."

With his right hand, Heiring made the sign of the cross. "May God bless you and keep you," he said. "In the name of the Father, the Son, and the Holy Ghost. Amen and good-bye."

Most people ignored the priest's blessing, their attention by then focused on struggling through the panicked crowd to retrieve terrified children, then dragging the youngsters by the hands, fighting to get through the doors and outside.

It was closing time at Williams' Confectionary, so young Bill Williams wiped down tables and stacked chairs. But his mind was scarcely on his chores. For the only time he could remember, the popular hangout at Greenwood and Archer had been deserted most of the night, its usual customers crowded into the streets of Deep Greenwood, wondering like the rest of black Tulsa about the fate of that Negro boy in jail. The only reason Bill Williams wasn't among them himself was his mother's insistence that he remain inside.

John Williams had joined Greenwood's leaders on their first trip to the courthouse around nine o'clock, and the boy was greatly relieved to see the party return a few minutes later. But then they left again only an hour after they had returned—John Williams and an even larger group of men, off on another mission downtown. Just a few minutes later, Bill Williams heard loud popping noises from the south, as if every jalopy on the white side of the tracks had backfired at the same time. The boy recognized the sounds from hunting trips with his father. It was gunfire that filled the night, and Bill Williams shuddered when thinking that his father might be in the middle of the fusillade.

It was a night of rumors, most of them untrue. But this rumor, which began to circulate about ten o'clock could not be ignored, because too many in Greenwood seemed to be saying the same thing: the white mob had finally launched an assault on the court-house to get Dick Rowland.

As it turned out, someone had probably confused the assault on the armory with the supposed attack on the courthouse. But the Negro defenders of Dick Rowland could not wait to sort things out. They piled back into their cars, about seventy-five men in all, more than twice the number of the first trip, and once again grimly headed south across the Frisco tracks. Additional squads of blacks started south on foot, shouldering their rifles, shotguns, and garden tools, marching in military formation toward the courthouse.

A white college student named Mary Jo Erhardt encountered one such squad marching west on Sixth Street.

"All were armed," she wrote years later. "Army rifles seemed to predominate, then hunting rifles of various caliber, then handguns. Were I an artist, what graphic studies I could still paint of the faces of those men—anger, resentment, fear, desperation, despair—all were there, and on each face, dogged determination. A dangerous army of men who would be extremely hard to stop if one wrong move or word occurred."

At the courthouse just ahead, the Negroes in cars continued their dramatic penetration into what had become enemy territory. They parked near the courthouse and marched single file to the west entrance, weapons over their shoulders. Once again McCullough met them at the steps and assured them that he had things in hand. The white mob had grown and was now heavily armed, but it was obvious even to the Negroes that no assault on the jail had taken place, at least not yet. Again the Negroes agreed to retreat, returning to their cars and leaving the way they had come, or walking in single file.

It was then, at 10:15 P.M., that the passions of the night finally boiled over. An old white man, short and frail, went after the largest Negro of them all, the famous black veteran O. B. Mann. The white barely came to Mann's belt buckle.

"Nigger, what are you going to do with that pistol?" the old white man demanded.

"I'm going to use it if I need to," Mann replied.

"No, you give it to me," the white man said.

"Like hell I will," Mann replied.

The old white man was in no mood for insolence. He lunged for Mann's pistol, and the gun discharged in the brief tussle that ensued. A hundred other shots rang out within seconds, sending the panicked mass of men, women, and children fleeing in all directions at once, diving into or behind empty cars, behind oak trees and shrubbery, pounding furiously on the doors of nearby homes, begging for shelter from the flying bullets. Scores of others, finding no sanctuary, fell to the street and buried their heads beneath their arms. Hundreds attempted to escape in their cars, which careened wildly down the streets, narrowly missing fleeing pedestrians.

Within seconds of the outbreak, the Negroes rushed north toward Greenwood on foot, most of them dashing up Main and Boulder Avenues toward the safety of the Frisco tracks. Behind them, at least twenty people, both whites and Negroes, lay dead or wounded. The old white man who had confronted O. B. Mann was among the first to die. A stray bullet had killed another white man who observed the melee from a block away.

McCullough took cover himself after the first shot, rushing into the courthouse. He sprinted up the stairs to the jail, expecting an immediate assault up the narrow staircase. He would remain in the jail for the rest of the night. At least he could make good on that much of his promise to the Negroes. Rowland would be protected or McCullough would die trying. Otherwise, the sheriff's worst fears had been realized. The nation's worst race war was on, and neither the sheriff nor anyone else had the power to stop it.

CHAPTER 6

BE READY AT DAYBREAK

He had never seen Greenwood like this, all those agitated Negroes, a good number of them crazed on choc beer and recklessly brandishing every manner of weapon, firing blindly into the night air as if whatever had made them so angry flew up there, someplace among the stars.

For several years, Henry C. Sowders had worked for Mrs. Loula Williams as a Dreamland Theater projectionist, a white man toiling each day amidst all those coloreds, but never once had he felt threatened, at least not until that night, May 31, 1921, when the devil himself seemed to be dashing up and down Greenwood Avenue.

Sowders noticed the stirring in the street before the first show, unusual for a Tuesday night, but not necessarily a matter for concern. Then the big Negro fellow barged in and made his announcement on the Dreamland stage, screaming about whites trying to lynch that Negro boy downtown, which pretty much cleared the place out. The Dreamland was nearly empty when Sowders screened the second feature. Then, at about 10:00 or 10:30, the Dreamland's manager, Mr. Cotton, poked his head into the projection room. Cotton was a quiet, peaceable man who always seemed happiest with eyeglasses sliding down his nose, working on the Dreamland accounts for Mrs. Williams. But now Sowders saw that Cotton had a .45-caliber pistol strapped to his thigh.

"What are you doing wearing that gun?" Sowders asked him.

"Looking out for number one," Mr. Cotton replied before disappearing again.

With that, Sowders figured enough was enough. He shut down the projector and made his way downstairs to the front door.

Outside, he heard the Negroes chanting, "It'll never happen here!" like a battle cry. He heard one fellow breathlessly describing to a group of others the terrible gunfight that had broken out just a few minutes before at the courthouse, a war between an army of whites and a few blacks who had gone to save that Negro boy from being lynched. Now there was blood on the streets and Negroes lying dead on the white side of town, and the white folks would pay, wouldn't they?

"It'll never happen here!"

The crowd seemed more frenzied with each passing minute, and thus more likely to turn its rage against the only white person who was handy. Henry Sowders. So Sowders pushed his way through the roiling humanity toward his car, which he had parked a few doors down from the Dreamland, on Greenwood Avenue. No one had laid a finger on his car on any night before, but now he was stunned when he saw it. Someone had turned back the ragtop and car was full of Negroes. About nine of them were crowded into the Sowders' prized auto, several of them bouncing around on his backseat.

"Let's go!" one shouted to the fellow behind the wheel. "Let's get on downtown."

"Hold them horses," the other man said. "Didn't you hear what happened? You wanna get us all killed?"

Sowders had saved for years to buy that car, and his anger got the better of his good judgment. He walked right up and insisted that the Negroes step out immediately so he could drive home. The Negroes laughed and playfully pointed their guns in Sowders' direction, then laughed some more as the projectionist threw up his hands and took a few frightened steps back.

Just then Sowders felt a huge hand take hold of his shirt collar from behind. He felt sure he was about to be killed. Instead, he was lifted from his feet by that one large hand and deposited on the flatbed of an old Ford truck parked a few yards away. Sowders then saw that the man who had grabbed him was the same massive Negro who had created the ruckus on the Dreamland stage earlier that night. O. B. Mann had managed to retreat across the railroad tracks after the shooting at the courthouse. Now, as much as anyone, he seemed to be calling the shots with the black mob on the street.

"If you know what's good for you, Mr. Sowders, you'll sit right here, nice and quiet," Mann told him.

Sowders just nodded. He watched as Mann stepped away from the truck and approached another big Negro, handing the second man a dollar bill.

"You better hurry up and get this fellow to the other side," Mann said. "This is no place for a man of his color now."

The second black man nodded and climbed into the cab of the truck, fired up the engine, and began to inch through the people. As Sowders looked down at them from the bed, every last man seemed to brandish a gun. He recognized almost all of the faces from the Dreamland—friendly, peaceable people, for the most part. But now they yelled up at him, murderously waving their weapons because Sowders was a white man and a race war was on.

The truck turned right off Greenwood Avenue onto Archer Street, heading west, past the small wooden homes of black people and the neat brick buildings that contained the Negro dry cleaners, lawyers' offices, blacksmith shops, and restaurants. The sound of gunfire grew louder. Sowders had the feeling that he was a reluctant soldier moving toward the front lines of a great battle. On the south side of Archer, he recognized the black police officer, the fellow named Pack, who was pleading with another group of angry Negroes, begging them to stay away from the Frisco tracks, where the bullets flew back and forth between the two worlds. But the black men swept by Pack as if he were invisible; those boys wanted a piece of the fight.

At Cincinnati and Archer, the Ford truck nearly ran over a black man in a starched white shirt and dark pants who was firing blindly toward the south with his rifle. Sowders noticed two other

Negroes, both in overalls, lying motionless in the street, blood staining the dirt beneath them.

"Afraid that's as far as we go, Mr. Sowders," the black driver called out to him from the cab. "Off you go now."

Sowders jumped from the bed of the truck as it pulled away, crouching low as shots from both sides of the Frisco tracks thundered in his ears. The heaviest fighting was now just a few blocks away, two armies of Tulsans massed on either side of the railroad. He dashed from building to building, from tree to tree, timing his movements with brief lulls in the shooting. He slipped around the Frisco and Santa Fe Passenger Depot and finally made it to First Street, where he saw a large mob of white men standing outside Dick Bardon's sporting-goods store. Sowders was relieved to see them until he realized what was happening. Bardon's front door had been kicked in and all the windows were broken. Every few seconds, another man emerged from the store with a new rifle or shotgun or pistol and his pockets bulging with ammunition. Some of the looters were uniformed Tulsa policemen.

"What in the world is going on here?" Sowders asked one man standing in the group.

"Young fella, you better get on home to your family, if you got one," the man said. "Either that or go on in and get yourself some arms. For the niggers have done it. The thing is coming on."

As he observed the faces around him, Sowders saw that if anything, the whites were more frenzied than the Negroes had been up in Greenwood. He left Bardon's and hurried around the corner to the police station at Second and Boulder, but virtually the same scene greeted him there. Just across the street from the station house, another group of white men had kicked its way into MeGee's Hardware and were emptying the place of its guns and ammunition. Officers had joined the looters at MeGee's.

Sowders turned from the store and pushed his way inside the police station, where he was jostled around in the loud chaos until he found a man in uniform. He tried to tell the officer that his car had been commandeered by the Negroes up in Greenwood and that he wanted to make a report. The cop laughed.

Just then another young man approached the officer, saying his name was Laurel Buck, a bricklayer who wanted to be deputized like the hundreds of other fellows now wearing special badges or ribbons.

"Get a gun and get a nigger," the police officer told him, and Buck disappeared into the crowd.

Sowders forced his way back outside. He paused in the street, listening as another man spoke excitedly of whites who were chasing down any Negro they found downtown, whether he had been part of the fighting or not. The mob had pursued one unarmed black down the alley between Boulder and Main, the man said, until the old boy ducked into the rear entrance of the Royal Theater, his final mistake. The whites followed him in and shot him dead right by the orchestra pit. That must have been worth the price of a movie ticket, don't you think? Men roared with laughter.

Sowders started walking home, wondering about his car. Other autos, full of heavily armed whites firing into the air and yelling, careened past him up and down the street. He had never been so relieved to get through the front door of his house, where he lay on his bed the rest of the night, listening to the guns.

Helen Donohue had pestered her older sister for days, begging to come along on her sister's date to the Majestic Theater on Main Street. This time, for some reason, her sister relented. So on that gorgeous Tuesday night, Helen put on her nicest dress and rode in the backseat as her sister's date drove the three of them downtown, parking on Main between Fifth and Sixth. The young man paid for Helen's ticket, too, and they found their seats near the front for the movie *Snowblind*. Helen tried not to notice that her sister and the boy were holding hands, for that would be impolite. She imagined she was on a date herself, holding the hand of a handsome boy sitting next to her in the dark, listening to the orchestra and watching the wonderful story of that handsome character Hugh Garth, who fled from the law into the Canadian Northwest and fell in love with a beautiful girl who was blinded in a blizzard.

When the movie ended and they returned outside, Helen's happiness was such that she scarcely noticed the noise of the crowd gathered around the courthouse just a block away. Helen's sister and her date took her to Getman's Drug Store across the street, where they discussed the movie and drank tall, cold sodas through straws. Then a breathless young woman in a large, dark hat rushed into the drugstore.

"There's a race riot!" she screamed. "Everyone get home as fast as you can!"

Shooting could now be heard outside. Helen's sister's date threw down a dollar on the front counter for their sodas, and the three of them rushed into the night. The street had seemed tranquil only a few minutes before, but Helen was almost paralyzed by the terror of what she saw there now. It was like another movie unfolding before her eyes. Negro men in open touring cars raced north along Main Street, firing behind them at armed whites giving chase in their own vehicles.

Helen's sister grabbed her hand and pulled her along as the three of them tried to run up Main Street toward their car, not knowing they were heading directly toward the place where the battle had broken out. Hundreds of men and women, even a few terrified children, all stampeding south in the opposite direction, nearly trampled them. Helen would never be able to forget the looks on those faces, the eyes so filled with terror, the desperation as they fought each other to pile into cars on the street, searching for any kind of sanctuary. Others cowered in alleyways or around the corners of buildings or just kept running into the night.

Helen's sister's date looked around for a place where the three of them might hide, then pulled them off toward a part of the Mayo Building at Fifth and Main, an addition to the skyscraper then still under construction. They felt their way in the dark, stepping around stacks of lumber, grasping bare studs, listening to the shots and the screaming that continued in the street. Helen tore her dress on a protruding nail. Well away from the street, the three of them held each other, shivering with fear, listening to the mayhem as it moved off to the north. After an hour, sounds of the shooting had grown faint and it seemed safe to inch their way back out of the Mayo Building. As they held hands and ran to their car, Helen noticed that all the street lamps along Main Street had been shot out. She tumbled into the backseat and cried as her sister's date raced them home.

W. R. Holway knew about the Klan's influence in Tulsa from personal experience, from the day when three men had invited themselves into his Tulsa office saying they represented a certain benevolent fraternal order. Holway's firm had just won the contract to design the Spavinaw Water Project, the massive public-works venture that would provide Tulsa's future drinking water. For that, Holway was to be congratulated, the men said. But there was a problem: Eighteen of the forty engineers on Holway's payroll were Catholics.

"We want you to get rid of them," one of the men said.

"I wouldn't even know who they are," Holway replied. "I didn't ask their religion when they were hired."

"Well, you're going to find out now, aren't you?" the man said, smiling. "You're going to let them go."

"Like hell I am," Holway insisted.

The men had laughed as they left the office, like they knew something Holway didn't. Sure enough, the very next day, Tulsa's mayor, Thaddeus Evans, and two members of the Water Board had called him, saying they'd heard that Holway had been a little unfriendly to those three fellows, which probably wasn't a good idea. Holway would be wise to follow their advice. He could always find good Protestant engineers, couldn't he?

Holway had assumed that the mayor and the Water Board members belonged to the Klan, too. By then, most of Tulsa's most powerful people did. There was no escaping those people. But this time, they had gone too far. To hell with them. Last time Holway checked, this was still a free country. His Catholic engineers, whoever they were, would stay right where they were. Nobody, whether they wore white hoods or not, would tell him who he could hire and who he couldn't.

But the Klan would have its way in Tulsa, if not with the Catholics, certainly with the blacks. Holway saw the terrible evidence of that for himself on the evening of May 31, when he and a friend attended the second show at the Rialto, *The House that Jazz Built*, featuring Wanda Hawley. Halfway through the feature, someone rushed in and shouted, "Nigger fight! Nigger fight!"

Women screamed and people rushed for the exits like the place was on fire, pouring out onto Third Street. By the time Holway made it outside himself, gunfire was echoing from all directions. No place seemed safe, and Holway considered returning to the theater to wait out the trouble inside, but curiosity got the better of him. He dashed across the street instead, shielding himself behind the big white pillars of Younkman's Drug Store, where he could poke his head out and get a look at what transpired.

The desperate young Negro appeared seconds later, sprinting down an adjoining alley. He was a short, wiry fellow wearing a dirty denim shirt and denim pants and work boots; he panted as he stopped, looking both ways as he came to the mouth of the alley. Then he tore off onto Third Street, trying to make it to the alley on the other side. But as he ran, a dozen guns fired as one, a barrage so thick it was a wonder the whites didn't end up shooting each other. The Negro's body jerked several times as the bullets struck him, and he dropped heavily onto the asphalt before he could finish three strides. Dark stains spread across his shirt and pants, and for a few seconds, a stunned silence took over the night. Gun smoke hung over the street like fog, and the world smelled of sulfur, but then the mob recovered its wits and a loud cheering replaced the sound of the guns.

The black man clutched a pistol. He was still alive, and writhing in agony. A man in a bow tie and crisp straw hat approached and kicked the gun from the Negro's hand, allowing the crowd to safely surround the fallen man and taunt him from up close.

A man in a dark suit whom Holway supposed to be a doctor approached the mob with his medical bag and tried to push through to the wounded man, but was cursed and thrown back. The doctor shook his head and reconsidered, starting down the street as the mob began to hack at the prone Negro with pocketknives.

Three ambulances roared down the street toward the fallen black, and the mob turned its attention on them. "Get the hell out of here!" one man yelled. "Don't touch that filthy nigger!" another screamed. The stunned ambulance attendants shut off their engines and watched.

The crowd grew as blood pooled in the street around the young Negro, and he called for his mama. Whites fought their way through the mob to get a better look. Holway recognized many Klan members among them. A billboard over at the Rialto caught his eye while he observed the ghastly scene, a sign featuring the winsome face of Mary Pickford, America's sweetheart, smiling down on the dying Negro and all those people so filled with glee at the prospect of his slow and painful death. Holway wondered whether his Catholic engineers might eventually face the same fate, whether his next visit from the Klan might not end so peacefully.

He started home about eleven o'clock a few minutes after the Negro's moaning finally ended. His telephone rang almost the moment he stepped in the door.

"Get your guns! Get your guns!" his neighbor yelled to him over the phone. "The niggers are coming!"

"I know," Holway said.

Don't kid yourself, Tulsa grocer Hugh Gary would say. That's what everybody called those folks, *niggers*. Hell, the niggers called *themselves* niggers. So there was nothing wrong with that. Now, the more highfalutin darkies—you might call them *colored*. But the average run-of-the-mill nigger was just a nigger. If you wanted to insult him, you called him *black*.

And no, Gary didn't hate Negroes. To the contrary, he and his family loved them. Negroes were like children—simple, uneducated people who couldn't have survived a month without the help of the white folks. So it was the responsibility of good people like Hugh Gary to take care of them, and if anyone did his part in that regard, it was he.

Gary always had plenty of Negroes on his payroll at the grocery store he owned just a few blocks from the colored section itself. Darkies stocked his shelves, washed his windows and kept his floor clean. The big Negro named Old James washed Gary's delivery truck every day. Old James sure took a lot of pride in the appearance of Hugh Gary's truck—definitely a good nigger, as niggers went.

Which wasn't even to mention the old mammy who had suckled several of Gary's children when his wife Annabelle was too ill to tend to them. That mammy pretty much moved in with his family at their new home at the corner of Sixth Street and Yorktown Avenue. Everyone in the Gary household loved her, and that nigger mammy loved them right back.

So why did those uppity, belligerent coloreds across the tracks try to make trouble for the peaceful, happy Negroes like Gary's employees at the grocery store, make trouble for his beloved mammy at home? Hugh Gary's Negroes damn sure knew their place. They didn't have any of these fancy ideas about equality. The troublemaking coloreds were trying to get the good Negroes to bite the white hands that fed them. What sense did that make?

Well, enough was finally enough. Now the niggers had finally crossed the line and it was time for lessons to be taught, as a parent would teach an unruly child. Late that night, Gary's neighbor called from two doors down, telling him of the melee at the courthouse. A full-scale black uprising had begun, Gary's neighbor told him, so maybe they ought to get their guns and see what they could do to help.

The neighbor carried a rifle and Hugh Gary a shotgun as they sped off downtown in the neighbor's car, parking near the courthouse. Then they followed the dozens of other excited white men also carrying weapons, walking north on Main Street toward the sound of the shooting. At Second Street, they turned east, toward Cincinnati, where the gunfire seemed loudest. Gary and his neighbor walked gingerly in that direction, hiding behind cars, then behind the corners of buildings. The louder the shooting became, the more Gary entertained second thoughts about the necessity of personally teaching the niggers any lessons firsthand.

He and his neighbor hid for a few moments behind a building, listening to the shooting nearby. Then his neighbor poked his head around the corner of the building to see what was happening, and the second he did, he took a bullet straight through the throat. Blood gushed from his neighbor's punctured artery as he crumpled to the ground, which is where Gary left the fatally wounded man fighting for his final breath. Gary ran back in the direction he had come from and was home by midnight. He put his shotgun up for good and joined his wife in bed.

"That's no place for a married man with kids," he told her.

At midnight, a small crowd of whites gathered again at the steps of the courthouse. Sheriff McCullough and his deputies, still barricaded inside the jail, heard them screaming from the street.

"Bring the rope! Get the nigger!"

McCullough and his men braced themselves once more, not knowing that the danger to Dick Rowland was past. By then, Rowland was an afterthought for most of the white mob, which eventually grew to ten thousand men and boys, and even included a few women. Tulsa people, terrified by the opening exchange at the courthouse, had quickly recovered their wits. When the Negroes were pushed north, the white mob recongregated downtown. Rowland—and whatever he might have done to some white girl on an elevator—was no longer their concern. The night had been transformed into something much larger. This was war. White folks were dead. As sure as God was in his heaven, the Negroes would rue the day they spilled the blood of the superior race.

The Negroes, meanwhile, had scattered in every direction after the outbreak at the courthouse. Many were hunted down and killed before they could escape downtown Tulsa. Three more died in pistol duels at close range. Other blacks made use of their military training and retreated in a more orderly fashion. They knelt and fired at the pursuing whites, laying down cover for their black comrades who sprinted north toward the Frisco tracks. But each Negro knew that the retreat would end at the tracks. They would die before allowing the white mob to come charging into their beloved Greenwood, into the world so many had worked so long and hard to create, the world of which they were so proud.

Many of the black fighters were thrilled by the outbreak. Brothers were wounded and dying in the Tulsa streets, and bullets flew all around. But unlike in Europe—where men had been slaughtered for principles that didn't apply to the American Negro—on that night in Tulsa, the point of their sacrifices was clear. Three centuries of enslavement and abuse boiled up inside of them. Finally they could strike back, if not to save Dick Rowland, then to defend their very homes and businesses against the white oppressor.

The first major stand came at the intersection of Second Street and Cincinnati Avenue, on the northern edge of the white downtown. The Negroes stopped and fired from alleys, from behind cars and trees, from around the corner of buildings, unleashing a barrage at the whites who were hunkered down to engage them in bloody urban warfare. The battle unfolded just outside the luxurious Hotel Tulsa. White guests with rooms on the upper floors observed the fight below them, but not for long, because every few seconds, bullets splintered another hotel window. Spectators were much bolder two blocks away. About five hundred people, scores of them women in long dresses and Sunday hats, crowded along Main Street to observe the thrilling exchange, feeling safer because most of the bullets traveled north and south, while the crowd stood a bit off to the west.

In the middle of the fray, shots ricocheted from the brick walls of the hotel and other nearby buildings such as the Axelson Machine Company, Right Way Cleaners and Laundry, Nixon and Nixon law offices, and the Manion Ness Piano Company. Late-night diners at the Carroll and Huddleston Restaurant dove for the floor as bullets shattered the café windows above them. Others scattered out the back door into an alley.

A noncombatant was among the first casualties. A. B. Stick, city clerk from the nearby town of Sapulpa, was a guest at the Hotel Tulsa that night, and loitering about the lobby when the battle broke out. Curious about the firecrackers popping in the street, he stuck his head out to investigate and was felled almost instantly by a bullet in the back. He died the next day in a Tulsa hospital.

The battle on Cincinnati raged for more than an hour, until ammunition ran low for fighters on both sides. In the lull, the Negroes, their numbers greatly reduced by casualties, sprinted to Archer Street, then to the Frisco tracks, where hundreds of reinforcements awaited them. Scores of whites pursued them to the tracks, which became the new battle line, the place where the two sides traded heavy fire for the rest of the night. Bullet holes pierced both sides of the cars of a passenger train that pulled into the Frisco Station, causing unsuspecting passengers to dive for the floor in terror.

It was into this surreal maelstrom that the unfortunate white motorist drove. He traveled west on Archer Street from the direction of Deep Greenwood, which was a fateful error. The white mob, inflamed by its own casualties from the battles downtown, was in no mood for discernment when the car came rumbling along. The mobsters assumed that the driver was a Negro and unloaded.

"Death was instantaneous," the *Tulsa World* said of the white driver in the following day's editions. "He was hit so many times, his body was mangled almost beyond recognition."

"Sheriff! It's me."

William McCullough recognized the voice of the cop reporter from the *Tulsa World*, a fellow with whom the sheriff had spoken almost every day since taking office a few months earlier. Finally someone he knew. It was well after midnight now, June 1, 1921, and every few minutes another voice had called up to him from the stairway of the courthouse, desperately yelling about papers McCullough needed to sign so the governor would send in the National Guard from Oklahoma City. To McCullough, that sounded like the ruse of a desperate mob, who knew that its only way to Rowland would be to overpower or trick the sheriff. But then he heard the reporter's voice and allowed the lad to come on up to the door of the jail. The reporter slid a sheet of paper through the steel bars as McCullough kept his pistol handy. Sure enough. The sheriff recognized the signatures of the police commissioner and a state judge on a letter requesting troops be sent to assist the beleaguered Tulsa authorities.

McCullough added his name and handed the document back to the reporter, who dashed down the steps. At 1:46 A.M., Tulsa authorities dispatched a telegram to Oklahoma Governor J. B. A. Robertson, formally requesting National Guard assistance to put down what was later described in Guard action reports as a "Negro Uprising." More than three hours later, at 5:00 A.M., more than one hundred soldiers piled into boxcars in the state capital of Oklahoma City for the hundred-mile journey east.

By then, however, Tulsa-based Guard members had long been involved in the fray. Guardsman began to congregate at the Tulsa armory about 11:00 P.M., and just after midnight, crowds of Tulsans cheered as Lieutenant Colonel J. F. Rooney and his heavily armed, khaki-clad outfit rumbled in an army truck past the courthouse on their way toward the police station.

"Now let the niggers come if they dare!" one man cried.

Tulsa police immediately deferred to the Guard commanders, who found a frenzied army of civilians in the street when they arrived at the police station. Only hours before, many of those civilians had been part of the Rowland lynch mob. Now at least five hundred were newly deputized law officers with a legal mandate to "get a gun and get a nigger," folks who had armed themselves by looting Tulsa's hardware stores, sporting-goods stores, and pawn shops, all of which had been ransacked and cleaned out by midnight. The civilian army ranged from preteens to men in their eighties, from taxi drivers and oil roughnecks to the wealthiest oilmen and entrepreneurs, people united in the unruly passions that Guard officers needed to marshal to some lawful end. One of the officers, Major Charles Daley, was also a commander with the Tulsa Police Department. With the authority of both positions, he stood on the steps of the police station shortly after midnight, pleading for quiet.

"If you wish to help us maintain order, you must abide by my instructions and follow them to the letter, rather than running wild," Daley yelled, and some in the mob seemed to nod their assent.

Daley recognized several World War I veterans among them and enlisted them as his assistants. He further attempted to impose order by separating the men carrying pistols from those armed with rifles, and by ordering that all boys twenty-one and younger be immediately disarmed, instructions that were promptly ignored.

Elsewhere, to prevent further Negro incursions, Guard officers ordered roadblocks at all the major thoroughfares running in and out of Greenwood. Units composed of volunteers and Tulsa police were detached to protect the public-works plant on West First Street, and the water works on Sand Springs Road. The Guard assigned squads of volunteers to patrol downtown Tulsa on foot, with instructions to preserve order, watch for snipers, and gather up any Negroes on the street. The white patrols had orders not to fire unless fired upon, which were promptly ignored as well. A machine gun was dispatched with Guard members to the top of Standpipe Hill, and other soldiers established a skirmish line just west of Detroit Avenue, thus sealing Greenwood off in that direction. Triage stations were organized, first at the police department, then at the National Guard Armory, where the wounded of both races were ordered taken for medical treatment.

But whatever the intentions of the local Guard officers, keeping order was the last thing on the collective mind of the mob now so loosely under their command. By 2:30 A.M., a hundred cars, some of them luxury sedans driven by some of Tulsa's most prominent citizens, raced through the city's streets. The bravest of them undertook wild sorties into Greenwood itself, firing indiscriminately into the homes of the Negroes. Others converged on white residences known to harbor Negro domestics. Dozens of blacks were pulled from their beds on the white side of town, dragged screaming from their homes in their nightclothes. Negroes who resisted were beaten severely before being hauled off to internment at Convention Hall. Other Negro servants were hidden by their white employers beneath beds or in cellars or attics, temporarily spared from the ugly passions that had taken over the night.

The great burning began well after midnight, long after the Negroes had been pushed back across the railroad tracks and the first members of the white mob had finally penetrated the black community, flushing Negroes from homes and businesses along Boston Avenue and on the western end of Archer Street. It was later said that the first fires were set for tactical reasons, to flush Negro snipers from buildings where they fired over at the whites. But it soon became evident that the whites would settle for nothing less than scorched earth. They would not be satisfied to kill the Negroes, or to arrest them. They would also try to destroy every vestige of black prosperity. It was in those early morning hours that the whites first engaged in a ritual so common over the next several hours: the liberal spreading of kerosene or gasoline inside Greenwood's homes and businesses, which were then put to the torch. Fire-department crews rushed north as the first fingers of black smoke stained the night air above Tulsa, but like the ambulances on Third Street, they were met by the weapons and bad temper of the white mob, and forbidden from dousing the flames.

It was probably during those first hours on Boston and Archer that one of the burning's most infamous atrocities took place. An old black couple refused to be displaced when the mob stormed down their street that night, so when the whites burst through their door, they found the man and his wife kneeling side by side in prayer at the foot of their bed. Each was immediately shot in the back of the head. Their home was looted and set on fire, incinerating the bodies of the couple inside.

By 4:00 A.M., flames had consumed two dozen Negro homes and businesses, including the Midway Hotel on Archer Street. A small house on Boston Avenue, a few blocks north of Archer, was among the last to go. It was there that Negro gunmen were holed up inside, fighting furiously to fend off the advancing mob. The dwelling was torched when the blacks ran out of ammunition. The white mob listened to the tortured bellows of four Negro gunmen who burned to death inside. A fifth was shot down as he attempted to flee. A handful of whites surged forward, retrieved his body from the yard, rushed it through the front door and tossed the Negro back into the flames.

Thus passed what a historian later called "Tulsa's longest night." The armies of blacks and whites continued to mass, but by the rosy dawn of June 1, the white mob outnumbered Greenwood's Negro defenders by ten to one or more. The whites also enjoyed an overwhelming advantage in weaponry and ammunition, and they made plans to exploit it. Sometime that morning, a light-skinned Negro who could pass for white had mingled among the mob at the police department and learned what most in Greenwood already expected: The whites were discussing a full-scale invasion of the black quarter sometime in the next few hours.

Casualties mounted as the night wore on, particularly on the Negro side. About five o'clock that morning, five hundred whites near the Frisco station engaged in a furious exchange with Negro snipers on the rooftop of a two-story building just across the railroad tracks on Archer. White marksmen hit one of the blacks just as he rose up to fire, and the Negro tumbled off the roof onto the ground below. Two other blacks hiding in buildings nearby met a similar fate. At least six black corpses lay between the warring forces, the place that came to be known as "no-man's-land." The whites cheered raucously as the body of a fallen Negro fighter was tied behind a car and dragged through downtown Tulsa, a macabre trophy. In the next several hours, Negro corpses dragging behind the cars of whites became a common sight in the streets of the city.

Young Choc Phillips and his friends were members of the same barbershop quartet, all of them boys who grew up to be fine citizens. Choc himself became one of the finest detectives the Tulsa Police Department had ever known. But that night, they were everywhere, and could you blame them? They were teenage boys, after all, and all of a sudden in Tulsa, Oklahoma, adventure beckoned on every street corner.

The night had begun like so many others; Choc and his buddies singing on the steps of Central High School as the sun went down. Then Choc saw a group of Negro men walking in a long column down the street toward the courthouse with what appeared to be hoes and rakes over their shoulders. As he sang his tenor part in the quartet, Choc remembered thinking it was strange that a road crew should be out so late. But the singing stopped when the boys realized that it was no road crew carrying rakes and hoes, but a determined Negro platoon with rifles and shotguns hefted over their shoulders. The night's singing forgotten, Choc and his friends headed for the courthouse, staying in a safe distance behind the Negroes. Their hearts pounded when white confronted black at the courthouse, and they ducked for cover when the first shots were fired and bodies began to litter the street.

Their adrenaline still rushed a few hours later, well after midnight. Who could possibly think of sleep? So Choc and his friends set out for an all-night restaurant to jabber about everything that had happened. The Negroes had been driven back over the tracks, but white Tulsa still seemed up in arms, which became more apparent when a man rushed into the restaurant and shouted, "Everybody go to Fifteenth and Boulder!"

The boys were out of their chairs before the sentence was finished, rushing to their car and speeding off, realizing as they did that scores of cars and trucks were heading in the same direction. Someone had spread the word in a hurry. The closer they got to Fifteenth, the thicker the traffic became. They had to park a few blocks away because the street was now fully clogged, so they left their car and dashed off toward the throng of people that had congregated at the corner, murmuring, as if waiting for instructions. Then a man stood atop a car and yelled to get the crowd's attention.

"We have decided to go out to Second and Lewis and join the crowd that is meeting there!"

And the crowd was off again.

The caravan headed east, horns honking, men hanging from the sideboards of touring cars, angry yells filling the night. The boys parked again and ran toward the mob, jostled about in an even larger throng of about six hundred that smelled of rage and whiskey. Choc noticed that scores of the men had gone home and put on their war uniforms. There were some who seemed to be the leaders, standing on cars and working the crowd into even more of a lather.

"Men, we're going in at daybreak," one man said as the crowd roared. Another man ordered an ammunition exchange in prep-

aration for the coming assault. "If any of you have more ammunition than you need, or if what you have doesn't fit your gun,
sing out." The crowd buzzed as men checked their pockets for
ammo and passed bullets back and forth. Then a third man spoke.
"Be ready at daybreak!" he yelled. "Nothing can stop us, for there
will be thousands of others going in at the same time," and this
time, the roar that greeted his words was deafening.

As the insanity continued to escalate, the Negro police officer
named H. C. Pack could not help but feel partly responsible. He
had lived in Tulsa since 1916 in a small house at 603 East Archer,
and for several years had patrolled Greenwood as one of Tulsa's
two black officers, enforcing the laws of the whites as best he
could. Two days before, he and Officer Carmichael had arrested
that boy Rowland in the naive belief that he would get a fair
hearing in the courts downtown. Now, as dawn approached, Pack
conceded the truth: There was no law where blacks were concerned. The hotheads of Greenwood had been right all along. The
only justice for Negroes was the justice they would earn by fighting for it.

Pack saw the fires on Boston and Archer and knew it was probably just a matter of time before his home would also go up in
flames. About five o'clock that morning, he met a friend named
Charlie Williams on the corner of Archer and Elgin and as they
spoke, Charlie took a bullet in his arm. While Pack tried to attend
to him, a gunshot from across the tracks caught another Negro in
the head a few yards away, and the man dropped dead.

As the horizon lightened in the east, Pack found his way down
to Greenwood Avenue and there he saw the people pouring out
of the Stradford Hotel, scurrying north in flight as gunfire continued to crackle along the railroad tracks. Many homes in the
Negro quarter were already empty, their occupants part of the
growing river of refugees stumbling north down Greenwood Avenue toward the country, or down the Midland Valley Railroad

tracks. Maybe daylight would bring back a bit of sanity, Pack thought, but his better judgment told him that was not likely to be the case.

Sure enough, just before dawn on the south side of the tracks, a small band of white sharpshooters hauled a machine gun and thousands of rounds of ammunition to the top of the granary of the Middle States Milling Company on First Street. From there, they enjoyed a clear shot at most of Deep Greenwood, the place certain to be the target of any white assault. On the ground, the whites were anxious to get on with it, their restlessness embodied by the five men packed into a Franklin automobile. The men in the car sped up to the white crowd behind the Frisco freight depot.

"What the hell are you waiting on?" one of the men inside hollered. "Let's go get 'em!"

When the crowd did not budge, the men tore off alone toward Deep Greenwood. A few hours later, when the attack finally came, their five bodies were found slumped inside the car, rifles still pointed out the windows, the bullet-riddled carcass of their Franklin smoking in the middle of Archer Street.

CHAPTER 7

THE ATTACK ON GREENWOOD

There was disagreement later about whether the whistle came from a steam engine parked in the Frisco rail yards or from one of the white factories on the south side. In any event, the shrill noise pierced Tulsa's predawn quiet at precisely 5:08 A.M. on Wednesday morning, June 1, 1921. And whatever its source, there could be no doubt as to its meaning: The whistle was the signal for the white invasion of Greenwood to begin.

In the hours before, mobsters had combed restaurants and homes, dispatching men and boys to strategic locations around the black quarter, where they were somehow restrained from attacking until the whistle sounded. But then the historic signal was heard across Tulsa before the sun rose, and a lusty cheer welled up among the thousands of whites poised at various locations on the edge of Greenwood. Choc Phillips saw men pour out from behind boxcars and the freight depot. "From every place of shelter up and down the tracks came screaming, shouting men to join in the rush toward the Negro section," he wrote years later. "Mingled with the shouting were a few Rebel yells and Indian gobblings as the great wave of humanity rushed forward, totally absorbed in thoughts of destruction."

Yet for all the planning and all the bravado, the white mob's initial advance was slow, especially as the whites attempted to attack across the Frisco tracks into Deep Greenwood. Several white corpses from the night before attested to the fact that the Negroes would not surrender Little Africa meekly. So at the sound of the whistle, the machine gun at the top of the Middle States Mill laid down a withering barrage, firing north across the tracks onto Greenwood Avenue, while whites on the ground opened up with their arsenal of stolen guns and ammunition. But after the first whites fell, the others took to firing from behind the cover of trees, boxcars, and locomotives, buildings and automobiles, advancing yard by yard if they advanced at all, absorbing heavy fire from the Negroes. The fighting was the most intense along the Frisco tracks, and on the west side of Greenwood, where local members of the National Guard joined civilian whites to fire down on the Negro quarter from Standpipe Hill.

But on Greenwood's east side, the blacks offered only token resistance, allowing roving bands of white mob members to penetrate the Negro quarter with near impunity, and it was there that the white boy named Walter Ferrell lived with his family. The Ferrell house, in fact, sat right on the border of the black community, so close that the Ferrells and other white families took up the east side of the street and Negroes lived on the west. In happier times, white and black adults exchanged neighborly pleasantries, calling greetings back and forth on warm evenings. And almost every day after school, Walter played with the three Negro boys, brothers about his age, who lived with their parents across the street and two doors down.

In Walter's mind, the black children were perfectly acceptable companions. The color of their skin didn't mean a thing when you needed a few more boys to fill out the sides for baseball, or when playing hide-and-seek, or when confronting the imaginary monsters while on youthful excursions into the hills and creek bottoms of the nearby countryside.

Each day, Walter and his friends marched off to their separate schools—Walter to study with the white children, his friends to learn with the Negroes. But their segregation ended with the afternoon bell, when Walter and the three Negro youngsters joined up to play until their mothers called them in for supper, then again after supper until dark.

At least they did until the morning the whistle awakened everyone in Walter's house, followed by the spasm of gunfire that echoed heavily less than a mile to the west, which the boy at first mistook for an approaching thunderstorm. His mother and father seemed nervous over breakfast, though they wouldn't tell him why. When he had eaten, he walked outside and stood on the corner of his block, looking toward the sounds of fighting and at the cloud of black smoke that climbed to the sliver of a pale moon lingering in the brightening sky. It was then, as Walter stood outside, that a big black sedan roared up the street and screeched to a halt in front the house of his three Negro friends, roared up as if the white men who were packed inside the vehicle had urgent business there.

All the men carried rifles or shotguns as they jumped from the car and ran toward the house. Walter watched two of the men kick in the front door. The first gunshot rang out seconds later, followed closely by a shotgun blast, then three more gunshots. Walter flinched with each one. His friends were somewhere inside that house, and he imagined how afraid they must be to have those white men in the big black car busting through the door so early in the morning, then shooting off their guns in there. Why would those men do such a thing? Walter's frightened musings were soon interrupted by the reappearance of the whites, who scurried back outside through the front door. He thought he heard them laughing as they lit torches and splashed liquid on the wooden walls of the house, which exploded in flame when touched by their torches. Then the white men ran back to their car and sped off.

Walter felt the heat from the flames within seconds, and it caused him to retreat a few steps. He ran back inside his house, where he realized he had soiled his pants in his terror. He watched from a front window for the rest of the morning, waiting for his friends to escape from the flames, praying that they and their parents would appear through the smoke. Sometimes Walter's own parents stood at the window with him, looking out without speaking. Walter waited at that window until the house across the street was nothing more than a pile of smoldering cinders, but his friends never came out.

Whenever the teenage Bill Williams asked, and over the years he asked often, the answer from his father was always pretty much the same. Why did you and mother come to Oklahoma, anyway? the teenager wanted to know.

"Well, Oklahoma was the Promised Land," John Williams would answer, winking. "We had to come to the Promised Land."

But his son always knew there was more to the story. That's why Bill Williams kept asking. He knew from the dark glances exchanged between his parents whenever Greenwood Negroes learned of another racial atrocity perpetrated against blacks somewhere else in the nation. Young Bill knew from snippets of conversation between John and Loula Williams, hushed discussions about the past that their teenage son wasn't supposed to hear. No. The lure of the Promised Land was only part of it. The other part was the evil that had driven them to Tulsa. John Williams and his wife were capable, ambitious Negroes, which served to mark them among Southern whites as uppity. Thus, if the couple hadn't come West, their lives might very well have been ended by a white man's bullet, or by a white mob's rope slung over a thick branch on some tree in Mississippi.

And despite his success in Tulsa, John Williams had never forgotten. White men, rich white men, lined up each day outside Williams' One Stop Garage in Greenwood. Williams fixed the white men's cars, and took their money, and built the Williams' Confectionary, and the Dreamland Theater just down Greenwood Avenue, then two other theaters in nearby Muskogee and Okmulgee. He and Loula became wealthy even by white standards. But John Williams had not forgotten what had driven him to Oklahoma in the first place. Bill Williams saw it in his father's eyes that morning as the sun came up.

The night before, Bill's father had finally returned home about midnight, after the shooting at the courthouse, unhurt but looking unusually weary and somber. He would not answer his son's questions about what had transpired downtown, insisting instead that the boy go off to bed. So Bill had gone to his room and lain down without removing his clothes and listened to the intermittent shooting as the night passed. Then, before dawn, he heard the whistle, immediately sensing its dark portent, and rushed from his room on the second floor. He found his father crouched in the second-floor bathroom that faced south, still dressed in overalls stained with grease from the previous day's toil at the garage. Only now, John Williams held his prized Savage rifle in both hands, like he did when waiting for pheasant to be flushed from the bushes, or geese to fly overhead. Bill saw his father's shotgun leaning against a nearby wall and a pistol tucked into John Williams' belt. Ammunition was piled around him in boxes, on the commode, and lying loose on the floor. Every few seconds, as he crouched there in the dark, John Williams peered out the window toward what looked to be thousands of whites on the other side of the tracks, firing wildly toward the north.

"Well, now they're shooting at us," John Williams said as if to himself as he drew up the screen on the bathroom window.

He rested the barrel of the Savage on the windowpane, squinting over the gun sight, and calmly squeezed off six shots, the noise echoing in the small room and causing Bill to throw his hands over his ears. Three white bodies fell in dark heaps, near the railroad tracks, and when they did, a dozen others scurried for cover. Bill Williams crawled up next to his father as he shot, and he saw that John Williams' jaw was grimly set. But when his father glanced over at him, Bill saw that his eyes were glinting as they did when he was happy or excited. His dad emptied the spent cartridges onto the floor and loaded several more bullets into the Savage, sighted the rifle and squeezed off six more shots, because he had not forgotten what had brought him to Oklahoma. John Williams had swallowed his rage all those years, the rage of having his fate and that of his family depend on the dark whimsy of hateful whites, the rage that now poured out through the barrel of his expensive rifle.

Behind them in the hallway, Bill's mother and the teenager who lived with the family, the lad named Posey, peeked around the corner as John Williams took on the white army. Other Negro gunmen fired at the whites from the windows and rooftops along Greenwood Avenue, but the Williams Building, at the intersection of Greenwood and Archer, was the closest to enemy lines, the southern gateway to the Negro quarter; thus the bullets of John Williams were the most strategic in keeping Greenwood from being overrun, and John Williams knew it. He emptied the Savage again, then grabbed the shotgun and unloaded both barrels out the window, then pulled his pistol from his belt and fired that at the whites, too. It must have seemed to the whites like fifteen men were raining bullets down on them from the Williams Building.

"Bill, help me defend Greenwood," John Williams said, holding the shotgun toward his son. "Grab some of that buckshot there on the floor. Loula, I think it's time you headed on off to your mother's."

Loula Williams nodded from the doorway. She crawled into the bathroom to hug Bill, still crouched next to his father at the window. She touched her husband's shoulder, then crawled back into the hallway, where she hugged Posey and disappeared down the stairs. Posey stayed in the hall while Bill loaded the shotgun the way his father had taught him on lazy weekend afternoons when they hunted for Sunday supper. He handed his father the shotgun, grabbed the empty Savage and loaded that, too. There was something thrilling about it, working with his father that way. For the first time in his life, Bill felt like a man. Windows shattered around them and bullets chipped away at the sturdy brown brick of their building. A pile of spent shell casings built at their feet. The air in the bathroom was thick with the smell of sulfur, but the boy was at his father's side as they defended Greenwood. For the rest of his life, Bill Williams would believe that more whites than blacks were killed that day, because of all the whites he saw fall outside their bathroom window.

But the numbers arrayed against them were too great. And when the sun came up, the whites unleashed another weapon.

"My Lord, Bill, would you look at that," John Williams said.

A biplane appeared from the east, circling high at first, like a vulture surveying its prey, then diving low over Deep Greenwood, its engine a loud, terrifying moan. The plane roared close enough that John Williams could see the man in the strange headgear and goggles in the plane's second seat, firing a rifle toward Greenwood Avenue. A second plane followed soon upon the first, attacking in the same manner. Seeing their destructive intent, John Williams fired several shots at the planes before they disappeared to the north, but for the first time that morning, Bill's father seemed unnerved, shaking his head and muttering to himself as his son handed him the loaded shotgun.

The appearance of the planes had the opposite effect on the whites. More cheers welled up among them, and dozens rushed over the tracks as John Williams was distracted by the assault from the air. They managed to take positions within a hundred feet of the Williams Building, and a platoon of white gunmen trained its weapons on John Williams' bathroom window, splintering the windowpane into a thousand tiny slivers.

"I guess we better get outta here now, too," Bill's father said. "Come on, fellas. Let's go."

He handed Bill the shotgun and carried the Savage himself. All three filled their pockets with bullets and shells. Then John Williams, Bill, and Posey scurried down the stairs, out the front door of the Williams Building and onto the sidewalk of Greenwood Avenue. They clung to the buildings on the west side of the street, inching their way north until another burst from the machine gun perched at the top of the mill on First Street caused them to duck into the Bell and Little Restaurant.

On any other Wednesday morning, the restaurant would have been filled with the aroma of frying bacon and grits, and men in well-worn old hats and faded overalls would be loitering around the tables covered with red-and-white-checked tablecloths before making the hike south across the tracks for work. Now the place was deserted, the lights dark. From the sanctuary of the restaurant, John and the two boys surveyed the terrible scene in the street. They saw scores of black people, including elderly folks and women dragging children, screaming and crying as they stumbled north, bullets from the machine gun in the mill kicking up sparks on the asphalt around them. Several of the refugees were hit and crumpled to the pavement. Bill saw the Negro undertaker, S. M. Jackson, step out from under an awning down the street and fire several shots with his pistol at another plane that had appeared overhead. Smoking rifles and shotgun barrels protruded from the second-story windows of the *Tulsa Star* and from the apartments above Carter's Barbershop. In one of the windows, Bill Williams recognized the big veteran, O. B. Mann, blasting away toward the whites.

After a few minutes, John Williams spotted a young Negro man with a shotgun standing in the door of the pool hall across the street. The young man waved at them and tried to yell over the gunfire.

"Why don't you boys come on over here, so you can get a better shot at those fellas up in the mill?"

"Okay," John Williams called back. "Hold your horses."

He looked at Bill and Posey. "You ready?"

The boys nodded.

"Let's make this snappy," John Williams said.

He dashed out into the street with Bill and Posey at his heels. Bullets zipped around their heads as they scrambled toward the pool hall and dove inside the door.

"Sure glad to have some company," the man with the shotgun said when they arrived. "I figure the best shot is from one of the windows upstairs."

John Williams nodded. The four of them raced to the second floor, into a bedroom with a window that looked out onto Greenwood Avenue. From there, it was a long but clear shot toward the top of the mill, and toward the place around some boxcars where the whites were still pinned down by the Negro fighters. John Williams sighted the Savage and started to fire, but after a minute, he realized that he was the only person in the room doing so. The other man just stood away from the window in the middle of the room, holding his shotgun over his shoulder, looking sheepish.

"What are you waiting for, brother?" John Williams asked.

"I'm afraid I don't how to load this thing," the man replied, tapping the shotgun.

"Lord Almighty," John Williams said. "Bill, give the man a hand."

Bill took the man's shotgun and loaded two shells from his pocket, then handed the weapon back.

"Thank you kindly, son," the man said, moving tentatively to the window next to John Williams. He pointed toward the street, pulled the trigger, and was knocked off his feet by the recoil. The butt of the shotgun had also kicked up into his teeth, and he lay stunned on the floor, blood gushing from his mouth. He finally pulled himself to his knees, then staggered up to his feet.

"I guess I'm not cut out for this sort of thing," he mumbled. "I think I'll be leaving."

He disappeared through the door and lumbered down the steps. John Williams and the boys watched from the window as the man joined the throng of refugees who were running up the street. Then John Williams turned his guns back toward the south and resumed firing. But now the white mob was breaking into the buildings of Greenwood Avenue from an alley to the west. White guns were soon poking out and firing back at John and the boys from windows of the Negro-owned buildings across the street. John Williams could even see white men in the windows of his own building on the corner. Greenwood Avenue was lost.

"Well, let's go," he said, heading out the bedroom door and down the stairs.

Bill and Posey followed him into an alley behind the pool hall.

John Williams tossed his Savage to the ground, pulled out his pistol and did the same with it. He told Bill to drop the shotgun and both boys to empty their pockets.

"It's probably best if we split up," Bill's dad said. "Head north and I'll meet you in the country. Hurry off now."

But Posey followed John Williams, so Bill set off alone, running north up the alley. He stopped to rest after two blocks, looked around to see if any whites pursued him, and reached into his pocket for his handkerchief. To his alarm, he felt two shotgun shells hidden there and quickly tossed them into some nearby bushes, which was a good thing. A few seconds later, he and two white hoodlums arrived at the next corner at the same time, nearly bumping into each other. The whites, who looked to be only a few years older than Bill, were dressed alike in denim shirts and denim pants soiled to the knees with dust. They both wore crisp, matching brown caps.

"Gotcha, nigger," one said, pointing a shotgun at Bill's head. "Hold it right there."

Bill stopped and threw his hands in the air.

"Where's that gun of yours, nigger?" one of them asked.

"Don't have no gun," Bill said.

"I know you do. I seen you throw something back in those bushes. Why don't we go have a look?"

One of the whites guarded Bill as the other trotted down the alley and poked around in the bushes. Bill knew he would be killed if the white boy found those shells, so he whispered the words of the Twenty-third Psalm. *Yea, though I walk through the valley of the shadow of death, I will fear no evil; for you are with me. . . . The Lord is my shepherd. I shall not want.*

In a few minutes, the white boy returned from the bushes after a fruitless search, and Bill sighed with relief.

"You're lucky," the young hoodlum said to him. "Now march."

They herded Bill up the alley another block to Easton Street, where a handful of whites held about forty other Negro men and boys captive beneath a stand of oaks. Bill recognized most of the prisoners. They were customers from the confectionary, or class-mates in school, or friends of his parents, but he was ashamed to see them in such a state of subjugation and despair. He walked toward a tree without speaking or making eye contact and slumped to the ground, listening as the whites taunted their pris-oners, turning his eyes away as they prodded the Negroes with their guns. He was consumed by his own rage then. Angry tears spilled down his face. He wished he hadn't left his father's shot-gun behind.

He had tried to warn those Negroes. If the blacks persisted in trying to help that Negro boy in jail down at the courthouse, they might just get everyone in Greenwood burned out, O. W. Gurley had said the night before until he was out of breath. That should have been plain to everyone. Those boys knew as well as Gurley did what had been the fate of Negroes who got uppity in other American cities. Had they forgotten East St. Louis, Chicago, Houston, Washington, D.C., Omaha, Duluth? Didn't Deputy Barney Cleaver and the sheriff both assure them that Dick Row-land was safe behind bars? And even if he wasn't, was the life of one nigger worth all this? Now they would see: The price of pride was fire.

Gurley stayed awake that night with his wife Emma, sitting up in their rooms on the top floor of the Gurley Hotel. The smell of smoke grew stronger by the hour, smoke from the first fires set by the whites on Boston and Archer, just to the west. At daylight, he looked out a window and saw that the inferno was much closer than that. Flames had begun to spit from the roof of Sattie Par-tee's place on Archer Street only a few yards south, launching red cinders into the morning air that were landing within a few feet of Gurley's doorstep. He ran downstairs and outside in his shirt-sleeves, hearing the crackling of the fire at Partee's place, gunfire booming all around him, and the air so filthy with smoke that he gagged and put a handkerchief to his mouth.

Six white men emerged like ghosts from one corner of this hell, walking toward Gurley through the smoke from the direction of Sattie's place. They carried shotguns and rifles, burning torches, and five-gallon containers. All of them wore khaki outfits, but Gurley couldn't tell if they were soldiers from the National Guard or white World War I veterans who had dusted off their old uniforms for that morning's attack on the Negro quarter. They marched up to Gurley when they saw him standing outside.

"You better get out of that hotel because we're gonna burn all of this goddamn stuff," one of the men said. "You better get all your guests out."

Then the men moved on to the next building, pounding on the doors of the restaurant, then to the pool hall next to the restaurant, screaming for anybody inside to get the hell out, because those buildings were marked for the torch.

Gurley ran back inside and found his wife as he had left her, in a bedroom rocking chair, rocking furiously, as she stared at the window, quaking with fear.

"We need to go, Emma," he said. "The fire's going to get us, too. The fire's going to get everyone."

"But where will we go if the fire is everywhere?" she asked.

"I don't know," he said.

As they stepped onto Greenwood Avenue and saw all the people rushing north, Gurley had an idea. He and his wife would run in the other direction and try to make it south across the tracks, back to white Tulsa, where O. W. Gurley was known as one of the reasonable Negroes and a man of means. He and Emma would be safer with the whites than with the blacks. So they rushed south on Greenwood Avenue to the corner of Archer, pausing at the Williams Building to look around the corner. It was then that Gurley learned how Tulsa whites were in no mood that morning to make distinctions between the Negroes who were reasonable and those who weren't.

Two white men with pistols came around a building on Archer and fired at the Gurleys. Emma moaned and fell heavily to the street.

"Emma!" Gurley cried as she fell. "Lord help us."

Her eyes were open as he bent over her, searching her body for a wound.

"Gurley," she said to her husband. "Don't worry about me. You need to run."

So he did. Gurley ran without saying good-bye. He left his wife and ran as fast as his fifty-three-year-old legs could carry him, back up Greenwood Avenue, running north now with the rest of the Negroes, passing women, children, and old people who were flee-ing from the whites and their torches and their guns. Only one man ran faster than Gurley, a young black fellow who sped by like Gurley was standing still. But the young man's haste did not serve him, for the second he passed Gurley, a bullet from the mill caught him square between the shoulders and spun him around. He landed on his back in the street, groaning as Gurley ran on by.

Gurley legs carried him down Greenwood a few blocks more, until he saw a black man with a rifle who was struck by a bullet and fell from a second-story window of the Masonic Hall to the sidewalk below. That sight finally convinced Gurley to abandon Greenwood and run east for several blocks, where he found him-self panting at the playground of the Dunbar Elementary School. His age finally overtook his terror and he could flee no more. He stumbled toward the school and slipped into the crawl space be-neath the new wooden building, hiding there for what seemed like hours, silently panting and sweating, weeping for Emma, and for a life of dreams and hard work gone to ruin because Negroes couldn't leave well enough alone.

Every so often in his distress, he peered out from his hiding place, and eventually he saw that the flood of black refugees had trickled to nothing. Now hundreds of whites filled the streets, all of them carrying guns and several of them hefting torches. He saw one white teenager point toward the school, and a group of whites walked in that direction.

"I swear I saw him go under the school right about there," the teenager said, standing only a few feet from where Gurley hid.

"Well, let's just see," a man replied.

The barrel of a rifle was thrust into the crawl space and fired several times. Gurley nearly screamed with terror, clawing his way as far as he could beneath the building, the bullets missing him by inches.

"Ah, hell," the man's voice said. "He must have crawled out the other side."

Gurley then heard a pounding noise and glass breaking, and feet shuffling in the building above him. He smelled smoke a few seconds later and realized that the school building was on fire, too. So he knew he was dead if he stayed beneath the school, and dead if he didn't. He crawled out from his hiding place, opening a deep gash on his hand on a piece of broken glass from one of the windows. Blood stained the sleeve of his pressed white shirt, already badly soiled with sweat and dirt, but Gurley scarcely noticed the pain.

Smoke poured from the school's broken windows as he stumbled away from the building, but it was his great fortune that most of the white mob had been distracted by events farther north. The street in front of the school was almost quiet. Gurley walked to a place nearby where an old white man with an antique shotgun held fifteen black men captive. Gurley threw up his hands and surrendered, telling the white man he meant him no trouble.

As the whites advanced across the black quarter, a Tulsa motorcycle cop named Leo Irish strung a long rope through the belt loops of six black men, hooked one end onto his motorcycle, then hopped on his machine and double-timed the prisoners on a mile-long trot from Greenwood to Convention Hall. It was among the more infamous means of transporting black prisoners on that morning when thousands of Negroes—men, women and children of all ages and from every strata of Greenwood life—were captured and marched by the whites to the Convention Hall; then, when the hall was full, on to the local baseball stadium called McNulty Park. Whites stepped from their houses and businesses

Deep Greenwood in 1917, site of the happy promenades on the maid's day off.
PHOTO: TULSA HISTORICAL SOCIETY

Leading Greenwood entrepreneur Bill Williams behind the wheel of black Tulsa's first automobile, with wife, Loula, sitting next to him, and son, Bill, in the back seat.
PHOTO: TULSA HISTORICAL SOCIETY

Tulsa Tribune owner Richard
Lloyd Jones, the Lincoln
devotee whose editorial
touched off a conflagration.
PHOTO: McFARLIN LIBRARY,
UNIVERSITY OF TULSA

O. B. Mann, World War I
veteran and Greenwood's
most feared warrior.
PHOTO: OBERA
MANN SMITH

Dr. Andrew C. Jackson, hailed by
the Mayo brothers as America's
finest Negro surgeon.
PHOTO: JACK ADAMS

Tulsa county sheriff William
McCullough, Dick Rowland's
last line of defense.
PHOTO: TULSA COUNTY
SHERIFF'S DEPARTMENT

A young mobster poses for a snapshot, as the Dreamland Theater burns in the background. PHOTO: TULSA HISTORICAL SOCIETY

Spectators heading toward the burning, while weary mobsters head home after a night of blood and fire. PHOTO: McFARLIN LIBRARY, UNIVERSITY OF TULSA

Prisoners share a flatbed with a dead man outside Convention Hall on June 1, 1921.

Tulsa whites gather at the railroad tracks to view the Greenwood
inferno. PHOTO: McFARLIN LIBRARY, UNIVERSITY OF TULSA

The ruins of the Dreamland. PHOTO: TULSA HISTORICAL SOCIETY

The Negro Alamo. Mount Zion Baptist Church in flames after black fighters are finally routed. PHOTO: MCFARLIN LIBRARY, UNIVERSITY OF TULSA

A Greenwood resident views the body of another black victim of the burning.

Women and children under guard in the aftermath.
PHOTO: McFARLIN LIBRARY, UNIVERSITY OF TULSA

A Greenwood resident stands in the rubble where his dreams used to be.
PHOTO: McFARLIN LIBRARY, UNIVERSITY OF TULSA

Death by fire. PHOTO: McFARLIN LIBRARY, UNIVERSITY OF TULSA

Nowhere to go. An old woman ponders her circumstances in the hours
after the burning. PHOTO: BOB HOWER

The procession of Negroes down Main Street on June 1, 1921.

Another Negro arrested as whites look on in the background.
PHOTO: TULSA HISTORICAL SOCIETY

and cheered at the sight of all those Negroes under guard with their hands in the air.

The humiliating march to the detention camps was also a source of amusement for some in the mob, who fired into the dirt near the feet of Negroes deemed to be moving at an unsatisfactory pace. Several times, the bullets ricocheted from the ground and struck prisoners in the leg, which caused the Negroes to collapse into the street, screaming in pain.

Young Bill Williams was forced into one of those processions in mid-morning. The whites marched him and scores of other Negroes back down Greenwood Avenue, as if to make them see the consequences of their revolt, make them watch as the whites raped the spiritual heart of their community.

They passed several bodies lying motionless in the street, Negro women and children among them. Bill noted with some satisfaction that a few of the casualties were white men. At one point as they walked, he saw a black man slip down the back steps of a brick business on Frankfort Avenue, just one block over. Smoke billowed from the building, and Bill assumed that the Negro had tried to fight off the whites until forced out by fire. The man now ran in a panic across an alley toward Greenwood Avenue, but before Bill could warn him, a group of whites spotted the fleeing Negro and shot him on the spot. Bill turned away and looked straight down the street.

Rage had left him by then, had evaporated somehow as the shock of his circumstances settled over him while he waited with the others beneath the oaks. Now, as he walked, he observed the world around him with a curious detachment, careful to keep his hands high and thus avoid a painful prod in the ribs from a white man's gun barrel. His mind wandered to the happy Thursday-night crowds along Greenwood Avenue—to all their customers at the Dreamland and the confectionary. He compared those nights to what he saw on Greenwood Avenue now: white men and women walking in and out of the Stradford Hotel as if they owned the place, one man carrying Mr. Stradford's Victrola, two others a cash register, yet another a chair from the lobby. The scene was the same at Mr. Ferguson's drugstore up the street, and Mrs. Walker's beauty parlor, and J. T. Presley's restaurant.

Then the procession reached the Dreamland. The Negroes marched by just in time for Bill to watch two white men smash rifle butts through the windows on either side of the theater's front door. A half-block farther down, whites swarmed the Williams Building like ants on a lump of sugar. A stool from the confectionery came flying through a window on the first floor. Upstairs, white men busted out the windows of the Williams' family living quarters from the inside.

Of all the terrible things he witnessed that day, what he saw next remained his most vivid memory: a short white man with a dark mustache emerging from the Williams Building wearing his mother's leopard coat. Her matching leopard handbag was strung over his shoulder. A leopard belt dangled from the purse. Other whites whistled at the man. As he marched past with his hands in the air, Bill Williams tried to memorize the white looter's face.

They were marched across the Frisco tracks to First Street, where the procession turned west, through a gauntlet of jeering whites standing in groups on the sidewalks. Whites ordered the Negroes to turn north again at Boulder and walk several final blocks to Convention Hall. Just as they arrived, Bill saw a black man spin in anger as a white poked him with his gun. When the protesting Negro turned, the white shot him in the head at close range, splattering blood against the brick wall of Convention Hall, sending the dead man's hat flying through the air. Standing near the hall, several white women, in bonnets and floor-length dresses, screamed and recoiled in horror, holding handkerchiefs to their mouths as they wept.

Then Bill was marched inside with the others. Thousands of black people sat silently in the artificial light, strewn about on the floors, or slumped in folding chairs that had been set up for the

Catholic school's graduation program the night before. The Negroes wept softly, or visited quietly among themselves. When Bill
saw them, he thought of the excitement on Greenwood Avenue
just the night before—the resolve, the pride. Greenwood Negroes
would not stand idly by while a black boy was lynched in Tulsa.
Now—huddled as they were in the Convention Hall just a few
hours later—Bill saw only their weariness and defeat. The air
inside the hall was thick with the smell of too many frightened,
despairing people too close together.

After a night at the Gurley Hotel, Green E. Smith let himself into
the Dreamland Theater before dawn. With any luck, he would
have the fan installed where Mrs. Williams wanted it by nine
o'clock and be on the first train back home to Muskogee. But
then Smith, a Negro carpenter, heard the whistle from the south
side of the tracks, and gunfire popping in the darkness, and for
the next four hours, he forgot his work to observe the surreal
battle unfold from the theater's second-floor window.

He was amazed by what he saw. In the years before, Smith
had made regular trips to Tulsa to help out Mrs. Williams with
various projects, and every time he came, he found Greenwood
a peaceable, friendly place where white folks were never a bother.
In fact, Smith knew that a couple of white fellows worked for
Loula as projectionists. But now Greenwood looked like the Battle
of Bull Run, with the weapons of the whites flashing in the predawn like lightning bugs and the Negroes' guns responding from
different places along Greenwood Avenue.

Smith had no clue to what had started the fighting. He had
gone to bed early and discounted the shooting he heard overnight
as part of the general Greenwood rowdiness. But then the sun
came up and he watched the war.

Part of him figured that whatever the problem, he should be
out there fighting with the Negroes, too. God knew, there was
plenty for American blacks to be riled up about. But Tulsa wasn't

Smith's home. This wasn't his fight. He had a wife and children back home in Muskogee to think about. So he stayed by the Dreamland's second-floor window and watched.

Which wasn't to say he was neutral. Not by any stretch. His heart certainly sank as the hours passed and he could see the battle turning against the Greenwood folks. The whites inched across the tracks, and airplanes zoomed so low over Greenwood Avenue that Smith was sure one of them would land right there on the pavement. He saw the black people routed, running down the street, falling as they went. Then the whites appeared behind them, walking in groups of twelve and fifteen, knocking on doors and splashing what was probably gasoline on the familiar brick buildings, then setting the buildings ablaze.

Smith was sickened even more as he watched what happened down the block on the corner. He saw a group of white men rush into the Williams Building, and a few minutes later, smoke poured from the windows on all three floors. He prayed that John and Loula and young Bill were no longer inside.

Smith stayed at the Dreamland window until the mob made its way to the theater itself. He saw that many of the men and boys in the mob wore civilian clothes, but also had the badges and ribbons of special deputies pinned to their shirts as they stormed into the Dreamland. He hid behind a door as a group of them climbed to the balcony and set the curtains on fire with their torches.

Clearly, everything the Williams family owned in Tulsa would be destroyed. Smith loved the family and was certainly sad about that. But his own life was Smith's top concern at that moment. He slipped down a back stairway and out into the street, where he surrendered to the first white he saw. Within minutes, he had his hands high in the air, just another Negro prisoner in another procession marching south.

CHAPTER **8**

A SINGLE RUTHLESS ORGANISM

Scholars and journalists attempting to reconstruct the great burning in the decades after it happened bumped up against an almost impenetrable conspiracy of silence among Tulsa whites, one inspired by shame in some cases, in others by the lack of a statute of limitations for murder. In any event, within hours of the catastrophe, the mobsters had disappeared back into the fabric of local life, their atrocious tales to be whispered in the secrecy of the Klan meetings, or bragged about in speakeasies when a mobster was overly drunk, or recounted on deathbeds when the prospect of hell finally compelled the guilty to unburden themselves.

Great remorse indeed plagued some white participants as the years passed. Two members of Tulsa's KKK conceded as much when talking confidentially to a magazine writer in the early 1970s. The wife of another mob member remembered the day, decades after the burning, when she and her husband heard the tragedy briefly mentioned on a local radio station. The woman said that her husband, then an old man who once had spoken obliquely of a day he killed Negroes, rose from his seat on a sofa, took down his hat and coat and disappeared without a word into the cold outside for a solitary walk that lasted the day. He did not speak to his wife for days afterward, seemingly lost in the past.

Others regretted that more Negroes weren't killed, that every last building owned by a black wasn't burned.

"I would do it again," one Tulsa Klansman, speaking confidentially, said a half-century after the event.

And though the worst culprits remained anonymous, there was no shortage of white apologists in generations to come. Most white Tulsans blamed the tragedy on the Negroes, viewing the blacks' attempted defense of Dick Rowland as an unforgivable act

of provocation. To this day, the catastrophe is generally known as
the Tulsa Race Riot, a gross misnomer.

Other whites blamed white ruffians almost exclusively—oil
roughnecks, cab drivers, bootleggers and the like—the lower class
of caucasians who poured from the boardinghouses along First
Street to give their drunken hatreds free rein. But Tulsa hardly
contained enough white rowdies to man an army of ten thousand.
Photographs of the tragedy also showed that many in the white
mob drove the most expensive cars and dressed in clothes beyond
the means of the average roughneck. Women who eagerly observed the fighting wore the finest floor-length fashions and the
most stylish bonnets offered at Lerner's Department Store downtown.

Tulsa authorities, meanwhile, chiefly police commanders and
local officers of the National Guard, later insisted that their only
purpose on the night of May 31 and the morning of June 1 was
to protect white Tulsans from the Negro uprising. While conceding that airplanes were used that morning—six two-seat World
War I trainers had been dispatched from Curtis Field, outside of
Tulsa—leaders insisted that the aircraft were limited to recon-
naissance missions over Greenwood. White newspaper accounts
of the time, based on interviews with Tulsa authorities, reported
that the aircraft were assigned to circle the embattled area to note
the spread of fires and the location of refugees.

Tulsa authorities and civic leaders also denied organizing or
otherwise encouraging the multipronged white attack that began
before dawn and didn't end until the last Negro fighter had been
either captured, killed, or driven north into the countryside, and
the last black family had been driven from its home.

That contention was also contradicted in several ways, among
them the later testimony of Tulsa firefighters, who said they were
forbidden from responding to calls in Greenwood by Tulsa Fire
Chief R. C. Adler, who was no doubt under orders from Tulsa's
highest councils. Firefighters instead were ordered to protect

white-owned homes and businesses located near the Negro district.

A former Tulsa police officer, Van B. Hurley, described a downtown meeting between Tulsa authorities and its top civic leaders at the height of the crisis. There plans were made to dispatch the planes that scores of witnesses later insisted had fired down on Greenwood. Hurley added that the leaders "never put forth any effort at all to prevent [the burning] whatever. [And they] said if they [the blacks] started anything at all, to kill every damn son of a bitch they could find."

Others recalled that uniformed Tulsa police officers not only failed to prevent atrocities, but openly participated themselves. In the days after the burning, the daughter of a Tulsa detective passed out fistfuls of Black Jack chewing gum to her neighborhood friends, bragging that her father had snatched a quantity of it from one of the looted stores in Niggertown.

"I saw men of my own race, sworn officers, on three occasions search Negroes whose hands were up," said Thomas Higgins, a white resident from Wichita, Kansas, who was visiting Tulsa when the catastrophe broke out. "And not finding weapons, [they] extracted what money was found on them. If a Negro protested, he was shot."

A black sheriff's deputy, V. B. Bostic, later testified that a white police officer rousted his wife and himself from their home, poured oil on the floor and set a match to it. Another white policeman was known to have raced home at the height of the attack to change out of his uniform, then hurried back to Greenwood, where he led a group of looters through Negro homes and businesses.

In yet another case, the young bricklayer, Laurel Buck, later testified that he had tried to join the assault on Greenwood early on June 1, but was restrained by a single policeman at the corner of Cincinnati Avenue and Archer Street. As Buck lingered there with several hundred others, he saw two uniformed officers walk up the east side of Cincinnati breaking windows of the Negro buildings with pool cues. Smoke poured from the shattered panes seconds after the officers entered.

Yet an overarching mystery remained eighty years later. Who masterminded the attack that destroyed Greenwood, and who led the impressive mobilization of white Tulsans that preceded it? Who recruited mob members by the hundreds from Tulsa's homes, theaters, cafés, and businesses and so efficiently dispatched them to the most strategic points on the edge of the Negro community? Was it the Klan? The police? Both?

Ultimately, only the participants knew for sure, and they weren't talking. But one thing was certain. The infamous whistle sounded at 5:08 A.M., and when it did, the white mob moved forth as a well-trained army, like a single ruthless organism, its passions harnessed to a terribly efficient result.

The destruction generally went like this: When the last Negro fighters had been vanquished, mob members moved from house to house and business to business, ordering Negroes outside, or blowing the locks from buildings already abandoned. Blacks who resisted were shot, as were men in homes where firearms were discovered. At dozens of places, blacks rushed from burning buildings with their hands in the air and screaming, "Don't shoot! Don't shoot!" The whites then systematically ransacked the residences, ripping telephones from walls and trampling family photos and other belongings that had obvious sentimental value. White women hefting shopping bags sometimes followed the mob into black homes, sifting frantically through closets, bureaus, and trunks to snatch clothing, jewelry, silverware, and curtains. Whites tore into straw-filled mattresses. White men and boys hefted Victrolas, furniture, and pianos from Negro homes, often loading the Negro possessions onto waiting trucks. One was heard to complain as he did that "these damn Negroes have better things than lots of white people do." Black-owned automobiles that could not be driven away were stripped of their tires. An office boy at a Tulsa oil company bragged that day about driving off with a luxury sedan owned by a Negro doctor.

"You're crazy, man," a coworker told him. "That's stealing."

"Well, if I didn't take it, it would have burned up," the office boy replied.

The arson commenced when the looting was done. The mob piled flammables such as bedding and wooden furniture into one room, sprinkled them liberally with kerosene or gasoline and lit the pile with a torch or a match. White-owned rental properties were virtually the only exceptions, and they were bypassed if the owner was present. So the wall of flame moved steadily northward, family pets, chickens, cows, horses, mules, and pigs all perishing in the growing inferno.

The efficiency and thoroughness made it seem like the thousands of mob members spread across Greenwood worked from the pages of the same depraved manual—with an efficiency that could be explained, at least in part, by the plethora of World War I veterans, who employed military tactics against the black enemy at home.

Some historians later suggested that the attack was not at all premeditated, but a spontaneous act born of pent-up hatreds that, once released, have their own predictable methodology, one on common display across world history. It happened again in the Jewish communities of Germany and Poland two decades later, and in the Balkans and Rwanda decades after that.

Thus the Tulsa mob advanced, either under orders or not—terrorizing, killing, stealing, and burning—forging a legacy of atrocity that rivaled the worst of wartime, a legacy difficult to believe if the horror was not so common.

One of the most heinous incidents, ironically, did not take place in Greenwood at all. The blind Negro man had been a fixture on Main Street for years, an old fellow so pathetic that until the burning, even the most racist whites regarded him with sympathy. For the Negro was also missing both of his legs. He inched around on the sidewalks of white downtown on a small wooden platform with wheels, propelling himself with hands cushioned by old catchers' mitts. One of his stumps, longer than the other, dragged along on the pavement as the old black man slid around on his board, singing and selling pencils while sympathetic whites dropped coins into his tin cup.

On the morning of June 1, the old beggar was at his accustomed place on Main Street, apparently unaware of what was transpiring in Greenwood. At about 8:00 A.M., four white men in a new car spotted him and roared up to where he sat on his piece of wood. One of the men was a known bootlegger. That morning, he and his companions rolled the old beggar off his platform and tied a rope around the longer of his two stumps while the old man begged for mercy. Several bystanders did nothing to help him as the mobsters secured the other end of the rope around their car's bumper and the men roared off, speeding down Main Street as the whites in the car howled with delight. The old Negro screamed, his head bouncing off the streetcar rails and the rough cobblestones, and he was never seen in downtown Tulsa again.

So many stories. All of them alike in important ways, but all of them different, too; stories that by and large were too terrible to repeat in polite company. So as the years passed, the particulars of the great burning were pushed into the hidden parts of broken hearts, memories that eventually took on the hazy tint of a dream. People often tried to convince themselves that none of it had really happened, that nothing so terrible could have taken place right there in Tulsa, that people could not hate that much, that it was all just a particularly awful nightmare.

But then an offhand remark made while rocking on a Greenwood porch swing, sipping lemonade with friends on a hot summer night, would cause a terrible story to come bursting out. Then came another, and another, because so many people had them. Porch swings rocked faster and faster as the stories came forth, and there could be no more denial of what had happened.

Old friends, Kinney Booker and George Monroe, had two of those stories.

Kinney was a boy of eight when it happened, huddling with four siblings in the attic of the family's place on Frankfort when the mob came and called their father "nigger" and took him away at the end of a gun.

"Please don't set my home on fire," Kinney's father pleaded.

But the whites ignored him and did just that, causing five children in the attic to choke from the smoke. Kinney and his siblings managed to escape, but bullets were zinging everywhere when they got outside, and flames shot out of the walls of their home, and telephone poles burned and toppled over up and down the street.

"Kinney, is the world on fire?" his younger sister asked as they looked around that morning.

"I don't think so," Kinney replied. "But we are in deep trouble."

A few blocks away on Easton Avenue, young George Monroe and his family were in deep trouble, too. George was only five then, the son of a man who owned a skating rink and a rental house next door to the big place where the family lived. From the window of the rental house, George could touch the handsome brown brick of the Mount Zion Baptist Church, the huge sanctuary the folks had just finished building. When it was done, George enjoyed watching the Negroes in their finest clothes as they came walking past on Sunday mornings and seeing how they parked their cars up and down the gravel street out front on their way to worship.

But then the trouble started downtown on that Tuesday night. The next morning, four white men carried burning torches toward the house. George's father was away someplace, so his mother shooed her children beneath a bed and ran off to hide someplace herself as the whites barged in and set the curtains on fire. One mobster stepped on George's fingers as he walked by the bed, and the boy would have yelled if his older sister hadn't slapped her hand over his mouth. When the men left, George and his siblings scrambled from beneath the bed and escaped with their mother while their house went up in flames.

One of her daughters was mentally retarded, the other daughter so sick with the flu that she could scarcely move. So what was Callie Rogers to do? The white men came up the street shooting, looting and burning, so Callie tucked an extra blanket around her feverish daughter, kissed her hot forehead, prayed that the Lord would be with her, then grabbed the hand of her retarded child and rushed out the door, tears streaming down her face, and headed north with the rest of them.

Mobsters found the sick daughter, moaning in her bed. They put her in a chair, covered her in blankets, then set the chair in the street, where the sick girl watched her house burn down. Red Cross workers found her toward evening, still slumped in the chair in the street, dazed from the fever and the shock of what she had seen.

The first whites hauled Susie Williams' husband off early that morning, marching him down Archer Street with the rest of the men. A second white gang came strutting up the street a few minutes after the first, pushing right past Susie, stomping into her house and setting her curtains on fire. Then they marched right back out and moved to the place next door, like burning homes was a job they did every day.

Susie grabbed a pail of water from a well and managed to extinguish the fire on her curtains . . . at least until one of the whites returned to her place for some reason and found Susie with her pail empty and her curtains no longer burning.

"You come on out here," the man said. "We set this house to burn."

So Susie dropped her bucket and ran outside. The white kept an eye on her until flames were shooting through her roof.

———

The old Negro man was eighty years old and paralyzed. Surely the mobsters could see that. If there was even an ounce of mercy left in their hearts, surely they would spare the fellow and his wife, and their little plank house along the dirt road. But the mobsters came busting through the door, while the old man and his wife sat shivering in shock and terror.

"March, old nigger," one of them said.

"I can't," the old man said. "I'm crippled. But I'll go if you can carry me."

"We ain't carrying no old nigger," the mobster said. "Lady, you come with us."

"But I can't leave him here alone," she said, weeping.

"Like hell you can't," the mobster said, grabbing the old woman by the birdlike arm and hauling her from the house.

Another mobster shot the old man, and within a few seconds, the old couple's home was consumed in flame.

Coach Seymour Williams was a gruff fellow, a World War I veteran who insisted on bending his players to his own fierce will with military-style discipline. But as a result, his football teams at Booker T. Washington High School always won more games than they lost. To think that his illustrious coaching career, spanning a half-century, was nearly snuffed out just as it began.

Seymour was a first-year teacher and coach at Washington High when the burning happened; he and his wife were living in a rented place on Detroit Avenue, where they watched several of the pricier homes nearby torched by the mob. Seymour Williams' pride and temper served him well as a coach, but nearly got him killed that day. Watching the other houses burn, he decided that the whites would not take his home without a fight.

"Come on out of there," one white man called from outside Seymour's house. "We won't bother you if you come now."

Like hell, the coach thought, his .45-caliber pistol loaded and ready. He damn sure knew how to use it, too. Those whites out there might get him eventually, but they would pay a dear price in their own blood.

His wife knew him well enough to know what he was thinking. "Don't you dare take that gun out there," she said.

"I'll do as I damn well please," Seymour replied.

He started toward the front door, pistol in hand, ignoring his wife and several of her hysterical friends who were with her in the house. The women wept, pleaded with him, tugged at his arms. As a last resort, his wife stuck out her leg and tripped her husband. The women pounced like cats when he stumbled to the floor and snatched away his pistol, which Seymour's wife immediately tossed out the back window.

"Where's your gun?" a white asked him when Seymour finally obeyed his wife and walked outside with his hands up.

"Don't have one," he replied, which was the lifesaving truth.

For years, the man named C. R. Gabe had swabbed the floors of the Tulsa Police Department, cleaned the commodes, and emptied the trash baskets. In that way, he had come to know the faces of the officers and the hundreds of others with business in the place, a familiarity that saved his life that morning, not once, but twice.

Gabe had watched in disbelief as two black men were shot down in front of his house. As guns still crackled outside an hour or two later, two white boys and an older white fellow started pounding on his front door. Gabe opened up so they wouldn't kick the door down, and threw up his hands the second he saw them point shotguns at his chest. The eyes of one of the youngsters blazed like a rabid dog's.

"Can we kill him, too! Can we kill him, too!" the boy begged.

"Hold on, son," the older man said. "I think I know this fellow. Where do I know you from, nigger?"

"You might have seen me at the police station," Gabe said. "I wash the floors down there."

"Damned if he's not right," the white man said, smiling in recognition. "Boys, I guess we'll leave this one alone."

Gabe saw the boys' shoulders sag in disappointment. But they weren't finished with him.

"What you got in your pockets, old man?" the wild-eyed boy said. "Let's have a look."

Gabe pulled ten dollars in rumpled bills and a silver quarter from his pockets. The boy laughed as he snatched the money, taking a few steps toward the door before stopping and turning. He flipped the quarter back to Gabe.

"You keep that, old man," he said, howling with glee while heading outside.

Gabe slumped in a chair when they had gone, quivering with fear and anger, until he heard more pounding at his front door a while later. Three more young whites with shotguns stood outside. Gabe recognized one of them, a civilian wearing the badge of a special deputy. The two boys with him wanted to shoot Gabe, too.

"Nah," the man in the badge said. "That's old Gabe. He's all right."

"You better be careful," one of them told Gabe. "We just killed that old porter at First National Bank, and we might just go ahead and kill you."

Instead, they ordered him from his house with his hands up and marched him to the place down the street where several other Negro prisoners had been collected. Gabe watched his house burn from there. A little later, he heard that John Wheeler, the popular porter at the First National Bank, had been shot down that morning by three boys in the mob.

The wealthy Negro woman stayed with her home until the walls and ceilings were all ablaze, then stumbled up the side of Standpipe Hill. She saw that scores of white people had gathered at the top of the hill, hiding behind trees and cars to observe Green-

wood's destruction—men, women, and children, even infants—
many snapping away with their cameras.

The awful panorama below was forever burned into the Negro
woman's memory. Black people scurried around like ants, obviously confused and running in circles. Bodies lay in dark heaps
in the streets. Flames and smoke were everywhere. The constant
noise of gunshots. Fire trucks arrived and hosed down the white
homes on the east side of Detroit Avenue, protecting them from
the shooting cinders. Her home just a few yards away on the west
side of the street, ten glorious rooms plus a basement, disintegrated before her eyes.

The hatred born in her then lived as long as she did. An old
white man in a fancy straw boater and red suspenders came by
as the woman slumped on the hillside, exhausted and too angry
to cry.

"It's awful, ain't it, Auntie?" the old man said to her.

He offered her a dollar so she could buy some dinner.

CHAPTER 9

THE NEGRO ALAMO

God and Satan waged a long and spirited tussle for Greenwood's soul, and what with the prostitutes who tempted from the shacks along First Street and the folks who were dazed on opium and the drunk young men who brawled up and down Greenwood Avenue on Thursday nights, it often seemed that Beelzebub had gained the upper hand.

But the faithful folks in Tulsa's Negro quarter were also up to the fight. In 1913, one particular group of Baptists bought a large vacant lot at the corner of Easton and Elgin, just below Standpipe Hill, with the intention of building a sanctuary so imposing that the devil himself would cower when it was done.

Come to think of it, maybe it was the devil that made their journey so long. Why otherwise would it have taken those Baptists eight full years to build their grand tabernacle, eight years of gathering for Sunday services in a converted dance hall near the church property, or on an empty lot outside when the weather was nice? Eight years of slipping pocket change into the collection plate, or taking ten percent of the profits from the family store, or from the money earned doing a white family's laundry, and adding it to the building fund of what would be called "Mount Zion Baptist Church."

The congregation no doubt would have faltered somewhere along the way had it not been for Pastor R. A. Whitaker. He was their Moses guiding them through the wilderness with his vision of grandeur and his oratorical gift. Lord, that man could preach. Brother Whitaker could stand with his Bible on a street corner in hell to proclaim his vision of Jesus' love on one hand and God's righteous vengeance on the other, and within ten minutes, all the fallen angels would be ready to reenlist in the army of the Almighty. Some Sunday mornings in Greenwood, Pastor Whitaker climbed atop the back of a truck and began his sermon to the curious crowd that was sure to gather. Once Brother Whitaker had them hooked with his words, he'd slyly signal to the driver and the truck would slowly pull away. The glassy-eyed converts followed like they were a bunch of ducks and Brother Whitaker was leading them along with bread crumbs. The next thing those ducks knew, they were inside the converted dance hall, firmly in the clutches of Jesus, and soon after that, adding their ten percent to the Mount Zion building fund.

As the years passed, and the lot at Easton and Elgin continued to sit empty, and the congregation grew frustrated and doubtful, Pastor Whitaker offered them a few more bites of rhetorical manna to keep his flock in step, turning up the volume of his preaching to help them keep faith with the dream of worshiping in the finest Negro sanctuary in all the Southwest.

And so, eventually, it was. In nickels, dimes, and dollars, the Mount Zion congregation saved about forty thousand dollars in seven years, only half of what was needed to complete the sanctuary, but enough to convince white lenders to kick in the rest. So beginning in 1920, the Mount Zion faithful finally watched beautiful red bricks mounted one atop another and marveled at the new bell tower that stretched toward heaven, and rejoiced at how sunlight played through the stained-glass windows imported from someplace in the East.

On the morning of April 10, 1921, new varnish on the pews smelled like heaven itself when 856 Greenwood people crammed into the pews of the Mount Zion Baptist Church, along with the dozens of others who fanned themselves while standing in back because all the seats in the pews were filled. That Sunday morning, the congregation knew the euphoria of Moses' people on their first glimpse of the Promised Land, for the Mount Zion people had wandered nearly as long, and the fruit of their efforts seemed just as sweet.

On that spring morning, Pastor Whitaker's words first echoed from the rafters of the new sanctuary. His people clapped and swayed and raised their hearts and their hands to heaven, and sang Negro spirituals and gospel music that spilled out onto Easton and Elgin every time someone opened the church door. It was rapture, a taste of the Second Coming. Brother Whitaker had been right. Every last penny saved, every last day they had waited, had been worth it in the end.

The great burning happened just six weeks following that glorious moment, only a few days after graduating seniors at Washington High and their families had convened at Mount Zion for a baccalaureate service. In the early morning of June 1, after the trouble downtown, whites massed on Standpipe Hill and formed a skirmish line down the hill to surround the Negroes on the west. Then they mounted a blistering attack from that direction, raining bullets down on Mount Zion, the nearby high school, and all the nice homes of the doctors, lawyers, teachers, and leading Greenwood entrepreneurs. If the dedication of Mount Zion had been a hint of heaven, that morning was surely a taste of hell. White bullets fell on that part of Greenwood like hail.

But the whites couldn't advance down the hill into Greenwood so much as an inch, at least not at first. Many died trying, because Mount Zion's belfry offered an unobstructed line of fire at the enemy. For an hour or more after the battle began, Negro marksmen trained to fight Germans picked off any white hoodlum foolish enough to expose himself trying to move forward.

Someone counted more than fifty Negro fighters inside Mount Zion when the sun rose, several of them up in the bell tower, others stationed with rifles and shotguns firing out windows closer to the ground. The smell of gun smoke had replaced that of new varnish, and the stained-glass windows were shattered in the fusillade and lay around the Negro fighters in large, colorful shards. But the Negroes inside continued to fight ferociously to save the House of God for which they had waited so long. They fought in Mount Zion like the Texas patriots at the Alamo, with a fervor that grew even higher when their most feared warrior dodged the white bullets and slipped through the front door into the besieged sanctuary. O. B. Mann stood inside the church with his rifle, bleeding from a wound in his right hand, but with a murderous look in his pale-green eyes.

It had happened sometime during the battle for Deep Greenwood, though Mann could never remember exactly when. It no doubt was a white's bullet or a shotgun pellet that had caught the little finger of Mann's right hand, causing the blood to come spurting out. But he barely noticed the dull, burning sensation and the wet warmth of the blood as it spilled over his hand, because his mind was fully engaged elsewhere and his adrenaline raced like water in a ditch after a spring thunderstorm. At some point, when the throbbing became too much to ignore, Mann looked down between shots and saw that his finger looked like raw hamburger, but he could fire just fine with his little finger all bloody like that, so fire away he did.

Mann killed several whites during the fight for Deep Greenwood, which satisfied him. It was a fleeting satisfaction under the circumstances, but satisfaction nonetheless. He'd killed German soldiers in the war, but then he was Private Mann under orders from white officers, and he'd had no particular beef with the fighters on the other side. But this enemy had tormented his people for centuries, and now it was launching an assault that rivaled the worst he had seen in France. Only now the attack was against the homes and businesses of the folks who bought their groceries from the Mann Brothers' store on Lansing. He had been born for this moment, all the ancient anger coiled inside, waiting for the time when he could strike back. His own blood was splattered across the starched white shirt he had put on for work the day before. He smeared blood across his face every time he tried to wipe away perspiration, blood that on his milky features looked like war paint. But otherwise, a pinkie turned to hamburger didn't distract him in the least. Mann took aim with the rifle he'd snuck home from the war and fired away even more.

For a few minutes in early morning, Mann also enjoyed the illusion that he and John Williams and the other blacks fighting from the buildings along Greenwood Avenue would actually defeat the whites, or at least turn them back across the tracks. The whites took heavy casualties on their first push before sunrise, when a cloud of Negro bullets greeted them and sent them scurrying in retreat. But Mann's hopeful illusions burned off with the morning sun when he could see that there was no end to the enemy. Kill one white and ten more sprang up in his place. The Negroes also didn't have the luxury of looting a dozen pawnshops and hardware stores. Their bullets had been purchased for hunting, and that ammunition soon ran low.

Then the planes attacked when the sun came up, and the whites began to break into buildings on the west side of Greenwood Avenue from alleys in the rear. When Mann saw them poking around inside Negro property, the rage made him dizzy. He wanted to toss away his rifle and go after those fellows with his bare hands, which he might have done if the boy hadn't come up the stairs, breathless from the excitement and his long run, to say the men needed help at Mount Zion.

Mann was incredulous. They were attacking where?

"At Mount Zion," the boy said. "Hundreds of folks firing down at us from Standpipe."

So they would attack a church, too. Mann squeezed off a few final shots at the whites across Greenwood Avenue and followed the boy down the back stairs, then out the door for the half-mile sprint to Black Tulsa's Alamo.

Young Ruth Sigler had never seen a dead thing until that morning, not even a pet. But she had never witnessed open warfare either, or an assault that approached genocide, or a whole community going up in flames. There were many things the first-grade girl had never seen until then, many things she hoped to never see again.

She was a child of seven, the daughter of a man who'd become rich in oil and real estate before his death a few years earlier. Ruth was therefore raised in the cocoon of privilege, a world of storybooks and new dolls and fancy ribbons for her hair. She was insulated from the coarser aspects of Tulsa life by her mother, by Aunt Jessie and Uncle Ross, and by the nuns at the Catholic school. No wonder that the shock of those days would never leave her system, that it would linger like a persistent virus that plagued her for the next eighty years.

Ruth's mother had been in the hospital for surgery at the time, so on the night before the burning, it was Aunt Jessie who dressed the little girl for the school program at Convention Hall, warning her against soiling her new white dress, which would cost nine dollars to dry-clean if it became dirty. But Auntie forgot about dry-cleaning costs when Father Heiring rushed onto the stage. In fact, it was Ruth's aunt who forced her and her younger brother, Jack, onto the dirty floor of the trolley that was packed with terrified people trying to escape south. The streetcar had been waiting near Convention Hall, which was only a few blocks west of the Negro district, and its windows had already been shot out. Several people cut their hands on the pieces of glass that lay about on the floor.

They rode in silence as the trolley clacked along, until Auntie yelled for the conductor to stop at Eighth Street and Main. Then she grabbed the hands of the children, and she, Ruth, and Jack sprinted for home a block away, where she pulled down the blinds as the priest had instructed members of his flock to do. Instead of putting on the electric lights, Auntie lit a candle to lead Ruth and her brother to their bedrooms, where she told them to remove their shoes but to sleep with their clothes on, though she didn't say why. So Ruth crawled beneath the covers in her once-precious white dress that was now wrinkled and smudged from the trolley floor. Her aunt closed Ruth's bedroom window against the sounds of gunfire and men shouting around the courthouse, which was only four blocks away. Ruth shivered in terror when Auntie left to look in on Jack.

Ruth wondered in later years how she managed to fall asleep that terrible night. But she did. She must have been asleep, because the loud bumping sound outside awakened her at dawn. She had never heard trucks in the neighborhood so early. In the thin morning light and in the shock of what she saw, it took a few seconds before she could comprehend the scene outside her bedroom window. Two slat-sided cattle trucks inched by in succession. Ruth assumed at first that the Negroes were only sleeping on the truck beds, but then she recalled the dire words of Father Heiring, and the sounds of the shooting, and it all began to fit together in her childish mind. It also dawned on her that no person could sleep like that, with people piled on top of one another. The corpses were stacked haphazardly, as if whoever put them on the trucks had been in a hurry. Negro arms and legs bounced through the slats with each bump in the road. A dead woman's legs dangled from the open tailgate of the front truck, and Ruth wondered what kept the woman's body from toppling onto the pavement altogether.

Some of the bodies were naked. Others wore only pants. A few dead women wore colorful kimonos. There were dead children on the trucks, too. Well, at least one. A young Negro boy lay spread-eagled atop the pile of dead Negroes on the second truck. He was barefoot, but otherwise dressed in a neat plaid shirt and dark-colored pants, as if he was getting ready for school when the end came. The truck bumped over another pothole and the boy's arms flounced. The bump in the road also caused his head to roll toward Ruth's window. The dead boy's eyes were wide open and seemed to look straight at her, somehow pleading with her. His mouth was open, too, as if to scream, but no sound came out. By the terrified look on his face, Ruth thought the boy had been scared to death.

Her mind raced and her stomach tumbled. She had overheard

previous conversations between Uncle Ross and Aunt Jessie about how the Klan hated Negroes, so she naturally figured that the Klan had killed that little boy and the rest of those Negroes on the trucks. But the Klan hated Catholics, too, didn't they? Ruth was a Catholic and about the same age as that boy on the truck. Might she someday end up on a pile of dead people?

The trucks were well down the street before she found her voice. "Auntie!" she screamed.

Aunt Jessie rushed into the room and gathered the hysterical child in her arms. She looked out the window to see what had frightened her niece, but by then, the trucks were long gone. Even when she had calmed down, Ruth had difficulty explaining what she had seen, had so much trouble untangling her words, that she began to wonder whether the dead bodies had been there at all. Auntie encouraged her in that regard, patting Ruth's head and dismissing her vision as a particularly bad nightmare. Then she brought the children to the breakfast table, lit another candle, and set steaming bowls of porridge in front of them as if it were any other Wednesday morning. After a few comforting spoonfuls, Ruth had almost convinced herself that despite the dirt on her dress, the whole chain of events had been nothing but a nightmare—Father Heiring on the stage, hiding on the trolley, those bodies on the truck, and the face of that horrified Negro boy. It wasn't possible that such terrible things could happen in Tulsa, Oklahoma.

But then Uncle Ross came bursting in through the front door, holding a folded newspaper, looking like he hadn't slept.

"The *Tulsa World* says an army of blacks are coming from Muskogee and they're gonna burn the whole place down," he told Aunt Jessie, gesturing with the paper.

"My Lord," Auntie said.

"The *World* says those Negroes are gonna start at Central High School and work their way out from there," Uncle Ross said.

"But Ross, that's only a block away," Auntie said. "What will we do?"

"I'll tell you what we won't do," Ross said. "We won't stay here. You and the children get out to the car. We need to get to the country place. My guess is that we'll be safe there."

The four of them, Uncle Ross and Aunt Jessie, Ruth and Jack, rushed outside and climbed into the Ford. Ross fired up the engine and sped off east on Eighth Street. Suddenly he turned north.

"What on earth are you doing?" Aunt Jessie said.

"I want to have a look at what's causing all that smoke," Uncle Jack replied.

"But what about the Negroes coming from Muskogee?" Aunt Jessie asked.

"It couldn't hurt to take a quick look, could it?" Ross said. "My God, I've never seen smoke like that. I'll just take a minute. Then we'll go. I promise."

Auntie sulked in the passenger seat but didn't argue after that. Uncle Ross drove north on Main Street as the wall of black smoke towered above them. Then he turned right on Easton and drove up the backside of Standpipe Hill, which extended into Greenwood like a long, fat finger. He stopped the car and they all sat speechless, struck mute, almost paralyzed by the otherworldly spectacle unfolding around them.

Dozens of other cars were already parked in the grass at the top of the hill. Some of the occupants were spectators, including several women who stood behind the thick trunks of oaks and cottonwoods to look down on what was happening in Greenwood. But there was an army up there, too. Several men in the khaki uniforms of World War I veterans, and other men wearing civilian clothes, lay on their bellies at the crest of the hill, firing with rifles and shotguns into the Negro neighborhoods below. Some of the men had turned their caps backward so the bills wouldn't affect their aim.

Ruth could look down into Greenwood from the backseat of the Ford. She saw the source of the smoke: orange flames flickering from dozens of homes and larger brick business buildings.

Groups of Negroes dashed away from Standpipe through the black haze, many of them adults dragging children along by their arms. Some Negroes fell as they ran and didn't get up. White puffs of smoke billowed repeatedly from the windows of a huge brick church at the bottom of the hill, smoke from the guns of the Negro men who fired back up at the whites.

Then planes roared in from the east, circling over the church. Ruth was afraid that the planes would swoop in their direction and shoot down at them, too, but in a few minutes, the machines circled again and disappeared.

A large brown dog raced up the hill toward their car, yelping in pain from the flames shooting up from its tail, until the man in the car next to them pulled out a pistol and shot the dog in the head. A white hen, its feathers singed black, cackled wildly and died.

Several khaki-clad veterans manned the machine gun that spit bullets from the top of the hill just south of Uncle Ross's Ford. One man aimed and fired toward the Negro church while another fed a string of bullets into the gun, and other men crouched nearby. One of the veterans at the machine gun spotted Ruth and her family, who were still sitting stunned in their car, and broke away from the others, running toward them. He waved a shotgun over his head, screaming to be heard above the noise. Ruth couldn't hear what he said until the man had almost reached their car.

"Dammit to hell!" he yelled. "Get out of here! You're in the range of fire."

Then he dropped his shotgun, and a dark red stain sprouted on the left shoulder of his uniform.

"Oh, my God!" he cried. "Oh, my God!"

He staggered against the Ford, clutching his wound with both hands. He tried to steady himself with a hand against the car, leaving bloody prints near Ruth's window. He bent to retrieve his weapon, but fell over into the dirt. Ruth instinctively leaned out her window to help him and Jessie pulled her back, but not before the man's blood had stained Ruth's white dress, which sickened her. It was a good thing that Uncle Ross had gathered his wits and begun to pull away. Soon they were racing back down the hill, which was the last thing Ruth remembered for a while. The world turned black and she heard a shrill scream that came to her from a long distance.

"Jack, slap her!" Aunt Jessie yelled. "She's hysterical."

The sting of her brother's palm brought Ruth back around, but her stomach immediately began to tumble. As they raced toward the country, she stuck her head out the window and vomited down the side of the Ford.

The standoff made the whites around Mount Zion impatient, and angrier each time one of their own fell dead or wounded. They cheered when the machine gun was moved from the top of the mill on First Street to the place where it was really needed on Standpipe Hill, and before long, the gun rattled away at the snipers in the Mount Zion belfry, splintering the new red bricks of the church. But the Negroes would still not budge. The whites charged the church in a series of frontal assaults that were blunted before any of them could get near Mount Zion's front door. Many whites were killed in the attacks. Inside the church as the battle wore on, Negro casualties numbered seven men killed or wounded.

Then the whites turned to deception.

"Hey, fellas," one man shouted toward the church. "Enough blood's been shed here. Let's talk."

A few whites waved a white sheet, walking slowly toward the front door of the church, apparently unarmed and with their hands in the air. O. B. Mann immediately suspected a trick and kept his rifle trained on the whites as they inched forward. But the Negroes were desperately low on bullets and his comrades figured it wouldn't hurt to listen, so they held their fire until it was too late.

Mann's suspicions had been correct. While the Negroes were

distracted, whites snuck up to the sides of the church with kerosene and torches, and the massive sanctuary was engulfed in flames within minutes. The battle for Mount Zion was effectively over, and with the church went the last great vestige of Greenwood life. The Negro fighters convened in the sanctuary, choking from the smoke, holding handkerchiefs over their mouths while they considered their options. They could stay in the church and burn to death, or join ranks and dash for freedom out the front door and maybe kill a few more whites as they did, which was no choice at all.

The men loaded the bullets that remained. O. B. Mann shouldered one of the wounded Negroes and moved toward Mount Zion's front door with the others who gathered in the thickening smoke. Hell itself could not have been worse than it was inside that church, so forty Negroes went charging out the door, firing as they went. Mann and about thirty others somehow penetrated the white ranks, then raced north along Easton. They fought final losing battles at a place farther north called Sunset Hill and then, about noon, at a Negro store at the northern boundary of Greenwood. After that, Mann and the few surviving fighters fled into the hills.

Ten other Negroes never made it off Mount Zion property. The whites emptied their weapons into the bodies of the fallen blacks, then kicked the corpses when their guns were empty. Smoke poured from the Mount Zion windows, and finally the belfry collapsed as the whites cheered.

The Negro battalions never arrived that morning from Muskogee, or from anyplace else. Neither Central High School nor any other white institution in Tulsa was ever threatened. In fact, classes at the sprawling school went on that morning as scheduled, though a sizable portion of the student body was absent because frightened parents had kept their children home, or because of the number of teenage boys who had joined the white mob.

Not that the school day proceeded with anything approaching

normalcy. A visiting professor from France was livid when in the middle of her lecture on French poetry, her students insisted on rushing to the windows to watch trucks and wagons loaded with dead bodies rumble past. Several boys climbed to the roof of the high school to watch corpses trucked away, or to get a better view of the explosions that erupted periodically in Greenwood, or of the flames that shot up from the Negro buildings. A history teacher named Mrs. Whitham discovered the boys on the roof and insisted they return to their rooms and study for final exams. The students reluctantly complied, then spent most of the morning at the windows anyway. Some of them, particularly the girls, became ill at the sight of the bodies and asked to be excused.

For others, the corpses, and the sound of gunfire that lingered throughout the morning, inspired a different reaction. A large gang of teenage boys decided that they would like to join the action after all, and headed down the corridors toward the front door.

The principal intercepted them on the front steps, ordering them to go home immediately, but the boys ignored him and struck off down the street to the north. Most of the shops along the way were closed. "Closed for Nigger Day," read signs in some of the windows. On the way, the boys encountered dozens of weary whites heading home after the eventful night. One of the men handed the delighted boys a new rifle and pocketfuls of ammunition.

"I've had enough shooting," the man said. "I'm going home and going to bed."

Then he shuffled off and the boys raced happily in the direction of the smoke and the flames.

CHAPTER 10

ARE YOU DR. JACKSON?

She was a beautiful old lady, with the same cream-colored skin as her grandfather, Captain Townsend D. Jackson. That day she wore her thin gray hair pulled neatly behind her head in a bun, and a new dress purchased specially for the occasion. The infirmities of eighty-two years caused Wilhelmina Guess Howell to shuffle to the podium of the crowded Tulsa community center, and the applause had faded by the time she finally arrived at the microphone. But her mind was as sharp that day in 1989 as it had been on her first day of teaching elementary school a half-century before, her recollections as clear and precise as they were terrible. For Wilhelmina's speech in Tulsa that day did not concern the generations of Negro children who had passed through her classroom. Her topic instead was that moment in history when it seemed that the final specks of human decency had disintegrated. Her topic was a dimension of cruelty and hatred that would have been unbelievable if not for people like herself, people who had lived through it, people who could testify about the great burning, down to its last ugly detail.

Until that day in the Greenwood community center, only a handful would have known that Wilhelmina was a survivor of that infamous event, and those people, like her, would have been very old. They were the folks who belonged to the same grim society, a club without dues or meetings, just knowing nods and a shared sadness between people who had seen too much. Wilhelmina Howell, for all her kindness and good cheer in her decades as a teacher, had that look. So did Bill Williams who had grown up to become a beloved high-school teacher; George Monroe, the veteran of the Battle of the Bulge and Tulsa's first black deliveryman for Coca-Cola; the lovely housewife, Eldoris Ector McCondichie;

Coach Seymour Williams; and the gregarious city employee, Robert Fairchild. They all had that look, and they nodded to each other with a special deference, like they were passing a secret signal back and forth. Because whatever else they had become in life—mothers and fathers, grandmothers and grandfathers, lawyers, doctors, merchants, taxi drivers, maids, teachers, coaches, barbers, dentists, street bums—they were also survivors of the great burning. Above all, they were survivors.

As the decades passed, fewer and fewer in Greenwood even knew the club existed, for the burning was not something regularly discussed in black Tulsa. The Negroes who survived were muzzled by fear, by the possibility, however remote, that it could happen again. They were also silenced by shame, by the memory of how their proud community had been so ruthlessly and completely subjugated.

So generations of children passed through Wilhelmina Howell's classroom until her retirement in 1971, most of them, particularly in the later years, completely unaware that the burning had happened at all, much less that their teacher was one of the survivors. Not until after her retirement, not until those days in the 1970s when journalists and historians finally began poking around and asking questions, did Tulsa blacks start to publicly tell their stories, and then Wilhelmina added her own voice to that remarkable testimony—which led to her appearance at the Tulsa community center on October 18, 1989, when she put on her new dress and nervously fixed her hair and shuffled to the podium in the expectant hall.

When she began her talk, the horror of her words was difficult to believe, but everyone knew that Wilhelmina Guess Howell was not the sort to lie or exaggerate. Heaven knows, enough students in her classroom had been disciplined over the years for those same sins. But the audience was thunderstruck just the same, which explained one woman's rather tactless question at the end of Wilhelmina's speech. How had she felt, the woman asked, hiding with her mother and sister beneath the back porch of her family's home while white mobsters ransacked her house and scuffed angrily about on the porch just above her head? Wilhelmina seemed a bit perturbed at first.

"How would you have felt?" she replied. Then she paused. The silence in the room became oppressive, broken only by an occasional cough, until Wilhelmina spoke once again.

"I was only fourteen years old and I was scared," she continued finally. "I have no doubt that's where the word 'horror' comes from."

Many in Wilhelmina's audience were too young to remember the time in America when Negroes were regularly lynched. But there was such a time. That, in fact, was what had started the whole business in the spring of 1921. The whites talked of lynching the boy named Dick Rowland, who supposedly had been messing with a white girl downtown, and Greenwood's blacks, a very proud people, would not stand for it. Wilhelmina's father, the lawyer H. A. Guess, had been one of the Negro men who drove down to the courthouse to confront the whites there, and to make their resolve known. When they had heard the sheriff's assurances of Rowland's safety and had returned to the black quarter, Wihelmina's father spent the rest of the evening along Greenwood Avenue watching the crisis come to a boil. It wasn't until midnight that he returned home.

Despite the late hour, Wilhelmina met him at the door of their home on Elgin Avenue, which was just three blocks south of the Mount Zion Baptist Church and the Booker T. Washington High School, the two most impressive buildings in the black quarter. The night of May 31, 1921, had been alive with the sounds of gunfire and shouting, and filled with dreadful rumors, so Wilhelmina, her sister Bernice, and her mother Minnie Mae, were desperate to hear of the state of things. But H. A. Guess was not forthcoming. He smiled when he walked in, but he looked haggard and pleaded with his family to go off to bed so he could rest also.

"It's been an awfully long day," he said. "I'm sure this thing will blow over some way. Let's try to get some sleep."

So Wilhelmina lay awake in her room, listening to the gunfire most of the night, a noise not uncommon in Greenwood. Sporadic shooting had always been a favorite evening pastime of the young Negroes who were drunk on choc liquor. But in the early morning of June 1, there was nothing sporadic about the noise. A dozen shots seemed to echo every minute outside Wilhelmina's bedroom window, shots fired by the whites against the blacks, or blacks against the whites, or into the air by both sides in displays of anger and resolve.

It was still dark when Wilhelmina's house began to stir the next morning. The gunfire intensified after a sharp whistle sounded from the south. Then, just after daybreak, the Negro snipers in Mount Zion and surrounding buildings and the whites on Stand-pipe Hill began their furious battle. For some reason, H. A. Guess insisted on staying in bed.

"My God, would you listen," his frantic wife said to him. "Most of the neighbors have already gone, and we need to go, too, before it's too late."

"Sweetheart, I was up late," H. A. Guess protested. "Come back to bed for a little while. Then we'll decide what to do."

Just then, a bullet pierced one of their windows.

"Well," he said. "Maybe I'll get up after all."

He slipped on his trousers and pulled a clean white shirt from his closet. He had started to fashion his bow tie when his wife grabbed him by the arm and dragged him from their bedroom, but by the time the family reached the front door, mobs of heavily armed whites marched up the street from the south, going from house to house shouting, "Come out of there, niggers!" Seeing the whites just a few doors away, H. A. Guess shooed his family back inside and hurried them out the back door instead. He shoved his wife and daughters beneath the wooden porch, but there was no room for him, so he dashed to hide inside their backyard chicken coop.

Minnie Mae and the girls soon heard fierce rapping on the glass of their front door, then the sound of the glass breaking as the whites pushed inside. The whites stomped around in the house, then stomped around some more on the back porch just above them when they found the place empty.

"I swear they were here a minute ago," one of the men said.

Wilhelmina nearly fainted with fear. She buried her head in her mother's shoulder while Bernice held close to Minnie Mae on the other side. But the men left as quickly as they had come, ordered away by another white man, whose voice Minnie Mae and the girls soon recognized. It was a friend of their father's, a white fellow who sold ground beef for the chili at Negro restaurants, a man sent by God at just the right time to tell a glorious lie. They heard the meat man tell members of the mob that he owned this house and every other dwelling on the same side of the street.

"I'm looking you in the face," the meat man told them. "I'll prosecute you if you burn my property."

So the mob members grumbled and moved on. Wilhelmina, her mother and her sister silently thanked the Lord for their deliverance, then waited an hour before crawling from beneath the porch, squinting at a world transformed, at the smoke in the sky and the destruction all around. Wilhelmina ran to the chicken coop where her father hid, but found it empty except for a few terrorized hens. Minnie Mae cried when Wilhelmina told her.

Black smoke began to billow from Mount Zion's roof just down the street. Most of the shooting from that direction had ceased. Houses and businesses all around them were also in flames. Minnie Mae and the girls looked for the meat man to ask if he had seen Mr. Guess, but he had disappeared, too. They ran to the front of the house, where they saw whites marching columns of Negro men and boys south down Elgin. Wilhelmina's heart soared when she spotted her father walking in the second group, his hands in the air like the others, but obviously unhurt.

"Mother, look!" she cried, pointing toward the prisoners.

H. A. Guess glanced over and met the eyes of his wife and daughters. He winked and smiled weakly before walking on, prompting a brief celebration between Minnie Mae and the girls. But as they embraced, nearby flames showered them with hot embers, threatening to ignite their home and the few other nearby structures not already consumed.

So they grabbed a hose from their toolshed and a ladder from the garage and quickly dampened their roof and that of Miss Stovall, the teacher who lived next door. The three of them hauled their furniture, family photos, jewelry and other keepsakes from the house just in case the fire caught, and piled it all in the street out front. Then Wilhelmina and Bernice did the same with the possessions of Miss Stovall, who had fled long before. The girls had been working for a long time when Bernice snuck a peek inside Miss Stovall's icebox and discovered the prettiest lemon pie either girl had ever seen. They were reminded by the fierce pangs in their stomachs that in all the terror and confusion, they hadn't eaten that day. So they sat down at the kitchen table as the world outside burned. Between them, the teenage sisters devoured every last bite of Miss Stovall's pie.

Sixty-eight years later, Wilhelmina's audience at the community center laughed when she told the story of the pie. But anguished silence abruptly replaced the laughter when the old lady described what happened next. About nine o'clock that morning, Wilhelmina said, a Negro man dashed up to their house with some very bad news.

"Mrs. Guess, I'm afraid your brother the doctor has been shot," the man said. "I heard they hauled him down to the armory."

Wilhelmina felt dizzy when she heard it. Uncle Andrew? Shot? Just the afternoon before, she had seen the handsome doctor driving in his car with that pooch Teddy sitting in the passenger seat next to him. Uncle Andrew had saved Wilhelmina when she came down with scarlet fever years before. He was her guardian angel after that, an almost spectral presence in her life. Not Uncle Andrew. In the whirl of her thoughts, Wilhelmina almost didn't notice when her mother rushed off with the man who bore the bad news, leaving her daughters behind.

Then a group of veterans came by and ordered Wilhelmina and Bernice to march with the others to McNulty Park. They were reunited with their parents there, and spent the following night in the basement of Holy Family Cathedral, eating sandwiches and drinking coffee that the nuns had made.

At about the same time that Minnie Mae Guess heard the news about her brother, a train carrying 109 members of the Oklahoma National Guard pulled into Frisco Station from Oklahoma City. The soldiers were groggy after the trip and sweating through their mohair uniforms in the morning heat. Many were World War I veterans who had endured such discomfort before, but they had assumed they had left the most apocalyptic visions of war behind them in Europe. So their mouths hung open as the locomotive inched to a stop in the heart of Tulsa on the railroad tracks that had divided white and black fighters just a few hours before. The windows of Frisco Station had been shot out and the exterior walls of the building were pocked by bullets in hundreds of places. But it was the smoke that most reminded the arriving soldiers of the war in Europe, a dense black cloud in the north that transformed a brilliant morning into a premature dusk.

The troops were commanded by Adjutant General Charles Barrett, another war veteran dumbfounded by what he saw when the National Guard arrived in Tulsa.

"In all my experience," Barrett said the next day, "I have never witnessed such scenes as prevailed in this city when I arrived at the height of rioting. Twenty-five thousand whites, armed to the teeth, were ranging in utter and ruthless defiance of every concept of law and righteousness. Motor cars bristling with guns swept through the city, firing at will."

For most of black Tulsa, however, the arrival of Barrett and his troops had come far too late. The Negroes had long been routed from their homes and businesses along Greenwood Avenue, more recently from Mount Zion. Their desperate attempts to fend off the white invaders were essentially at an end, with the exception of brief but deadly firefights at the northern boundary of the Negro community.

If Barrett and his troops had acted promptly when they arrived, they might have saved the homes of Greenwood's leading doctors, lawyers, and businessmen along Detroit Avenue, dwellings that had been spared because the mob mistakenly believed that those substantial residences belonged to whites.

But Barrett and his troops were in no hurry to wade into the inferno. When they piled out of the boxcars, Barrett allowed his men to break ranks and eat breakfast while he consulted with city officials. A civilian who approached one of Barrett's Guardsmen to complain about that indulgence was promptly arrested.

John Oliphant was seventy-three, a prominent retired judge, and before that, a lawyer in Tulsa since the days of Indian Territory, a major local power broker acquainted with every politician and public official worth knowing in the state. He often bragged that he was responsible for Thaddeus Evans's election as Tulsa's mayor the year before, so it was only fitting that he would be notified early on that the National Guard was on its way from the capital. Oliphant was also pleased to hear that General Barrett, another of his cronies, would command the arriving troops. Barrett was a man of action and integrity, Oliphant knew, a fellow who would surely succeed where the Tulsa police and every other responsible authority had failed so miserably that morning. At nine o'clock, the approaching troop train's distant whistle was the old lawyer's first real hope that something resembling order might finally be imposed on the insanity that had swept across his city.

Oliphant had built his spacious home near the top of Standpipe Hill sixteen years before, an Easton Street address with a spectacular view of downtown Tulsa in one direction and the foothills of the Ozarks in the other. He had been living there for years by the time the Negroes began building equally fancy homes on Detroit Avenue just below him, an intrusion that rankled Oliphant at first. But to his surprise, he soon came to find his new neighbors quite agreeable—more so, in fact, than a lot of the whites he knew. They were educated, polished, and to judge by the size of their homes, had a good deal of money—men like the newspaperman Andrew Smitherman; Dr. R. T. Bridgewater; Dr. A. C. Jackson; and the high-school teacher, J. W. Hughes.

Those Negroes were a far cry from those choc-drinking lowlifes of the sort that Tulsa whites most despised, and with everything happening that morning, Oliphant couldn't help but feel sorry for his colored neighbors now. Yet sympathy was hardly his chief concern. Oliphant's house sat virtually next door to Negro property, and if the burning wasn't halted somehow, the morning's strong easterly breeze would ensure that the flames spreading across Greenwood would dance right up to his doorstep.

What a morning it had been, exceptional even by the lawless standards of boomtown Tulsa. Oliphant woke up thinking he had landed in one of those war movies, with soldiers from local units of the National Guard and veterans in khaki uniforms lined up along the crest of Standpipe Hill, just south of his home. They fired east toward the black gunmen holed up in the belfry of Mount Zion Baptist Church, or inside Booker T. Washington High School, or in the homes along Elgin, or inside the big brick grocery store nearby. The Negroes fired back with just as much gusto, some of their bullets landing almost at Oliphant's doorstep.

Just after dawn, as Oliphant observed the battle, one Negro neighbor, the friendly man who ran a grocery store down the way, poked his head out his front door.

"You better get on out of there and give up so you can get some protection," Oliphant yelled at the man, who waved at him and disappeared inside.

The Negro and his family emerged from their home with their hands up a few minutes later, heading toward the white soldiers at the top of the hill. Then Oliphant saw Professor Hughes and his wife, and several other men and their families, come out of their homes on Detroit to surrender, leaving their property at the whim of the white mob still hungry for Negro buildings to destroy.

That was not right, Oliphant knew. What's more, those homes were the last that stood between the spreading inferno and his place. So the old man telephoned the police department, reminding whoever answered the phone that John Oliphant was a very important man in these parts and insisting that officers be sent to his address.

"Send me ten police officers and I will protect all this property and save a million dollars' worth of stuff," Oliphant said. "And do it on the double."

"We'll do the best we can," was the answer he received, but the officers never came.

Oliphant called the fire department next, but was told that the firefighters had orders not to leave the station. So as the sun climbed through the smoke, an angry, frightened old man stood alone in the street to confront, at different times, four different groups of roaming mobsters who hefted jugs of coal oil, gasoline, torches, and guns.

"If you burn those houses, you'll burn me out, too," Oliphant pleaded with them. "I'm Judge Oliphant, and if you leave those houses alone, I'll make damn sure Negroes never live in that row of houses again."

Oliphant wasn't sure he could make good on the promise, but it seemed to satisfy the first few bands, which he managed to stave off until he heard the whistle of Barrett's train. Only then did the old lawyer allow himself a sigh of relief. He scribbled a note and signed it, dispatching a neighbor boy to meet the train and deliver his plea to the general. If Barrett could spare just fifteen troops, Oliphant could protect the last homes on Detroit. But they must hurry, because clearly the appetite of the mob had not yet been sated. Oliphant heard the locomotive hiss when the train pulled into the station to the south, and he kept glancing over his shoulder in that direction. But precious minutes turned into hours and no help came. It was eleven o'clock before Barrett and his well-fed soldiers marched over the hill, bayonets fixed. By then, the homes on Detroit were gone.

Women and children began to appear among the looters around the time the National Guard pulled into town. The fiercest fighting was finished, and Detroit Avenue began to resemble a street festival. Oliphant watched hundreds of jubilant whites empty the Negro homes of pianos, Victrolas, clothing of all kinds, and musical instruments. Many of the larger items were loaded onto trucks and driven away. The women emerged from the houses carrying linens and pillowcases filled with loot. One man sat down at a piano taken from a Negro home and tapped out a happy ditty that set others to singing and dancing in the street.

The actual burning was left to the notorious bootlegger named Cowboy Long and his crew. Oliphant had heard versions of the same statement several times from various bands of mobsters that morning: "Cowboy Long will fix these homes when he gets here." When the man finally appeared, Oliphant was stunned to see a shiny badge pinned to the chest of his dirty denim shirt. Two companions were dressed in civilian clothes and also wore badges. The fourth man with them was a uniformed police officer. This time, none were in the mood for Oliphant's protestations or his promise to keep the Negroes out of the neighborhood.

"We're going to make the destruction complete," one of the men bragged.

They took after Dr. Jackson's house first, barging inside with their torches and canisters of gasoline. Black smoke poured from the doors and broken windows as they emerged to repeat the task in the house next door.

Of course, Dr. Jackson was long gone from his home by then, shot down by those boys two hours before. Oliphant was standing twenty feet away when that had happened, and of all the miserable things he had witnessed that morning, the treatment of the kindly physician was easily the worst. But now, as he watched

Jackson's house burn, and the others with it, he wondered if Jackson wasn't better off dead after all.

Dr. Andrew Jackson noticed that Teddy was gone on another trip between the crowded Negro hospital and the buildings along Archer, where many of that night's Negro dead and wounded had ended up. Out of habit, he reached toward the passenger seat of his Ford to pet Teddy, but the three-legged dog was missing from his familiar place next to him, had vanished sometime in the noise and the chaos while Jackson was tending to the wounded inside the hospital.

Now, in the middle of Greenwood's worst night, as the prominent doctor took a break from his duties, he couldn't get the dog out of his mind. You would have thought he might have other things to think about, what with all the death and misery he had witnessed during the last horrible hours.

Many of Jackson's friends had served as Army surgeons during the War, and he had marveled at their gruesome but exciting tales of their adventures overseas. He often wondered what war must have been really like. Now he felt he knew: wounded men crying for drinks of water and for their mommas, limbs shot off, brains spilling from head wounds, the nauseating smell of burning human flesh, the equally terrible odor of intestines perforated by bullets. But this war was not fought in some distant, exotic land. This was Tulsa, Oklahoma. These dead and wounded were Jackson's friends and neighbors. Yet with all of that, it was Teddy that the surgeon thought about while driving toward his home, that mangy white mongrel he had nursed back to health after it was hit by a boxcar on the Frisco tracks. He wondered if the dog knew how to find his way back to Jackson's home on Detroit. The doctor considered turning around to take one last look for him in Deep Greenwood because there was a lull in the fighting, but he quickly decided against it. Whites were said to be massing for a major attack on Greenwood at dawn. If he wanted to check on his home and get some rest, this might be the only chance he would have.

Teddy would have to fend for himself, a thought that further saddened the weary doctor.

Jackson sped by the Elgin Avenue home of his sister Minnie Mae. The windows were dark, and he assumed that his sister, her husband, and the two girls had fled north with the rest of them. Jackson drove three blocks farther north and decided to park on Elgin, one block east of Detroit, because the whites had formed a battleline on Standpipe Hill, just up from the front of his house. Thank God he'd sent his wife Julia away the night before, Jackson thought. That was one less worry, at least.

Jackson grabbed his black-leather medical bag from the Ford's backseat and set off on the short hike home. He saw the shadowy silhouettes of whites milling atop Standpipe Hill, but was relieved to see that his home was undamaged and a dim light burned in the window of the basement apartment that he and his wife rented to the old fellow named Oliver. The doctor paused and surveyed his block. Dr. Bridgewater's house and most of the others were dark. Bridgewater had spent part of the night with Jackson, tending to the wounded. Most of the other families on the block were already refugees. In the other direction, lights burned in the home of Professor Hughes, which reminded Jackson of the house call he had scheduled there for eight o'clock that same morning. Hughes's wife had been running a fever for days, and Jackson had begun to fear the onset of pneumonia. But on a night when so many had died already, her illness seemed almost trivial.

Jackson knocked lightly on the back door to the basement apartment. Oliver answered in seconds, as if the doctor had been expected, though it was three o'clock in the morning.

"May I stay with you tonight?" Jackson asked. "It isn't a night to be alone."

"Of course, Dr. Jackson," Oliver said, flashing a toothless grin. "It is a good night for company, I agree. I've never seen such a thing."

By candlelight, they spoke about the developments, but not for long because both were exhausted. Oliver blew out the candle and lay down on a pallet on the floor, while Jackson settled into an old rocking chair, and within seconds, both men were sound asleep. But their slumber was brief. Gunfire awakened them less than two hours later, so they sat together until the sun came up, listening to what sounded like a persistent thunderstorm, though the brightening sky was without a cloud.

Jackson knew that the latest outbreak of shooting meant more Negroes wounded, but he was hesitant to leave Oliver and his house. When he finally picked up his bag, it was too late. He could see from the window that white gangs had taken over Elgin below his house in the east, which likely meant that the whites also controlled Detroit Avenue in the other direction. He and Oliver were trapped. Soon the smell of smoke grew more intense.

"Mr. Oliver, I think it's time you and I go on," Jackson said.

"If that's what you say, Dr. Jackson," Oliver consented.

Jackson walked out first and started around his house to the right, with Oliver following several steps behind. Jackson put his hands in the air when he rounded the corner of the house, leaning into the slight incline that led to the street in front, where several white men with rifles were milling about. He recognized one of them, nodding to the old white lawyer Oliphant, who lived just a few doors over on Easton. Oliphant had even sought Jackson's treatment for minor maladies over the years. The others on the street with Oliphant were much younger, just boys, really. There were seven or eight of them in all, a couple of them dressed in khaki uniforms, but most wearing civilian clothes. Jackson quickly glanced around for a uniformed policeman, but found none and figured the boys would have to do.

"Here I am," Jackson said to them. "Take me."

Two of the boys raised their guns.

"Don't shoot him!" Oliphant yelled. "That's Dr. Jackson."

But the boy with the biggest rifle, the one in the white shirt and cap, didn't listen. He fired two shots into Jackson's chest. When the doctor fell, a second boy stood above him and fired another shot into Jackson's leg. Old man Oliver, who had been walking behind, dove behind a telephone pole when the boys turned on him, firing a couple of errant shots in that direction before the other whites grabbed away their guns.

The smoke-blackened sky swirled above Jackson's head as white faces peered down at him.

"Is that true?" asked one of the men in khaki. "Are you Dr. Jackson?"

The voice came to Jackson as if from a long tunnel. He felt himself nod.

"Oh, shit," the soldier said. "Those boys have done it now."

The soldiers hailed a passing car and loaded Jackson into the backseat, where the world went black for him a minute later. He woke up to the faces of his older brother, Townsend, Jr., and Minnie Mae, and his father, the great captain, all of them shiny with tears as they looked down on him. Townsend, Jr. cradled his brother in his arms in the shade of a large oak. Jackson recognized the brick exterior of the National Guard Armory and wondered how he had gotten there. He noted the great commotion all around, trucks roaring past with the bodies of Negroes on the rear, and white men marching back and forth with their rifles. The smoke didn't seem as bad here. Jackson knew that his family tried to speak to him, because their lips moved, but he couldn't quite catch what they were saying. He wondered instead what had become of Teddy.

Dr. Jackson's final journey began a few days later when his family said their tearful good-byes at the Frisco Station and his casket was loaded onto a train. Only his father would accompany the body on that trip west to Guthrie, so Wilhelmina, her sister and parents, Uncle Townsend, and the scores of the doctor's friends and patients watched the train huff off past the towers of downtown Tulsa and disappear into the distance.

Dr. Jackson's relatives later collected his obituaries that had appeared in newspapers across the nation, stories that quoted physicians of both races who paid the slain doctor great tribute.

In the Negro and liberal white press particularly, Jackson's killing, more than any other single death, symbolized the broader atrocity inflicted on Greenwood by Tulsa's whites.

But none of the tributes comforted the old man who glumly watched the hilly prairie roll past his window in the train's passenger car. Once Captain Jackson had held his son up as the embodiment of Negro promise in America, an example of the limitless opportunities for people of his race if they applied themselves with the same fervor and grace exhibited by Andrew. Now, as the elder Jackson sat alone, shame mixed with his grief. How blind he had been. What a fool. The young Negro firebrands in Tulsa and elsewhere across the country had been right all along. Negro progress had been an illusion. Despite appearances, despite the gains of men like Andrew, white hatred burned with as much intensity in 1921 as it had in the years when Andrew's father was still the property of a white master. That was the cruel truth that the short life of Dr. Andrew C. Jackson represented now.

Captain Jackson was sixty-five at the time of the burning. Finally, after all those years of stubborn optimism, came the heartbreak that overwhelmed his resilient hopefulness. As he sat alone in the train, he retraced his journey across the hate-filled nation, from the Civil War Battle of Lookout Mountain when he was just a boy to Tulsa's marauding whites when he was old. Why, he wondered on the train, had he taken the trouble to learn Latin on those nights in Memphis? Why had he and his family fled from Memphis, thinking they could somehow outrun the mob? Why had they bothered to leave Guthrie? The years in Greenwood had been the most illusory, most falsely seductive, of all. Jackson had stood up before its citizens and proclaimed his gospel of self-reliance, and pointed to living examples of it on every street corner, none of those examples more compelling than the one of his own son.

But now he would finally concede that there was no outrunning hatred of the sort that still lived in the hearts of the whites. Men like W. E. B. Du Bois had been right. Perhaps the only solution to hate was hate. Perhaps America's only solution in matters of race was the sword; only now, Captain Jackson, the fearless Negro lawman of yesteryear, was too old to pick one up.

Back in Greenwood, he would eventually rebuild his home and barbershop on Cincinnati Avenue, which had been among the first Negro properties torched in the madness. But his view of the world would never be the same. Once, so long ago, he had put his son on a train headed east to medical school. Now he and Andrew traveled together on one final journey, west to Guthrie, where the old man buried his son in the family plot next to his mother, Sophronia. A lifetime of Townsend Jackson's dreams were buried with him.

CHAPTER 11

SICK FROM WHAT I SEE

Margaret Dickinson's mother was often too ill to care for her youngest child, so from the time Margaret was old enough to walk, the little girl accompanied her father to job sites, or to meetings with Tulsa power brokers, or to any of the other myriad engagements befitting the owner of the young city's most prominent construction firm.

Wilfred Dickinson's company put up the Tulsa Hotel, and the movie theaters, and the Drew Building, and the homes of Tulsa's millionaire oilmen and its most prominent doctors—success beyond the wildest imaginings of the man who came to the United States from Britain around the turn of the century. Margaret's father worked first in Pennsylvania coal towns, then in Kansas, before moving with his wife and two oldest children to Tulsa in 1907, lured like so many others by the miracle of the oil city that had appeared overnight. Margaret was born three years later.

Wilfred Dickinson was a godlike figure to his daughter, a dashing fellow in a bowler hat whose wonderful accent betrayed his British upbringing, which further distinguished him from any other man in town. His hair was brown, and he had a reddish mustache always neatly trimmed, and fair skin that flushed a deep crimson when he was angry, but that was not often. Margaret loved observing the way that Tulsa's most important men treated her father with deference. And she loved the way his workers revered him, the dozens of men—most of them husky Negro carpenters and bricklayers—who tipped their hats to Margaret's father when he approached on the job. In turn, the white owner called each of his workers by name and never failed to inquire about their families. One of the Negroes, in fact, a man named Charlie Mason, was both Wilfred Dickinson's foreman and his best friend. Margaret's father might have been well acquainted with the mayor, the city commissioners, the police commissioner, and Tulsa's business leaders, but when faced with a particularly ticklish concern, it was with Charlie that he consulted. A common memory of Margaret's childhood was seeing her father and the large Negro sequestered to the side of a construction site, carrying on a long and obviously important conversation.

None of that struck her as odd whatsoever, because for some reason, befriending blacks seemed as natural to her father as breathing was, something quite typical of his expansive spirit. Yet, over the years, Margaret came to think frequently about her father's relationship with Charlie Mason, and of his fondness for his black employees. She remembered his great satisfaction in knowing that he made life better for those men and their families. As time passed, she eventually came to understand that those feelings were largely responsible for her father's anguish on June 1, 1921, and in the days that followed. His violet eyes were ablaze beneath the brim of his bowler that day as he and Margaret first surveyed the stricken city, his skin blazing red from his forehead to the collar of his crisp white shirt. Even his mustache seemed to glow.

"Are you mad, Daddy?" Margaret asked him that day as they drove.

"No, I'm just sick from what I see," he said. "Margaret, this is the place hatred can lead."

Wilfred Dickinson had roused his wife and children about midnight the night before. It might have been an exaggeration to say that he looked horrified, but there was certainly distress on her father's face unlike anything Margaret had seen there before. His lawyer, Ernest Cornelius, had come pounding on their back door close to midnight. Cornelius had been working late downtown and thus was present at the courthouse at the outbreak of the violence there. Thinking of Dickinson's family, the lawyer had rushed eleven blocks north to their home on Cheyenne Avenue, which was precariously located just three blocks west of the Negro district. Someone shot Cornelius in the arm from behind a tree as he approached the Dickinsons' door—whether it was a white or a black, he never knew—so he was pale and bleeding when he finally managed to deliver news of the events downtown.

Margaret's father thanked him profusely, called a doctor for the lawyer's wound, and woke his family, hurrying them into the basement while insisting that everyone be silent. They need not ask why, because from the cold of the basement's cement floor where they huddled together in blankets, they listened to the gunshots that sounded like firecrackers, and the sirens that wailed continuously in the dark outside.

It was daybreak when Wilfred climbed the stairs to look around the neighborhood. He returned a few minutes later, convinced that they could return to their beds upstairs because the immediate threat appeared to be over. But sleep was impossible after the night they had spent, and they gathered for an early breakfast instead.

At midday, Margaret's father was informed that the National Guard had finally arrived to patrol the streets and that the governor had declared the city to be under martial law.

Force of habit caused Margaret to follow when her father left the house a few minutes later, and habit that prompted her to climb into the passenger seat of the Dodge. In decades to come, she could never decide whether she regretted going with him then and seeing things that human beings shouldn't. But there was a certain thrill to it, too, a sense of magnitude and excitement that was intensified by the fact that she shared those historic moments with her father.

So that morning they turned south on Main, stopping briefly at a fire station where her father was told about the catastrophe by acquaintances there. As they drove off again, Margaret was mesmerized by a black cloud of smoke so close it made her eyes water. All that smoke, yet so many people on Main Street, hundreds of them, maybe thousands, milling about on a Wednesday afternoon when everyone should have been working or at school.

And she had never seen so many guns. All the men seemed to have one, particularly those piled into the touring cars that raced up and down the street.

Then another strange sight. Margaret wondered why, in the midst of all the ruckus, that Negro man should be sleeping on the Frisco railroad tracks. He was a big fellow, dressed in overalls and a gray shirt with one sleeve ripped away to reveal a thick, brown arm. The men in the two cars just in front of them saw the sleeping Negro, too. They aimed their guns out the window and fired in his direction, and the prone Negro's torso twitched when struck by the bullets. Margaret realized then that the man was already dead. The men in the cars yipped and screamed as they fired at the corpse, then roared away, laughing gleefully.

"Don't look," her father said. "That is not a good sight to see."

But Margaret could not look away. She looked directly at the dead Negro, whose eyes stared imploringly toward the smoky sky. His jaw hung open like he was trying to shout. A terrible thought came to her as she studied him.

"Daddy, is that one of our boys?" she asked.

"No," he said, his face burning red.

They crossed the railroad tracks, passing the edge of the devastated Negro district. There the smoke was white by then because most of the fires were burning themselves out, leaving a dense fog that drifted over the piles of ashes and cement blocks where homes and businesses had been. All the leaves were burned from the trees, whose spindly, dark outlines looked ghostly through the smoke. A few old Negro couples sat on the front steps of places that had burned, or in chairs near the street, staring blankly at Margaret and her father as they idled past.

Margaret's father decided that Standpipe Hill was the best place to begin the search for his workers, and he turned the Dodge in that direction. That was when they saw the old woman, sitting on a low wall that ran along the road at the bottom of the hill. Her hair was gray at the temples, plaited in tight braids that were tied at the back of her head with white string. She wore a tattered robe and some old slippers, and she clutched a toddler to her chest, rocking back and forth, her face shiny with tears and contorted with sorrow. Wilfred parked nearby, stepped from the car and approached the woman tentatively, as if trying to keep from spooking a frightened animal.

"My home's burned," she said without looking at him. "Why'd you folks go and burn my home? I ain't done nothing to you."

"I'm very sorry," Wilfred said. "I'm not one of them. It was a horrible thing to do."

"Lord," the woman said.

"Can I help you with that baby?" he asked.

"This is my grandson," the woman said, her wrinkled face quivering like a person who was chilled. "He's my daughter's boy."

"Where is she now?"

"Lord, if I knew," the woman said. "She ran with the rest of them when the world went to burning. Left me here with this boy."

Margaret's father didn't speak for a long while, just stood over the woman, looking down at her and the baby. His lips were pressed together and he scratched the back of his neck like he did when he was thinking.

"Why don't you come with us?" Wilfred said finally. "That's my daughter in the car. We'll help you."

The old woman didn't resist when he stepped forward, gently taking the baby from her arms. She rose from the wall and shuffled toward the car, a vision of grief with sagging shoulders and tears streaming down her weathered cheeks. Margaret's father followed, carrying the sleeping infant against his chest. As they got close, Margaret saw that the little boy wore nothing but a tiny bathrobe and white diaper, which led her to guess he had been in his crib sleeping when the fires started. Margaret's father opened the car door for the old woman, who bent and slid into the backseat. When she was settled, Wilfred returned the baby to her arms, then got back behind the steering wheel and they inched off down the street in the Dodge.

"Where are we going?" Margaret asked her father.

"We've got to take care of this little baby," he said.

"Are we going to take it home?" she asked, listening to the old woman softly moaning in the backseat.

"No," he said. "We've got to take the baby to be buried."

"Why are we burying the baby?"

She noticed that the anger had drained from her father's face.

"Because the baby is dead," he said.

"Why is the baby dead?" Margaret asked.

"I guess because it breathed in too much smoke," her father replied.

Margaret had never seen a dead thing up close before, so she stole glances over her shoulder at the lifeless little form in the old woman's arms. They pulled into the funeral home's parking lot a minute or two later. Wilfred offered to carry the baby inside and make the arrangements, but the old woman said no, she would do it because it was her grandson. Margaret watched while she carried the dead baby from the car, walking so slowly toward the front door of the funeral home that Margaret worried lest the old woman's last bit of strength fail her and she would collapse right there in the parking lot. Her father appeared to be thinking the same thing, for he followed only a foot or two behind, his hat in his hand, poised to catch her if she faltered. He held the door for her when they reached the front. The old woman's arms were empty when they reappeared a few minutes later, but the tears still streamed down her face as she returned to her spot in the backseat.

Margaret's father drove home. She and the stricken woman sat in the car while her father hurried inside and talked to Margaret's mother. Mrs. Dickinson came out of the house and brought the woman inside, sat her down at the kitchen table and patted her head consolingly. Margaret's mother fixed coffee, a bowl of steaming oatmeal and two scrambled eggs, and set the food down on the kitchen table in front of the grief-stricken visitor. The Dickinson family's Negro maid also knelt to console the old woman, whispering gently into her ear and rubbing the back of her smoky nightclothes. The woman didn't speak, just cried and cried until Margaret's father coaxed her into eating.

"You've got to be strong," he said gently. "You've got to eat."

The old woman nodded, picked up a fork and ate a few bites of the eggs so she wouldn't seem ungrateful. A few minutes later, Margaret's mother and father walked the woman back to the car, one of them on each side, and the three of them drove away. The dead baby's grandmother was not with them when her parents returned.

The two white farmers saw dark shapes appear on the horizon about daybreak, moving slowly toward them out of the huge cloud of smoke to the south.

"What in hell is that?" one said to the other. "A herd of buffalo?"

"I'll be damned," the other said. "That's not buffalo. It's a big ol' bunch of niggers."

There were hundreds of Negroes of every age and description, carrying children or pulling balky mules or horses haltered to ropes. The Negroes seemed to move in a collective trance until they saw the white farmers standing at the fence along the road. Then the refugees snuck fearful, sideways glances at the whites, half expecting them to produce guns and resume the shooting. So the Negroes picked up their pace until they were past. Similarly, every time a car appeared down the road from the south, dozens of blacks disappeared into the nearby woods until the vehicle had gone by. Then they returned to the road and continued their trek to nowhere.

It was the same that morning and afternoon on every road and every set of railroad tracks leaving Tulsa: masses of people moving away from the inferno like characters from some passage in the Book of Exodus. Mostly, they walked in silence, but sometimes they commented on the day's growing heat, or asked for the whereabouts of loved ones. Or they asked this question: "How far had they burned when you left?"

They walked, and carried their children, and herded their animals from Greenwood all the way to the edge of towns like Sapulpa, Owasso, Broken Arrow, and Sperry, places twenty and thirty miles away. Whites in those towns had heard that Negroes had tried to take over Tulsa, and they met the refugees on the outskirts with rifles, but the Negroes rarely crossed the city limits and never caused the slightest disturbance. Instead, they were swallowed up by the hills and wooded hollows, congregating in places like the one called Flatrock, where five hundred refugees built a crude camp along the Delaware Creek.

With every step, they wondered when the whites would come back with their guns and torches and airplanes to finish what they had begun in Tulsa. One little girl, spooked by the sound of nearby gunfire, sprinted from the band of refugees, so fearful that she attempted to ford a fast-flowing creek near Sperry and drowned. A Negro man spent days searching for his two daughters, ages twelve and fourteen, who had rushed into the woods through the back door of an abandoned farmhouse when their hiding place was riddled by the bullets of some roving whites.

Sometimes they encountered kindly whites. Every day for a week after the burning, Merrill Phelps and his wife Ruth hid twenty or more Negroes in the basement of their new home in the country, a day's walk north of Tulsa. The white couple were teachers before they'd been lured to northeast Oklahoma by the higher pay of the oil refineries. Both believed that the Golden Rule applied equally, no matter whether a person was white, black, or purple. So Ruth put on extra pots of beans and sow belly, feeding the Negroes who hid in their basement during the day before they escaped toward the Osage hills under the cover of darkness. Each morning, another group of them appeared at their door, pleading for food and sanctuary, then huddling quietly in the basement to rest and eat their beans and cry and stare blankly into the shadows before setting off to God knows where when the sun went down.

The Negroes didn't talk much about what had happened to

them in Tulsa, and the Phelpses didn't think it polite to pry. The couple had heard about the Negro uprising, of course, but could not imagine what might have inspired such terror and despair in those colored people, at least not until Merrill Phelps and his wife drove into Tulsa to tour the ruins of Greenwood themselves several days later. The horror was self-evident then, and the couple was doubly glad to have offered the smallest comfort to the victims of those depredations.

By the afternoon of June 1, Red Cross volunteers had been dispatched into the countryside surrounding Tulsa to try to end the exodus, pleading with the Negroes they encountered to return to the city, promising that they would be safe there now. One black pastor finally convinced seventy-five members of his congregation to hike back into town, where they were promptly marched to the detention camp at the fairgrounds and treated like criminals or prisoners of war—women, children, and old people placed under the guard of soldiers who often added to their humiliation by taunting them.

Other blacks trickled back in small groups over the next several days. Or they never returned at all. Thousands moved to Chicago, or New York, or San Francisco, or Los Angeles, or smaller towns in Oklahoma and Arkansas, where they tried to put the great burning behind them. But most found that impossible, because Tulsa's disgrace followed them and insisted on ruining their sleep.

Several years earlier, white Tulsa grocer Hugh Gary's wife was too ill to nurse her second child, so the family's Negro mammy assumed the chore. The children never knew her real name and just called her "Mammy," but they came to love her like one of the family. Hugh Gary had to admit he was fond of the woman, too. On the night of May 31, 1921, Gary watched his neighbor get shot through the neck by a Negro. But that most certainly had been done by one of the bad Negroes who had taken over Greenwood that night. Mammy was a good Negro. So Gary went looking for her around noon on June 1 and found her huddled with the others at Convention Hall. He vouched for her with the white authorities that checked Negroes in and out of the place, and drove her to his home on Yorktown Avenue, where Mammy lived for several days because her place had been burned down. Gary's family was delighted to see her, and she them.

But those other uppity, murderous coloreds. They were another story entirely. Hugh Gary was the kind of father determined to make sure that his children knew the wages of sin. A few months before, in fact, when a white outlaw was hung in town, he'd taken his oldest sons, Hubert and Richard, to the funeral home and insisted they look closely at the purplish and yellow bruises the noose had left around the dead criminal's neck. Now the boys needed to get a view of the even higher price those Negroes had paid for their crimes.

So that afternoon, Gary loaded the boys into his Dodge and they set off driving north. The father pointed out the building near Cincinnati Avenue where his neighbor was killed the night before, then turned east on burned-out Archer Street, which had been part of the battle zone. From there, they turned north onto Greenwood Avenue, into the heart of the devastation. Gary drove a block at a time stopping so he and the boys could take it all in, then driving a few more yards before he stopped again. The jaws of the boys hung open and their eyes were like saucers, but Gary could hardly blame them, for the destruction surpassed anything in his own wildest imaginings.

Some walls of the larger brick buildings still stood in places, but the roofs were gone and the interiors were completely gutted. Skinny chimneys rose toward the sky, but the buildings to which they had been attached had disintegrated. Wooden homes were intact here and there, as were almost all of the outhouses, because the mob had not wanted to waste their coal oil and gasoline on those. But most of the homes were piles of smoldering gray ash, with metal bedsteads or stoves or pipes occasionally protruding from the mess. Mules, horses, and cows remained nervously tethered to naked trees, whose leaves had been burned away. Gary and his sons could scarcely breathe because of the white smoke.

At one point when his father had stopped the car, Hubert spotted something in the street and set off after it in his knee-length knickers. As he did, a piece of burning newspaper blew up against his bare leg, causing him to shriek in pain. Hubert would carry the scar from that substantial burn for the rest of his life. But his father was too caught up in the devastation to fret overly about his son's injury. The boy was still sniffling when they set off again, turning west toward Standpipe Hill to obtain a panoramic view of the destruction.

They drove to Convention Hall after that. Hugh Gary stopped and nodded toward several of the men who marched around with their guns. Blacks sat morosely on the beds of trucks that rumbled back and forth. Another group of Negroes was marched into Convention Hall every few minutes.

Hugh Gary had been visiting with one fellow for quite a while, then shook hands with the man and hurried the boys back toward the car. They sped south on Lewis Avenue, on the east side of town, until the pavement ended at Cedar Bluff Dairy. From then on, it was a rough dirt road that curved through the hills outside of town. After a few bumpy miles, they spotted the flatbed truck with the hard rubber tires, laboring back and forth to get close to the edge of a deep gully. Hugh parked his car nearby so he and the boys could get out and watch.

The boys were pleased to be away from the smoke, in the country where they could finally breathe. A stiff breeze blew, and a hot sun bore down on them, and birds chirped in the quiet. But it took only a few seconds for their attention to be riveted on the large truck. The bodies of about twenty-five dead Negroes were stacked like cordwood on the bed, arms and legs and heads dangling from the sides between two-by-fours stuck in the slats. Two men unloaded the dead Negroes, one of the whites grabbing a body by the arms or neck or hair, the other white taking the legs so they could swing the bodies off the truck and down into the gully, the corpses tumbling down the steep incline like rag dolls. When they had tossed three or four bodies to the bottom of the gully, another man went to work with a burro harnessed to a huge scoop shovel. But the soil was rocky, making his chore difficult. Before he could load a full scoop, the shovel would catch on a stone and turn over, disgorging the dirt before he could get it over the bodies. The man with the donkey swore each time that happened, whipping the animal even harder, causing Hugh Gary to chuckle at his predicament.

"It'll take a week to get them buried at this rate," he said. But humor aside, he was not about to let the boys miss the lesson. "This is the wages of sin," he told them as they watched the bodies being swung off the truck. "These niggers did something mighty wrong, so they deserve what they got."

They returned to the car after a few minutes and drove back to town. Hubert and Richard were particularly obedient for a long time after that.

The Stanley–McCune Funeral Home provided S. M. Jackson with a place to sleep because the white funeral parlor was swamped with bodies after the burning, both black and white corpses, but particularly Negroes. The white funeral directors thought it best that the blacks be embalmed by one of their own, so they offered Jackson twelve dollars and fifty cents a body to accomplish the task. That was half of what white undertakers were paid, but Jackson figured he was lucky to get it, the way things were in Tulsa at the time. His own funeral home was in ruins, after all, and he had no other place to lay his head.

The white mob had torched Jackson's funeral parlor at 600 Archer Street, also incinerating the four bodies he had been preparing for burial before the burning broke out, a fact that galled Jackson as much as anything. What a day it had been—watching the whites pour over the tracks with their guns; firing up at the planes as they roared over Greenwood; the old woman shot in the arm by the snipers in the mill as Jackson tried to pull her to safety; then finally the crowd of Negroes at Convention Hall, where everyone sat around like they had seen ghosts. Maybe it was easier for Jackson than most to stomach the horror because he was used to seeing dead people.

The white funeral owners had somehow found Jackson that afternoon in the mass of folks at Convention Hall and requested his help with the bodies. They first sent him on a truck with a bunch of white men to pick up the dead people all over Greenwood. They had a good truckload of corpses, more than twenty in all, by the time they got to McNulty Park to load up the Negroes who had died there. As they walked through the camp, a Negro woman fainted into the dirt.

"Take care of that nigger wench and get her back on her feet," shouted an angry white who wore some kind of uniform.

Jackson bent over the woman and was able to revive her by patting her face. Soon she was sitting up, and he was relieved that they would not have to load her onto the truck with the others.

They returned to the funeral home toward evening, and Jackson got to work, embalming twenty-six black bodies over the next few days, though he knew that was just a fraction of the number of Negroes who had been killed. A good number of the blacks were burned beyond recognition and therefore did not need embalming, and there were dozens of other bodies besides that. Some folks talked about seeing sixty bodies laid out on a sandbar in the Arkansas River. Others said they saw many others just dumped into the river itself. Or they ended up in common graves out in the country, where they couldn't be found. The only bodies that really needed embalming were those that came with an upstanding family seeing to them. For every one of those, Jackson figured there were five others that just disappeared.

Jackson was grateful that he knew only two of the people he worked on that week. One was the Negro fellow named Mr. Howard. The other was Dr. Andrew C. Jackson, the kindly physician who lived up on Detroit Avenue. S. M. Jackson, who was no relation to the doctor, had heard talk that Dr. Jackson had been shot down in front of his home, but he was nonetheless surprised and saddened to see the handsome young surgeon's body lying before him on the slab in the mortuary. Mr. Stanley, one of the establishment's owners, had known Dr. Jackson, too, and liked him quite well, and thus took a special interest in the doctor's arrangements.

"You reckon you could embalm him?" Stanley asked S. M. Jackson. There was some question about the case because the doctor's body was punctured by buckshot from one end to the other.

"Yeah," S. M. Jackson said. "I can do that."

When the Negro undertaker had completed Dr. Jackson's embalming, Stanley seemed quite pleased.

"I wouldn't want it any better, Jackson," Stanley said of the work done on the doctor's body. "He doesn't leak and he doesn't spoil. I wouldn't want it any better myself."

Margaret Dickinson and her father set out again later that afternoon, this time to survey the situation downtown. The two of them walked hand in hand up the street, eavesdropping on desperate conversations among restaurant owners and shopkeepers and hoteliers who, all of a sudden, had no Negroes to cook for them, or wash their dishes, or stock their shelves, or fix up their beds in the hotels. It was the greatest labor crisis in white Tulsa history because all of the Negroes were dead, wounded, burned, locked up in detention camps, or wandering around in the countryside like lost cattle. It was said that many white women in town had to cook their first meals in years and suffered the great indignity of having to hang their own laundry.

Near the courthouse on Boulder, Margaret and her father met the skinny, nervous-looking man with round glasses and a pointy nose. From previous meetings with his father, Margaret knew the man to be Mayor Thaddeus Evans. The two men gravely shook hands.

"We've got all these Negroes rounded up in McNulty Park, but we can't keep them there," the mayor said. "Some of them are sick, and some of them are hurt, and I don't know what in the world we will do when it rains. So we've got to get them out of there."

"That's true," Margaret's father said.

"I've seen a lot of your men in there," the mayor said. "I'll call you when I'm ready, and I'll release them all to you if you'll vouch for them. We're not letting any of those coloreds out unless a white will give the okay. We don't want them to get back to their old tricks."

"You let me know," Margaret's father said.

They shook hands again and Evans rushed off down the street. Sure enough, the mayor's call came shortly after Margaret and her father returned home. Wilfred Dickinson left by himself a few minutes later, saying he was heading for McNulty Park. The Dodge lumbered back up the street a few hours after that, weighted down with Negro workers and their families. Charlie Mason drove one of the two Dickinson Company trucks that followed the car, each of them also loaded with homeless Negroes. At the rear of the strange procession came a horse and wagon, usually used by her father's workers to haul bricks. But now the wagon was full of people. When the trucks and the wagon pulled up, the men hopped down from the beds, assisting their wives and the elderly to the ground. Children were handed down to their fathers.

Margaret's father glanced around at the neighboring houses, where people glared from their front doors or windows at the dozens of Negroes who had congregated in front of the Dickinson place. So Wilfred Dickinson quickly herded them inside. Some of the men recognized Margaret, tipping their hats to her and smiling sadly. Margaret's mother held the door for them as the Negroes made their way, jostling for places to sit on the floor of the basement, or in the garage, or in an apartment behind the house. Small children scrambled about the knees of women who moaned and wept. Some of the men cried, too. Some looked angry. Others ashamed. But all looked so weary. A few winced from burns or from minor gunshot wounds that hadn't been treated, so Margaret's father summoned a doctor, who spent hours in the house attending to their various injuries.

For much of the next week, Margaret's mother and the Dickinson family maid cooked around the clock. Margaret, her older siblings, and Wilfred Dickinson himself, carried tubs of food to the Negroes from morning until night—fried chicken, mashed potatoes, soups, stews, meat sandwiches, oranges and apples, lemonade, cookies for the children, cakes. When the people were fed, Margaret watched her father move from family to family, visiting with the Negroes, quietly commiserating with them. At other times, Margaret saw her father sitting alone behind the desk in his study, staring out the window with puffy sacks beneath his eyes.

The Negro children became Margaret's playmates. So she was sad when her father began loading families into the Dodge. He said that the Red Cross was erecting tents in Greenwood where the homes had been, which was where the Negroes would have to live for the time being. Margaret's father drove them to their new homes, promising to do what he could to get them back on their feet, but many were reluctant to leave. Margaret always remembered one of the men in particular.

"Don't send us back, Mr. Dickinson, sir," the Negro man said to her father. The man had tears streaming down his face. "My wife, she's afraid to go on back to Greenwood. At least we're safe here."

Wilfred Dickinson looked ready to cry himself.

"I'm sorry," Margaret's father told him. "There aren't any beds. There's no room. There's hardly anything for you here."

"Yes, sir, Mr. Dickinson," the man said. "Whatever you say. We thank you kindly for what you and your family have done."

Then the man herded his family toward the Dodge. He sat in the front passenger seat and took a young son onto his lap. As they drove off down the street, Margaret saw the little boy poke his hand out the window and wave.

CHAPTER 12

ASSIGNMENT OF A LIFETIME

Faith Heironymous never cared for baseball, so in her short time in Tulsa, she had never actually attended a game at McNulty Park. But she frequently walked or rode her bicycle past the stadium at Tenth Street and Elgin Avenue, and when she did, she was always pleased by the well-tended patch of green in the heart of the city; by the sight of eager young men in their baggy gray uniforms dotting the playing field, pounding their gloves and chattering expectantly; by the low hum of the crowds in the grandstand; by the smell of popcorn and cooking onions.

Which is probably why the sight of McNulty Park on that hot afternoon stunned her as it did, a contrast that amazed her to the point that the young newspaper reporter gawked at the scene for several minutes before remembering to take the pencil and notepad from her purse and start writing down some notes. The shouts of the National Guard soldiers were what finally jolted her back to her senses.

"Get back!" the soldiers shouted to the white curiosity-seekers crowded along the ballpark's outer fence like patrons at a popular zoo. "Please get back!"

The whites dutifully retreated because the soldiers carried drawn pistols and had bayonets attached to their rifles. Another group of Negroes arrived just then on the back of a truck, guarded by armed white civilians, and shuffled into the park with their hands above their heads as the white crowd parted to let them through. And Faith Heironymous finally went to work.

This was her big chance, after all. Tragedy translated into opportunity for young reporters like her—the greater the heartbreak, the greater the occasion for journalistic glory. So she had scarcely believed her good fortune when she reported for work at the *Tulsa World* on the morning of June 1, 1921. Coverage of the previous night's chaos downtown, and of the momentous battles and burnings in Greenwood that followed, had been reserved for the male reporters at the city's largest newspaper. But now the fighting was over, Greenwood was completely burned out, and the paper needed a front-page piece to tug at the heartstrings, a story to support the outrage of *World* publisher Eugene Lorton, whose editorial for June 2 would compare Tulsa's marauding whites with the German soldiers in Belgium.

"Members of the superior race," Lorton wrote of the burning, "boastful of the fact, permitted themselves to degenerate into murderers and vandals; permitted themselves to deal their home community the foulest blow it has ever received in history."

So the editors looked around the newsroom and picked Faith Heironymous. If anyone could capture the pathos of the moment, it was Faith. She was a woman, after all, thus sure to be more susceptible to the plight of thousands of homeless Negroes. She was also openly ambitious, primed for such an assignment, a woman in her late twenties who had come to Tulsa from the small paper in Enid, Oklahoma, the year before, desperate for the grittier journalistic challenges the larger city could provide. In the time since she'd been hired, Faith had demonstrated a nice knack for turning phrases, but her reporting had been limited for the most part to society news. That was about to change.

The city editor called Faith into his office late in the morning for a brief pep talk, said something about seizing the moment, about her story being part of history, about the necessity of capturing the small details that would make her writing come alive. Her heart pounded with a combination of anxiety and excitement as she rushed out of the newsroom. On the short streetcar ride south, Faith checked her purse three times to make sure she had sharpened her pencils, promising herself that she would do as her editor instructed—seize the moment, make her journalistic name. To think that she might never have to cover another debutante ball again. But then she jumped off the car a block from the ballpark and her resolve disappeared the minute McNulty Park came into focus, her youthful ambition melting away in an otherworldly sea of human misery.

Someone counted more than four thousand Negroes at McNulty Park that afternoon, three times more than had been interned at Convention Hall. Instead of eager young whites in baggy baseball uniforms that Faith had seen so many times before, thousands of Negro men and boys huddled in small groups on the diamond— one cluster on the pitcher's mound, another around second base, another in the dirt around home plate. Some wore white shirts and bow ties and expensive hats, suit coats thrown over their shoulders. Others wore baggy overalls over denim shirts or stood without shirts or shoes, their dark skin glistening with sweat on an afternoon when the sun bore down through remnants of the smoke, boosting the afternoon temperature into the humid mid-nineties. Others lay dozing in the soft grass of the outfield. Women filled the shaded grandstand, sweating like the men, fanning themselves with straw hats, weeping, staring, trying to placate howling infants and confused toddlers, sliding over to make space on the wooden bleachers for refugees arriving on the latest trucks. Young children clutching tattered dolls wandered through the throng, wailing and calling loudly for mommas and papas they had not seen since the white onslaught began at daybreak.

White soldiers and Red Cross volunteers worked frantically, facing a challenge comparable to that of Jesus on the day of loaves and fishes. They hauled tub after tub of ice, water, lemonade, and coffee from trucks parked outside the gates, and vats of soup, and boxes of cheese, crackers, and sandwiches that were rushed to the front of the food line that stretched from the backstop behind home plate to the foul pole in the right-field corner.

Faith wandered through the mass of Negroes, trying to get her bearings, jotting down observations here and there, but eventually she felt embarrassed by her pencil and notepad. She wanted to reach out to the refugees herself, to help as the Red Cross volunteers were helping, at the same time feeling constrained by the necessity of journalistic detachment, the words of her city editor ringing in her head. Yet how could any person, ambitious young reporter or not, remain the least bit indifferent in such a place? The last of her emotional remove finally dissolved at the sight of one old woman seated on the steps of the dugout, a gray handkerchief tied around her weathered face. In her hand she held a ration of hot vegetable soup that was being doled out by the Red Cross, but the soup was ignored as she stared blankly toward the remaining wisps of white smoke in the sky, as if waiting for a message to appear there.

Faith couldn't help herself. She sat down on the step next to the woman.

"Sister, why don't you eat your soup?" she asked softly.

The old woman turned her attention from the sky and looked at Faith. Single tears trickled out from each hooded eyelid and slid down the old Negro woman's face, tracing a crooked path through the dust on her skin.

"Oh, Lordy," she moaned, rocking back and forth. "Me an old woman who's worked so hard all her life, now everything gone. My house burned, my chairs burned, my chickens burned, my carrots and onions burned. Nothing I have but the clothes on my back. Oh, Lordy. That I should live to see such trouble come to me."

A beautiful young woman stood nearby, and when she heard that lament, added one of her own, something about she and her husband saving for years to buy their place in Greenwood, and now it was gone, too, with everything else they owned but these rags they wore. Just then, her husband approached through the crowd, carrying half a loaf of bread.

"Here's some bread, honey," he said. "Can't you eat it?"

The young woman angrily turned her back on him and crossed her arms in front of her chest, as if she blamed her husband for their predicament.

"Eat?" she asked. "And us paupers? I can't eat!"

Faith rose from the side of the old woman, fighting the urge to drop her notepad and run, ashamed of having intruded on such despair. She felt dizzy as she walked away, but there was no escaping the evidence of the great evil that had descended upon Tulsa, a misery that closed in around her, swallowed her up, made her breathing difficult. A few yards down the grandstand, a Negro woman in a clean white maid's uniform sat reading a Bible to a group of young children. The woman was one of the lucky ones— she lived in servants' quarters with the whites on the south side— so she had come to McNulty Park to tend to the children of her burned-out friends and relatives. Next to her, a light-skinned woman cuddled a beautiful mulatto baby to her chest. The baby cooed and gurgled and happily kicked its little bare feet. The mother looked up at Faith and smiled.

"He don't know what this is all about," the woman said. "My husband and I left before daylight and we don't know whether our home is standing yet or not. It doesn't seem possible that this thing is happening in Tulsa, does it, sister?"

"No," Faith said. "It doesn't."

Faith walked on for a few yards, then stopped to lean on the fence at the end of the grandstand. She noticed a group of shirtless Negro teenage boys throwing a football around on the outfield grass. With every passing minute, more whites drove up in limousines and long sedans, the men wearing crisp straw boaters and business suits, the women fine dresses and sunbonnets. They rushed from their cars into the park and began calling desperately at the top of their longs.

"Annie, are you here? Annie?"

Or—

"Luella? Where are you, Luella?"

Or—

"Aunt Lizzie? It's me, Mrs. Thomas."

Every so often, Negroes answered the summons, and the whites rushed to embrace them, and after the happy reunion, walked the baffled-looking blacks to a table near the entrance where some soldiers sat. There the whites signed papers promising to look after the refugees and to keep them out of trouble, then dragged them from the stadium as if worried the authorities would change their mind and insist that their Negroes stay behind at McNulty Park with the others.

Sometime in mid-afternoon, the soldier pointed at Bill Williams where the boy sat on a folding chair at Convention Hall and said, "Young fella, you follow me." Bill first thought he would be taken outside and shot as punishment for helping his father defend Greenwood. His heart thundered as he finished a bite of cheese and crackers the Red Cross had been distributing, rose from the chair and followed the soldier through the defeated multitude that filled the hall. But the friendly demeanor of the soldier, a young man with bright red hair and freckles, put him at ease.

"Looks like you could use some fresh air," the soldier said to Bill, which was certainly true, because the heat in the hall had grown more oppressive as the day wore on.

They passed through the front door and into the commotion outside, then walked toward a truck loaded with Negro men and boys; a few white men stood among them, holding shotguns. "Hop on, young fella," the soldier said, smiling cheerfully. "You're gonna get to play some ball."

So Bill climbed onto the back of the truck, squeezing in next to the rest of the Negroes, and in a few minutes, the truck rumbled off down Boulder Avenue to the south, back through the sea of white faces that still lined the road. A man slumped next to Bill on the truck looked vaguely familiar, probably from nights at the confectionary. He seemed to recognize Bill, too.

"Guess there wasn't no lynchin' after all," the man said.

"I wouldn't know," Bill said.

"Nope," he said. "No lynchin' at all. Some deputies snuck that Rowland boy out of jail and drove him outta town about eight this mornin'. That's what I heard. So all this for nuthin'. That's a shame, isn't it?"

"I guess it is," Bill said.

The truck pulled up to the front gate of a baseball stadium, and the whites ordered the Negroes off and marched them inside the fence. If anything, Bill saw more colored folks here than he did at the hall. Negroes filled the grandstand and milled about everywhere on the field, forming a long line for food and water. Bill wandered over to the outfield and sat down by himself, leaning on the fence, closing his eyes against the glare of the hot sun.

"Well, look who's here," said a familiar voice, laughing. "It's Bill Williams, the rich boy himself."

Bill opened his eyes to see a classmate named Archie standing shirtless above him with a grin on his face, juggling a football from hand to hand. "Guess we got plenty of time to throw the ball around some?"

"Don't really feel like playin' right now," Bill said.

"Well, suit yourself," Archie said. "But you know what coach says about practice."

In a few minutes, Archie had found two other boys to play with him, yelling and throwing the ball back and forth between them while stepping around the Negroes lying on the outfield grass. Bill watched them for a few minutes, then closed his eyes again, thinking of his mother and father and Posey, wondering where they had gone, or if they were still alive at all. A giant sob built in his chest and he swallowed hard several times to force it back, then opened his eyes to watch the boys throw the football, trying to put his mind on other things.

He sat there until evening, when he saw a familiar white face come heading toward him across the field.

"Come on, Mr. Bill," said Henry Sowders, the Dreamland projectionist. "Let's get you out of here."

Bill followed Henry through the crowd to a table by the front gate, where Henry signed papers handed him by some soldiers. The soldiers gave Bill a piece of green paper and told him to keep it with him at all times, because if he didn't, he would end up right back here with the others. Then Bill followed Henry out through the front gate.

"Those boys stole my car outside the Dreamland last night, Mr. Bill," Henry said. "You up to walking a spell?"

They walked to Henry's house. On the way, the projectionist said there had been no word about Bill's parents. That night, Bill put on clean clothes belonging to Henry, and Henry's wife fed him dinner and breakfast the next morning. Then Bill thanked the couple and walked back downtown, where he took a job washing dishes during the lunch rush because his pockets were empty. He was paid two dollars for the chore, and he left the restaurant without knowing what to do next. He decided he would try to walk to Greenwood, thinking he might find his parents there. Just then, as he turned the corner on Main Street, he almost bumped into his mother, who was on her way to the office of her white lawyer, hoping the attorney could help her find Bill. The sobs the boy had stifled for two days could be denied no longer. Loula Williams swept her son into her arms and he buried his head on her shoulder and cried loudly, white people averting their eyes as they stepped around them on the sidewalk. Loula Williams wept, too, patting her son's head, telling him that both his father and Posey were safe, staying with some relatives in one of the houses that hadn't burned. The theater and the confectionary were gone, true enough, but they were all alive, and wasn't that the important thing, after all?

O. W. Gurley knew the Negroes watched him, the pitiful old man with a bandage on his hand, a torn and bloody white shirt with silver cufflinks, fancy trousers with a hole in the knee. He was the richest man in Greenwood. For years, Gurley had cultivated that image. But the rain falls on the rich and poor alike, doesn't it. What good did Gurley's riches do him now? That's what those people thought when they watched him stumble from the medical area at McNulty Park, where doctors had patched up his hand. That's what the Negroes thought as they watched Gurley wander aimlessly across the ballpark, keeping his eyes to the ground. The mighty had fallen that day. Just like everyone else.

Then, in front of the grandstand, he heard that glorious noise. "My Lord, it's Gurley!"

It was his wife's voice. Gurley squinted against the shadows of the grandstand, and in a second he made out Emma, hurrying down the bleachers in his direction. She was alive after all, and right this moment, rushing through a gate onto the field and into her husband's arms. She had fainted that morning on Archer Street. That's all. There wasn't a mark on her, thank the Lord.

"Gurley, what did they do to your hand?" Emma asked him after they had embraced for a long time.

"It's just a scratch," he said.

For a long while, Faith Heironymous was lost in the ocean of faces at McNulty Park, seeing all of them, but seeing none of them. Then the intensity of a slender black woman in a white dress that was soiled with dirt and ash snapped Faith from her stupor. The woman stood near the gate leading into the grandstand, turning her head from side to side, desperately scanning the imprisoned throng. Faith observed her from a distance, then was drawn in the woman's direction, fumbling for words along the way.

"Excuse me," Faith said. "Did you lose something?"

She regretted the question the second the words left her mouth, knowing how ridiculous it sounded under the circumstances.

"Lose something?" the woman asked, turning to look at Faith fiercely. "You ask me if I lost something? I done lost my home. I done lost my clothes excepting these here on my back. And my shoes is burned." The woman held up one charred shoe as proof. "And I ain't seen my husband since we left this morning with our house a-burning."

The woman's anger gave way to weeping, then to a loud wail. She dropped the charred shoe and wrung her hands. "It seems to me," she said between sobs, "that nothing would matter no more if I could just see my husband."

Faith approached and touched her shoulder. "Is there anything I can do?" she asked.

The woman suddenly stopped weeping and looked at Faith. "There is if you can find my husband," she said. "Figure you can do that, young miss? Of course there's nothing you can do. Get away from me, if you please."

Faith backed away as the woman buried her head in her hands and again began to sob. Faith felt ill then, dizzy, her stomach tumbling. She thought she might vomit as she stepped over and through the dark bodies that were standing and lying and sitting on the ballpark grass. She grabbed the fence at the edge of the field to steady herself, then staggered toward the gate where she might escape from the misery and breathe again. A tiny old Negro lady sat on a cot just before the exit. She smiled as the reporter neared.

"Darlin', you look pale as a clean sheet," the old woman said. "Come sit here a spell."

She slid over, making room for Faith on the cot. Faith was baffled by the act of kindness, but in her condition, she had no choice but to sit.

"Take some of this," the old woman said, offering a tin cup half full of cold water.

Faith took a small sip and handed the cup back.

"Thank you," she said. "That's better."

"Surely, darlin'," the old woman said. "That sun getting to you?"

"No, ma'am," Faith said. "Not the sun."

"What then?"

"All this, I guess," Faith said, looking out at the ballpark. "All these poor people."

"It is a vision, ain't it, child?" the old woman agreed.

"I don't know how this could happen," Faith said.

"How could it *not* happen?" the old woman asked.

Faith looked over at her tiny face, where the skin was stretched tight across her fine old bones. She guessed that the old woman probably weighed no more than eighty pounds. *How could it not happen?* They sat silently for a few minutes, watching the people, passing the cup of water back and forth for small sips. The woman asked Faith her name, and what was she doing out amongst all these colored folks. Faith told her how she had moved to Tulsa the year before to work for the newspaper, which explained her notepad. The old woman said that was nice. Her name was Easter Smith, because that was the day she was born, a long, long time ago, though everyone called her "Auntie." Would Faith believe that Auntie would be ninety-seven years old in a few weeks? But she was still as fit as a young filly. In fact, she had hiked that morning from the home in Greenwood where she lived with her son and daughter, led along with a band of captured Negroes to Convention Hall. Then she was trucked to McNulty Park because the hall was full. The white men let her ride in front because she was so old. She hadn't seen her son and daughter since the burning began, but she had faith in the Lord they would turn up eventually so they could go home and start putting things back together. Auntie was impatient for that to happen.

"Me to be all stowed up like this," Auntie said, shaking her head. "At home, I packed water and did washin', even though my son and daughter both fussed at me. They says, 'Auntie, you're too old to be workin' this hard.' But I can't sit and fold my hands after all these years bein' so busy and a good cook. I began cookin' in my eleventh year. I cooked all the days I was a slave. In a hotel, I cooked some of the time, then after the War. I don't cook in hotels no more."

The old woman paused and drifted off in remembrance. Auntie was obviously saddened that she no longer cooked in hotels.

"I was born in Georgia," she said after a minute. "Did I tell you that?"

"No, ma'am," Faith said.

"I was born in Georgia, but my master, he lived in Arkansas," she said. "He was a nasty old man. Sold my mama and two of my

212 · THE BURNING

brothers to this other fella in Tennessee. But I did his cookin'
and his washin' 'cause I was told to. I was a young woman when
they fought that war to set us free. That was something, let me
tell you, child. The master comes and says, 'You niggers go on.
You don't belong to me no more. Go on before I shoot you.' But
I stayed there in Arkansas until my son come down here to Tulsa
'cause he heard about all these colored folks getting rich. So I
came, too."

The woman paused again, took another sip of water and offered
the cup to Faith. "I seen lots of trouble," Auntie said. "But in all
my born days, I never seen a day like this."

"Me either," Faith said.

Auntie looked over at Faith. The old woman began to quiver
with laughter, her tiny frame shaking.

"No, darlin'," Auntie said finally. "I don't suppose you have."

Faith rose from the cot, took Auntie's cup and stood in line to
have it refilled, then returned it to her. Both Auntie's kindness
and her laughter convicted Faith that afternoon, burdened her
with a shame that lingered inside her for the rest of her life. She
wept on the streetcar ride back to the newsroom, but walked
around the block a few times before entering the newspaper
building to make sure that her eyes were not still red.

Her story, which appeared on the front page of the *Tulsa
World* on June 2, 1921, would be remembered as one of the most
skillfully written, most heartrending articles ever published by the
paper. But it was years before Faith could read it again herself.

That same day, the *World*'s rival, the *Tulsa Tribune*, published
a front-page article that was every bit as masterful, but a story
whose tone could not have been more different. If the Heironymous account in the *World* gave voice to the shame that many
whites in Tulsa felt over what had been perpetrated on Greenwood, the *Tribune* story reflected a sense of triumph shared by
many other whites in the city. And though the *Tribune* article ran
without a byline, there was little doubt about the identity of its
author. The poetic cadence, the keen eye for detail, the lyrical

flourishes, exceeded the command of the typical Tulsa newspaper reporter. This was the work of an experienced writer trained at one of the nation's best journals. The article was most surely written by *Tribune* editor and publisher Richard Lloyd Jones himself.

Blacks Taken Into Custody Form Motley Parade to Ballpark

Tulsa, a city of ninety thousand people, witnessed this most unusual spectacle this morning when a motley procession of Negroes, on foot and in every conceivable kind of vehicle, those later being reserved mostly for women, wended its way over the city's most prominent thoroughfares and main streets to the ballpark. . . . The men walked. As they passed the city's most traveled streets, they held both hands high about their heads, their hats in one hand, a token of their submission to the white man's authority. . . . They will return not to their homes they had on Tuesday afternoon, but to heaps of ashes, the angry white man's reprisal for the wrong inflicted on them by the inferior race.

Two horse-drawn wagons, one a wobbly, non-descript affair on wheels drawn by a decrepit burro, were features of this strange procession. In the vehicles the occupants had evidently hastily piled all their earthy belongings. There were shabby worn trunks, boxes, articles of furniture, even young chickens. On the tailgate of one wagon there rode a dingy boy of seven or eight who surveyed the menacing guards and sidewalk throngs and tried vainly to figure out what it was all about. Tramp. Tramp. Tramp. Through the dusty streets the prisoners strode, ever under the watchful eye of the white man's authority and the white man's gun. Negro women, more brazen and unafraid than their men folk, tried at first to put a bold front on the entire affair, but as they ruefully gazed on the unfriendly street throngs, they seemed to sense it was a most serious epic in their lives, and most of the bravado had left them by the time they [reached] the ballpark.

Yes, the bravado had been squashed out of even the defiant women; Tulsa Negroes had been taught a lesson that they would never forget, a lesson for American Negroes everywhere; the events in Tulsa had convincingly affirmed the superior race—all of these developments were heralded in print by the paper of Lincoln devotee Richard Lloyd Jones, who wrote and otherwise directed the *Tribune*'s coverage of the historic episode, pausing from time to time for assignations in his room at the Tulsa Hotel with his assistant, Amy Comstock.

Little matter that from the moment the ashes began to cool, most authorities blamed the *Tribune*'s reckless and inflammatory coverage of Dick Rowland's arrest for inciting the courthouse confrontation and the much larger tragedy that came of it. Within hours of arriving in Tulsa, General Charles Barrett of the National Guard concluded that the conflagration was caused by "an impudent Negro, a hysterical girl and a yellow journal." In a *World* story published a few days after the burning, James Patton, Tulsa's chief of detectives, said officers investigating Sarah Page's accusations were doubtful that the case against Rowland would come to much.

"If the facts in the story as told to the police had only been printed, I do not think there would have been a riot what so ever," Patton said.

In a front-page story a few days after the riot, the *Tribune* defiantly denied any role in the catastrophe. But clearly, the paper and its publisher were not chastened in the least. If anything, Jones's racism became even more publicly virulent in the days immediately after the burning.

Never one to miss an opportunity for national exposure, Jones had somehow found time to write a long freelance account of the burning for the *New York Post*, which ran on June 2 under his byline that also noted he was "formerly of *Collier's Weekly*." In that story, Jones assured his Eastern audience that there are "good Negroes . . . who are kind and courteous. They are helpful, and the Southerner has an affection for them." Then he went on:

But there is a bad black man who is a beast. This is a physical fact that the traditional New Englander, for instance, does not know and cannot comprehend. That bad black man is a bad man. He drinks the cheapest and the vilest whiskey. He breaks every law to get it. He is a dope fiend. He holds life lightly. He is a bully and a brute.

Once again, Jones called forth the stereotype of the Negro buck Gus from the *Birth of a Nation,* the blockbuster film endorsed six years before by President Wilson as well as the chief justice of the U.S. Supreme Court. It was that type of Negro who had arrived at the Tulsa County Courthouse on the last night in May, Jones wrote, using the threatened lynching of a Negro boy as a pretext to make trouble. It was that type of Negro who bore the responsibility for the cataclysm that came afterward.

Jones did not mention, of course, that his own Tulsa publication had largely inspired the lynching threat, or that the contingent of blacks attempting to thwart it was made up of Greenwood's most affluent, literate, and respected citizens, hardly the choc-drinking malingerers to which Jones referred.

Little matter. The burning had heated Jones's blood to an editorial froth. Two days after the *New York Post* article was published, he struck an even more bellicose note with his local audience. In a June 4 *Tribune* editorial, he urged Tulsa to seize the opportunity presented by the catastrophe. In effect, he said, the white mob had succeeded where Tulsa police and other city leaders had failed. The mob had cleaned up Niggertown, and he wrote:

Such a district as old "Niggertown" must never be allowed in Tulsa again.

It was a cesspool of iniquity and corruption. . . . This old "Niggertown" had a lot of bad niggers and a bad nigger is about the lowest thing that walks on two feet. Give a bad nigger his booze and his dope and a gun and he thinks he can shoot up the world. Now these four things were to be found in Niggertown, booze, dope, bad niggers and guns. The *Tulsa Tribune* makes no apology to the police commissioner or the mayor of this city for having pled with them to clean up the cesspools.

Events in Tulsa in the following weeks and months, a time when the Negroes struggled to rebuild their devastated community with almost no assistance from the whites, demonstrated the degree to which whites shared Jones's sentiments. The publisher had again demonstrated his talent for capturing the zeitgeist of both Tulsa and the nation. He survived and eventually prospered in the newspaper business, in large part because he was not afraid to give voice, with considerable literate polish, to the hateful racist miasma clouding so many American souls. In that regard, Jones could legitimately argue that his own hatred, opportunism, and journalistic recklessness had not caused the great burning, but merely tapped into the racist jingoism so prevalent at that time. Many others would contend, also with some merit, that if it hadn't been for Dick Rowland and the *Tribune*'s incendiary coverage of the case, something else would have come along to ignite Tulsa, just as atrocities had been ignited in cities and towns across the nation in the several years previous.

Among them was Oklahoma Attorney General S. Prince Freeling. In Tulsa to oversee the grand jury investigation of the burning, Freeling said in a mid-June speech to Tulsa business leaders that "the cause of the riot was not Tulsa," and that—

It might have happened anywhere for the Negro is not the same man he was thirty years ago when he was content to plod along his own road accepting the white man as his benefactor. But the years have passed and the Negro has been educated and the race papers have broadcast thoughts of equality. Then came the war and the army and the Negro learned the value of organization. So with the continued tirades against the white race launched by Negro publications throughout this nation, the

Negro has come to look upon the white man as his oppressor, and so they have, in a large way, become organized since the war, and in this organization there lies a force that is liable to start trouble any minute.

In a comparatively short time . . . Tulsa and the world will forget the difficulties and Tulsa will have been aided by the occurrence, for it will mean stricter enforcement of the laws, and from the ashes of the Negro section will come a better Tulsa.

Mayor Thaddeus Evans, speaking at a City Commission meeting a few days after the burning, was equally sanguine. The catastrophe was probably inevitable, Evans agreed, adding that the belligerent Negroes were to blame. If so, he continued, "I say it was good generalship to let the destruction come to that section where the trouble was hatched up, put in motion, and where it had its inception."

So Richard Lloyd Jones's eloquent and unabashed hate-mongering resonated deeply, not only in the hearts of Tulsa's oil-field roughnecks, bootleggers, and the city's assorted white ruffians, but among its political leaders, lawyers, doctors, ministers, and businessmen, who, in the months after the burning, enlisted by the hundreds in the Ku Klux Klan.

Tribune readers also appreciated the paper's willingness to move beyond the hand-wringing caused by the burning, its insistence to once again write about life as it had been before the great event, its ability to even find some humor in the ashes. On June 22, for example, the paper detailed the quandary of James O'Bannon, "a coal-black senegalan [sic] with an old-fashioned German name." O'Bannon's marriage license had burned up with the rest of his belongings, the story said, leaving him without proof of recent vows with the "dusky maiden," Mattie Harris. Thus O'Bannon arrived at the courthouse one day demanding to know from officials there whether "he am or he ain't."

The burning otherwise was soon replaced on the *Tribune's*

front page by more-pressing local concerns. Jones abandoned his rants against "Niggertown" to take up controversies involving street paving and the city's water supply. A year later, when the publisher's affair with Comstock was exposed during the street-paving controversy, the burning had disappeared from the newspaper altogether, and would not be mentioned again in those pages for fifty years.

It was, in fact, just five days after the burning that the dominant photograph on the *Tribune*'s front page did not concern the event at all, but featured the winner of the newspaper-sponsored beauty pageant. The coronation of Mrs. Irene Moise, office secretary for a group of architects, had been delayed for a few days by all the trouble. But newspaper readers could not be kept in suspense any longer.

"I'm feeling a little dazed right now," the triumphant beauty queen said after her crowning. "I've never had this sort of thing happen before. It's fine to think of the future as having possibilities for me. I guess I'm building air castles already."

CHAPTER 13

SCORCHED EARTH

No matter what their disposition toward the burning, whether it was shame or a perverse sense of triumph, Tulsa leaders agreed that the city faced a public relations nightmare of staggering proportions, a sentiment articulated by the Reverend Charles W. Kerr, pastor of the city's all-white First Presbyterian Church.

"For twenty-two years I have been boosting Tulsa," Kerr said in the days after the burning. "And we all have been boosters and boasters about our buildings, bank accounts and other assets, but events of the past week will put an end to the bragging for awhile."

By Thursday morning, June 2, 1921, Greenwood's decimation dominated the front page of every major newspaper in the nation, including *The New York Times*, which termed the catastrophe "one of the most disastrous race wars ever visited upon an American city," describing Greenwood in the aftermath as "a smoldering heap of blackened ruins . . . Hardly a Negro shanty is standing throughout an area that housed upward of 15,000 blacks."

The *Times* story went on. "Domestic animals wandering among the wreckage give the only token of life over a desolate territory, extending from the Frisco tracks to Stand Pipe [sic] Hill on the north. Looting by lawless elements goes on, sporadically."

Even worse for Tulsa's reputation than those bleak descriptions were the published accounts of how the destruction had come about. Most arriving journalists concluded that the whites, though they had congregated in an apparent lynch mob, did not bear all of the blame for the initial outbreak at the courthouse, and that their actions throughout the confusing night that followed might also be seen as somewhat justified. But as dawn approached on June 1, the Negroes who came to Dick Rowland's rescue had been driven back across the Frisco tracks into their own community. The threat to white Tulsa—if there ever had been a threat—clearly was at an end, and the bloodshed should have ended there as well.

"It was then that bands of whites crossed the railroad district and began to invade and burn the Negro houses," the *Times* wrote on June 3. "The ruthless demolition of virtually the entire Negro quarter south of the tracks is condemned as indefensible violence."

Tulsa was thus skewered on editorial pages across the nation. A *Houston Post* editorial was typical of the condemnations. "Americans have been loud in the denunciation of pogroms in Poland, of the massacres in Armenia and Russia and Mexico, and they were ready to go to war to avenge the victims of barbarous German warlords," said the *Post*.

"But unless we can create a public sentiment in this country strong enough to restrain such intolerant outbreaks as Tulsa has witnessed, we shall be unable in the future to protest with any moral weight against anything that may happen in less favored parts of the world."

"If the Tulsa collision had happened in Vera Cruz," a *New York Times* editorial added, "the American people would have deplored the lawlessness of the Mexicans and found it shocking."

"The bloody scenes in Tulsa, Oklahoma," wrote the *Philadelphia Bulletin*, "are hardly conceivable as happening in American civilization of the present day."

Race riots and other racial violence, including widespread lynching, had become commonplace in the United States by then. But the Tulsa calamity seemed to shock the conscience of the nation to an extent greater than any of the previous outbreaks, calling to mind as it did the mammoth atrocities that Americans attributed to people in less sophisticated, less righteous, parts of the world.

The burning was indeed of a magnitude almost unimaginable in peacetime, destruction rivaling the worst that any of the visiting correspondents had seen during the recent war in Europe. Panoramic photographs of the decimation bore a haunting resemblance to those from Nagasaki and Hiroshima a quarter-century later: Thirty-five square blocks of the Negro community lay almost completely in ruin, save for hundreds of outhouses and a few isolated residences. As the whites had moved north on June 1, they put the torch to more than 1,115 Negro homes (314 more were looted, but not burned), five hotels, thirty-one restaurants, four drugstores, eight doctors' offices, the new Dunbar School, two dozen grocery stores, the Negro hospital, the public library, and even a dozen churches, including the community's most magnificent new edifice, Mount Zion Baptist Church.

Most personal belongings of the blacks were consumed as well, along with monetary savings that Greenwood families typically kept tucked away under mattresses or hidden in cupboards because no black banks existed on the north side of the tracks. Thus white curiosity-seekers poking around in Greenwood's rubble regularly plucked coins from the ashes, and dozens of Negroes later attempted to redeem charred currency at white Tulsa banks, unsuccessfully in most cases.

The toll of dead and wounded was even more staggering, but for a variety of reasons, the true extent of the casualties would never be known. Determining the exact number of injured was impossible, in part because so many Negroes fled from Tulsa to be treated for burns and gunshot wounds by doctors as far away as St. Louis or Kansas City. Many whites, on the other hand, were reluctant to seek local medical treatment for injuries sustained while engaged in looting, arson, or murder. Other whites presented themselves to Tulsa hospitals insisting they had been hurt as innocent bystanders. In any event, every Tulsa hospital was swamped with the injured. Surgical teams operated around the clock for days afterward, on both white and Negro casualties. Basements of white churches, the National Guard Armory, and a private residence were commandeered for the purpose of treating the wounded.

The Red Cross also converted the classrooms of the Booker T. Washington High School into a hospital, where the largest number of injured blacks were treated. Red Cross records reflect that the agency treated 531 men, women, and children in the week after the riot, only forty-eight of them white. Twenty doctors working for the Red Cross, half of them Negroes, performed 163 operations in the days after the burning. Among those beleaguered black physicians was Greenwood's first Negro doctor, R. T. Bridgewater, the friend, colleague, and neighbor of the slain Dr. Andrew C. Jackson, who had become the riot's most publicized victim. Bridgewater's home on Detroit Avenue was also pillaged and ruined by the mob.

"My piano and all my elegant furniture were piled in the street," he recalled later. "My safe had been broken into, all of the money stolen; also my silverware, cut glass, all of the family clothes, and everything of value had been removed, even my family Bible. My electric-light fixtures were broken, the dishes that were not stolen were broken. The floors were covered, literally speaking, with glass. Even the phone was torn from the wall." So after twenty-hour days spent treating his people in Red Cross hospital wards, Bridgewater was forced to return to a cot in a detention camp for a few hours of sleep.

Red Cross reports also attribute the death of eight prematurely born infants to burning-induced trauma, part of a death toll that was even more difficult to accurately quantify than the number of injured. In the burning's immediate aftermath, a Tulsa fire official estimated the dead at 185, saying that many of the victims had been incinerated in their homes. But Tulsa's official estimate was quickly revised downward to seventy-seven dead—nine whites and sixty-eight Negroes, and reduced even further in coming days to ten whites and twenty-six Negroes.

Anyone in Tulsa on the day of the burning knew that death estimate to be ludicrous. For hundreds of Tulsans, the most vivid memories of the tragedy were the surreal scenes of trucks rumbling through town in succession, hauling piles of black bodies through the city, apparently en route to burial grounds at unknown destinations out in the country. Dozens of other bodies were seen stacked like firewood onto railroad flatcars. A Salvation Army official told a visiting journalist that his agency had fed thirty-seven Negro grave diggers who had worked to complete twenty graves into which coffinless Negro bodies were placed and covered with dirt.

Thus, while Tulsa civic leaders clung to the most conservative estimates, the number of dead no doubt climbed well into the hundreds, making the burning in Tulsa the deadliest domestic oubreak in America since the Civil War.

That grim assessment was supported by the experiences of a white Tulsan named Ed Wheeler a half-century later. Wheeler, a writer and amateur historian who rose to the rank of brigadier general in the Oklahoma National Guard, spent seven months researching the destruction of Greenwood for a 1971 article published in the black Tulsa magazine *Oklahoma Impact*. For his article, which had first been rejected by the white publications in town, Wheeler interviewed about ninety elderly survivors and witnesses, both black and white. Five of them said they independently recalled watching National Guard soldiers lay out about sixty bodies on a sandbar in the Arkansas River, apparently using the hidden spot as an open-air morgue until arrangements could be made to permanently dispose of the corpses.

Most witnesses had spoken to Wheeler only with his promise of anonymity, but during their interviews, they pulled dozens of old photographs from scrapbooks and cigar boxes, pictures showing charred corpses lying in the street and in stacks on the back of trucks and railcars, scores of different bodies in all. At the end of his research, Wheeler concluded that the number of dead probably approached three hundred.

White Tulsans ridiculed Wheeler when his article was published, and it was his estimate of the dead that inspired the most derision. But shortly after the piece appeared, a man named Bill Wilbanks called Wheeler to say that he had come across some old documents the writer might find pertinent.

Wilbanks, then the retiring commander of the Tulsa Police Academy, had been cleaning out old files when, at the bottom of an old police-department cabinet, he discovered five yellowed pages stuck together with a rusty paper clip. The papers lacked headings or descriptions; but were filled with two columns of entries, fifty on each page, examples of which read as follows:

> Black female, mid-20s, shot
> White female, mid-30s, shot
> Black male, teenager, shot
> Black female, hanged from a lamppost.
> Black male, mid-forties, burned.
> White male, mid-20s, shot.
> Black infant, dead of unknown causes.

The roughly two hundred and fifty victims were listed by race, but not by name. Blacks outnumbered the whites by two to one.

"What do you think?" Wilbanks asked Wheeler after he had reviewed the documents during a meeting between the two men at the police academy.

"Any prudent person would probably think this was an informal body count," Wheeler said. "Somebody was keeping count of what they found, but didn't want to make an official report."

"That's what I thought, too," Wilbanks said.

As the national focus on Tulsa intensified in the days after the burning, a front-page headline in the June 3 edition of *The New York Times* captured the official posture of white leadership in the afflicted city: TULSA IN REMORSE.

In an emergency meeting of the Tulsa Chamber of Commerce on June 2, a gathering widely attended by national journalists, civic leaders competed to offer the most hyperbolic statements of regret. While blaming the riot on "some lawless [black] leaders," Alva Niles, president of the Tulsa Chamber, said the city "feels intensely humiliated and standing in the shadow of this great tragedy pledges every effort to wiping out this stain at the earliest possible moment."

Former Tulsa Mayor Loyal J. Martin was even more emphatic. "Tulsa can only redeem herself from the country-wide shame and humiliation into which she is today plunged by complete restitution and rehabilitation of the destroyed black belt," Martin said, to loud applause, then added:

> The rest of the United States must now know that the real citizenship of Tulsa weeps at this unspeakable crime. And will make good the damage, so far as it can be done, to the last penny. We have neglected our duties and our city government has fallen down. We have had a failing police protection here, and now we have to pay the costs of it. The city and county is [sic] legally liable for every dollar of the damage which has been done. Other cities have had to pay the bill of race riots, and we shall have to do so, probably, because we have neglected our duty as citizens.

Cheers also followed Martin's statement that the criminals (presumably he referred to the whites) responsible for the burning "should have been shot on the spot." The former mayor was then named to head a committee of influential Tulsans, all of them white, to lead the Greenwood recovery effort. Mayor Thaddeus Evans was hooted down when his name was proposed for the same committee. "He's failed already," a member of the crowd shouted.

In their efforts at damage control, Tulsa leaders were quick to point out to journalists that scores of white families were housing hundreds of Negroes in their homes and servants' quarters; that thousands of whites had donated food and clothing for the afflicted blacks; that white teachers had taken their black colleagues into their homes by the dozens. Even the incarcerated Negroes were described as being treated with the utmost humanity. By June 2, four thousand Greenwood residents remained in custody, having been moved from McNulty Park and Convention Hall into the shelter of pig and cow barns at the Tulsa County Fairgrounds. But while they waited for a white person to secure their freedom, eighteen hundred of the Negroes were vaccinated for tetanus, smallpox, and typhoid fever.

Yet, away from the headlines, Tulsa's white leaders treated the Greenwood Negroes as a hostile and vanquished force, subtly at first, then overtly. Negro men were ordered to dig latrines and repair roads around the detention camps. Whites securing the release of Negroes were forced to promise that the blacks would be kept "indoors or at the scene of their labor." Several days after the burning, Tulsa police decreed that white Tulsans could no longer provide shelter for Negroes who were not their employees, most likely because white neighborhoods had become overrun with homeless coloreds. Until July 7, 1921, any Negro who had secured his release was forced to wear or carry a green card stamped "Police Protection" on one side, with their name, address, and employer recorded on the other. Any black found on the street without his green card was subject to arrest.

Tulsa also benefited enormously from the national media's short attention span. By June 4, the burning was no longer front-page news in America, the Oklahoma tragedy replaced by a flash flood in Pueblo, Colorado, that killed hundreds. And with the national spotlight extinguished, white Tulsa's commitment to make amends, its promise to assist the Negroes in the rebuilding, evaporated just as quickly. Four days after the burning, Tulsa leaders decided they would not accept outside donations to help with the rebuilding, though such offers were pouring in from across the country. In one case, a thousand-dollar contribution was rejected from the *Chicago Tribune*, whose publisher was told "in theatric fashion that the citizens of Tulsa were to blame for the riot and that they themselves would bear the costs of restoration," one black journalist later reported.

Yet, in the weeks after the burning, the costs of restoration seemed the farthest thing from the minds of white Tulsans, whose leaders had washed their hands of any responsibility toward the afflicted Negroes by turning every facet of the recovery work over to the Red Cross. Civic leaders instead seemed more concerned with capitalizing on what was increasingly viewed not as a tragedy, but an opportunity.

NEGRO SECTION ABOLISHED BY CITY ORDER read a headline in the June 7 edition of the *Tulsa Tribune*. The story that ensued began: "Thirty-five blocks south of Standpipe Hill now in ruins following the fire Wednesday morning will never again be a Negro quarter but will become a wholesale and industrial center."

The story was based on meetings of the Tulsa City Commission that less than a week after the riot, proposed to transform the devastated area into the site of a new railroad station, white-owned manufacturing plants and warehouses. "Let the Negro settlement be placed further to the north and east," Mayor Evans said. It later became known that white businessmen had attempted to purchase burned-out property from stricken Negroes, generally for a few cents on the dollar, before the last fire had died out. Most blacks refused. But on June 7, the City Commission gave them further incentive to sell out and relocate. Fire Ordinance No. 2156 extended a stringent fire code over most of the burned-out area, mandating that rebuilt buildings be constructed of concrete, brick, or steel, and be at least two stories high, requirements clearly prohibitive to most Negroes. Under the new ordinance, wooden houses were permitted only on Greenwood's northern edge.

"Because of the building requirements laid on this district," the *Tribune* reported on June 7, "it is believed impossible that Negroes will again build homes there."

Many desperate Negroes ignored the ordinance and began to

put up shacks on their property anyway. Two months later, Negro lawyers sued the city, asking a state court to allow the blacks to rebuild in the restricted area, and to abolish the ordinance that might cause thousands to lose their property without due process. In September, a three-judge panel in Tulsa ruled for the Negroes, and the rebuilding of Greenwood began in earnest, but precious time had been lost. Nearly one thousand Greenwood residents spent the winter in Red Cross tents. The city's land grab also fueled rumors and suspicions that survived in the black community for eight decades; because white Tulsa, especially the downtown area, was hemmed in on the south by the Arkansas River, city leaders had actually planned and orchestrated Greenwood's destruction to gain access to the land north of the Frisco tracks. In the years to come, scholars found no direct proof of such official culpability, but the actions of Tulsa leaders in the burning's aftermath were almost as revolting. To them, the Negro property had seemed tantamount to the spoils of war.

On the morning of June 9, 1921, dozens of Negro survivors filled the halls of the county courthouse, jockeying to be the first to testify before a special grand jury that had been ordered by Oklahoma Governor J. B. A. Robertson. Each of the twelve men selected for the panel was white, but the governor had made clear that he wanted a thorough and unbiased probe, and the Negroes at the courthouse that day had apparently taken Robertson at his word. Finally came the chance to tell their side of the awful story, of how the whites had swept across the tracks before dawn, how they had stared down the end of white shotguns and rifles as they were rousted from their homes in their nightclothes, how they had watched their belongings being stolen, their homes being burned, their friends and loved ones being shot down like dogs or burned alive.

Whites, unsurprisingly, were much more reluctant to testify, and, in fact, there was such a dearth of witnesses of that race that authorities put out a plea in the local papers, begging for people who had knowledge of the burning to come forward, witnesses who might assist the panel in answering the following questions: Who led in assembling the mobs of whites and blacks? Who fired the first shot at the courthouse? Who headed the various factions of the mobs? Who set fire to the Negro district? Did police officers properly carry out their duty?

After several days of testimony, which had been elicited by Oklahoma Attorney General Prince Freeling, the grand jury returned eighty-eight indictments, including a charge of attempted rape against Dick Rowland, the famous bootblack still incarcerated at an unknown location outside of Tulsa. Dozens of whites were charged with rioting, arson, theft, and assault, including Cowboy Long, the notorious hoodlum bootlegger who led the burning crew along Detroit Avenue. Tulsa Police Chief John Gustafson was indicted for failing to take the action necessary to quell the disturbance, and on unrelated charges that he had conspired with a local car-theft ring.

But most of the indictments named Negroes, fifty-seven in all, including a known drug dealer named Will Robinson; Peg Leg Taylor, the one-legged veteran of the Spanish War who supposedly killed a dozen whites by himself while firing down from a Greenwood hilltop; and the massive Negro veteran O. B. Mann, who disappeared from Tulsa after the final battles against the whites on June 1. Those Negro men, the indictments said, "assembled together . . . armed with rifles, shotguns, pistols, razors and other deadly weapons," and attacked downtown Tulsa in cars, trucks and on foot, killing several peaceable whites and wounding many others.

Tulsa authorities singled out two men as the Negro ringleaders: *Tulsa Star* editor Andrew J. Smitherman and his friend John Stradford, whose years of proud belligerence had finally caught up with them. Both had long been recognized as the most uppity, contentious Negroes in Greenwood, so it came as no surprise when O. W. Gurley, the grand jury's star witness, testified as to how Smitherman and Stradford seemed to be giving the orders to the group of angry men gathered that night at the *Tulsa Star*, men determined to prevent Rowland's lynching. Gurley fingered O. B. Mann and many other of his Negro neighbors as well, men whose belligerence had cost the Greenwood pioneer the financial fruits of two decades. A short time after his testimony, Greenwood's first businessman moved to Los Angeles, branded a traitor to his race.

Stradford and Smitherman, meanwhile, had slipped out of Tulsa when Greenwood was overrun, Stradford fleeing to his brother's home in Independence, Kansas; Smitherman to points unknown. Lawmen caught up with Stradford on June 3. "They wanted me and now they have me," the Negro leader said when officers arrived at his brother's to take him into custody. But he quickly secured his release on bail and remained free while Tulsa authorities sought his extradition, efforts that included affidavits from Tulsa's leading whites promising the Kansas governor that the Negro defendant would be protected from the mob and receive a prompt and fair trial. But by the time the Kansas governor ordered his return to Tulsa, Stradford had vanished again, this time to his son's home in Chicago. Tulsa's attempt to find and prosecute him ended there. Smitherman eventually turned up in Buffalo, New York, where he edited another black newspaper. Neither man ever returned to Tulsa.

In most other cases, the grand jury indictments were empty gestures. One black was sent to jail, but for only thirty days on a charge of carrying a concealed weapon. After a raucous trial in July, Chief Gustafson was convicted, fined, and fired. But the rest of the indictments against white and black alike were either dismissed or ignored in a city determined to erase from its collective memory what had happened in Greenwood. Not one white was sent to jail for the burning.

More telling than the indictments, perhaps, was the grand jury report issued at the end of its deliberations, a document that offered another window into the heart of white Tulsa, and perhaps into the heart of all white America of that time. The report briefly criticized inflammatory local newspaper accounts for helping precipitate the tragedy. But once again, jurors reserved most of the blame for the Negroes. The catastrophe, the grand jury report said, "was the direct result of an effort on the part of a certain group of colored men who appeared at the courthouse on the night of May 31, 1921, for the purpose of protecting one Dick Rowland." The report went on:

> We have not been able to find any evidence, either from white or colored citizens, that any organized attempt was made or planned to take from the sheriff's custody any prisoner; the crowd assembled about the courthouse being purely spectators and curiosity-seekers resulting from rumors circulated about the city. There was no mob spirit among the whites, no talk of lynching and no arms. The assembly was quiet until the arrival of the armed Negroes, which precipitated and was the direct cause of the entire affair.

The report also cited a less-tangible cause of the outbreak, the same condition to which Attorney General Freeling had referred in his speech that month to Tulsa business leaders: The American Negro had changed, had become agitated by propaganda promoting ideas of social equality: "This agitation resulted in the accumulation of firearms among the people and the storage of quantities of ammunition," the report concluded, "all of which was accumulative in the minds of the Negro, which led them as people to believe in equal rights, social equality, and their ability to demand the same."

The panel's proposed solution had nothing to do with criminal charges or prison sentences. Instead, jurors recommended that "colored town be policed by white officers, that indiscriminant mingling of white and colored people in dance halls and other places of amusement be positively prohibited, and every law be rigidly enforced to the end that a proper relationship may be maintained between the two races."

The Negroes, in other words, must be kept in their place.

But in Tulsa after the burning, no white need have worried. The feisty heart and soul of black Tulsa had been ripped away. Its leaders had fled. There would be no more loud public debates about race in Greenwood, not for decades. Tulsa Negroes had learned in the most convincing fashion imaginable that they could not prevail against whites, who had both numbers and the law on their side. For decades after the burning, black Tulsans kept their collective eyes to the ground.

Tulsa whites seemed to take a different lesson from the dark episode. Much private sorrow no doubt afflicted members of white Tulsa households, where they were reminded of the travesty on a daily basis by the despair of their servants. But Tulsa's boomtown jauntiness soon returned. Oil prices once again soared, and even more impressive towers began to populate the young city's skyline.

And in the summer and fall of 1921, when Greenwood was a tent city shrouded by the white smoke of outdoor cook fires that burned continuously, white Tulsans joined the Ku Klux Klan by the thousands. The Tulsa Klan soon boasted an auxiliary for women, called the "Kamelia," and a junior Klan for boys age twelve to eighteen. White robes and hoods were for years the most popular costumes for children at Halloween. In 1922, the Klan, which officially referred to itself as the Tulsa Benevolent Association, built what would be one of the secret order's most impressive facilities in the nation. Beno Hall, a stucco palace at Main Street and Easton Avenue, contained an auditorium that could seat more than a thousand members, a place generally filled for the Klan's monthly meetings.

The name Beno was supposedly derivative of the word "benevolent," but among some in Tulsa, the building's name took on another meaning. It stood for Be No Nigger, Be No Catholic, Be No Jew. Klan opponents however hardly dared whisper such sentiments, because most of the important people in the city were members. Mayors, city commissioners, sheriffs, district attorneys, and many other city and county officeholders who were either Klansmen or Klan supporters were elected and reelected with regularity throughout the 1920s.

Almost immediately after the burning, the KKK had become the dominant reality of life in Tulsa, and it remained so until the end of the decade. Some of the order's most impressive downtown marches took place within weeks of the Greenwood tragedy. Hundreds attended initiation ceremonies around burning crosses on hilltops. There were Klan funerals and Klan fund-raisers. For whatever private sorrows that might have remained, the burning of 1921 had affirmed the superiority of the white race. At the same time, it was a powerful lesson to any colored person with ideas of tampering with the right order of things.

National Klan officials had certainly been correct when they had instructed their brethren from Tulsa. The best way to boost Klan membership was to have a good riot. On a night in August 1921, thousands of Tulsa men, women, and children crammed Convention Hall, the same facility that just two months earlier had been filled with homeless, terrorized Negroes. By contrast, the atmosphere that night in August was more mindful of a pep rally or tent revival. The crowd had gathered to hear the speech of a visitor from Atlanta, a man named Caleb Ridley, who would tell of the past and present glories of the Ku Klux Klan, its sacred principles, and the requirements for membership. Ridley was enthusiastically introduced that night by the prominent Tulsa attorney Washington Hudson, who numbered among his clients that famous Negro shoeshine boy, Dick Rowland.

CHAPTER 14

A CHRISTMAS CAROL

Only a few days after the Klan rally at Convention Hall, Tulsa attorney Washington Hudson drove across the Frisco tracks to deliver the happy news to Damie Rowland's tent on Archer Street. Sarah Page had decided to drop her charges. Damie's boy and Wash Hudson's client, Dick Rowland, was a free man, at that very moment probably strolling the streets of Kansas City, the place where Sheriff McCullough had hidden Dick since the burning. Damie nearly fainted. She made Mr. Hudson tell her the news again. Then she hugged him, weeping for joy in the musty shadows of the Red Cross tent erected on the ashes of her boardinghouse. It was her first glimmer of sunlight after three months of endless night.

Damie had lost everything in the burning—the boardinghouse, her clothes, her savings—but few in the Negro community extended her much sympathy. She knew instead from the averted glances and the whispers when she passed on the street that people in Greenwood blamed Dick for what happened, and they blamed Damie, too, for she had brought that troublemaker to town in the first place and had failed to keep him in line when she did.

Not that Damie didn't blame herself. Every day for weeks, she sat in a rickety wooden chair outside her tent and thought about her years with Dick, starting with the day the skinny orphan named Jimmie Jones appeared at her door in Vinita with a grown man's shirt draped over his bones, complaining of hunger. She remembered his laughter and sweetness then, the radiance of the boy's smile, then the move to Tulsa and Jimmie's new name and his diamond ring, and his rolls of cash, and the rumors that made their way back to Damie about Dick showing up in Greenwood's choc joints and brothels. Then Dick and Sarah Page. Where had Damie gone wrong? What should she have taught Dick that she didn't? Why hadn't he had the good sense to leave that trashy white girl alone?

And look at what happened. A whole community in ruins. Because of that, there were plenty in Greenwood who felt that the mob should have had its way with Dick Rowland that night at the courthouse, even if the boy was guilty of nothing worse than stupidity. Everyone would have been better off if the whites had satisfied their blood lust with one shiftless, choc-swilling young Negro who insisted on messing with a white girl. Instead, dozens of Greenwood mothers and wives and children wept for sons, husbands, and fathers who had disappeared into hidden graves in the countryside. The tents were everywhere in Greenwood now, and people still picked the ashes from their teeth and their clothes, and brushed them from their hair when the wind blew. The whole place still smelled of charred lumber. All those folks still wore donated clothes that didn't fit, and dirty bandages over their burns and gunshot wounds. The women still burst into tears for no reason, and the men stared into the distance. Dick had brought that onto his people. Dick and Damie.

If that weren't misery enough, Damie had still dreaded what would happen when they brought Dick back to town and put him on trial for trying to rape Sarah that day in the elevator. What chance did Dick have then, famous white lawyer or not? None, Damie knew. The whites would hang him anyway, which would be the final dagger in Damie Rowland's ailing heart.

But then on that day in September, Mr. Hudson rolled up in his expensive Ford, wearing a beautiful brown suit with a vest and bow tie, and a nice straw hat, which he tipped politely to Damie before bending to step into her tent. Then he delivered his wondrous news, which she made him repeat to make sure she wasn't dreaming. It was over. Dick was free. There would be no hanging, no more death. Before she could stop herself, Damie's tiny arms flew around the white lawyer's thick body. She grabbed Mr. Hud-

son into a big hug and pulled the tall fellow down to her height
so she could kiss his cheek, smelling his sweet cologne up close
when she did. She never forgot that scent. In the years to come,
on the infrequent occasions she caught a whiff of that cologne on
other men, Damie's insides tingled with the memory of Dick's
deliverance.

He came in the night, and then only once. Damie didn't recognize
him at first, thought him another young Negro beggar desperate
for some food or for a few pennies to buy choc beer with. Damie
heard the man whisper her name outside her tent, and when she
poked her head out the front flap, he stood to the side, outlined
in the shadows. The young man had put on a belly from the jail
food, and even in the dark, Damie could see that his cheeks were
shiny with tears.

"Isn't this an awful mess that I caused?" Dick whispered.

Damie nearly fainted again. She rushed the few yards toward
him and hugged him like she had hugged Wash Hudson, only
Dick smelled like several days of riding in boxcars. Then Damie
remembered herself, remembered what the other Greenwood
folks might say or do if they saw Dick, so she grabbed him by his
muscular arm and pulled him inside her tent. She fed him and
they talked some, and Dick said he was so sorry, but there were
only so many ways he could express his remorse. What was done
was done, Damie said.

She looked closely at her boy in the thin light of her gas lamp.
Dick's diamond ring was gone from his finger. A dirty piece of
string was tied around that finger instead, as if to remind him of
his flamboyant life and where that life had led him. Eyes that
once twinkled like the evening star on a clear night were now dull
and old, though Dick had just turned twenty. He asked Damie
about the folks around Greenwood, wondering who died in the
burning and who survived. He asked Damie what she would do,
with her boardinghouse and all her money gone. Damie said she
would find a way to get back on her feet, that Dick shouldn't

worry. Then, well before dawn, Dick hugged her one last time and disappeared into the night.

He wrote to her every month from Kansas City. Damie was surprised when he told her that Sarah Page had moved back to Kansas City, too, the place where she had grown up and divorced her husband before moving to Tulsa. By his letters, it sounded like Dick and Sarah saw a great deal of each other. Dick said that Sarah felt terrible that the police had arrested him for something he didn't do, but she never talked at all about the burning and killing set in motion by her lies. If Dick still loved Sarah, he didn't say. Then her name disappeared from Dick's letters, and not long after that, he moved to Oregon, where he found work in shipyards along the coast.

He continued to write from Oregon, telling Damie of his love for the ocean, how the sound and the smell and the hugeness of it made it easier to forget the bad things that he had done, letters that kept coming for forty years. Dick wrote to Damie about his work and the sea, but he never mentioned a wife or a family, or even a friend. Then a final letter came from Oregon, one delivered to Damie in the 1960s and written by a man who said he had been Dick's roommate there. He was sorry to inform Damie that Dick had been killed in an accident on a wharf. Damie was the only person that Dick ever really loved, the man said. Damie's new boardinghouse on Archer Street, the one she eventually had rebuilt after the burning, was closed for several days after she got the news.

Bill Williams first heard the sound about a week after the burning. He was working with his father near dusk, pulling charred metal frames of theater seats from the ashes of the Dreamland and piling them onto a truck parked in the street, when a blues melody someone was tapping out on a piano drifted toward them from a tent across Greenwood Avenue. It was the first music Bill and his father had heard since the trouble had happened, and they paused from their labors and smiled at the sound for a few minutes before getting back to work. Not long after that, Bill heard a sax wailing along Greenwood Avenue, and within a few weeks, regular crowds gathered along the street to eat ribs and greens cooked over open fires and to listen to the jazz and the blues, which expressed feelings that the Negroes of Greenwood couldn't otherwise put into words.

So somehow life in Greenwood continued. To be a slave before the Civil War, or to be a Negro in America afterward, was to learn endurance, how to move forward through terrible things that colored folks had come to expect out of life, things that would make members of a weaker people turn to dust. That's how it was in Greenwood after the burning. People moved forward. Life continued.

Vegetable stands sprouted among the tents within a week. Cows were milked, and eggs collected from nervous hens. The thousands of Negroes resumed their daily treks back across the railroad tracks to shine shoes, or hang a white family's laundry and do its cooking, or trim hedges and cut lawns, or drive limousines, or run elevators, or wash dishes in white restaurants. Then they came home to the tents across the tracks and made do, the rich Negroes and the poor Negroes alike, because after the burning, there wasn't much to distinguish the two.

Before the burning, the fellow named C. L. Netherland lived in a ten-room home with a basement, and cut hair in a Greenwood Avenue parlor with five enamel chairs, four baths, a set of electric clippers, an electric fan, two lavatories and shampoo stands, a double shine stand of marble, and an income of five hundred dollars a month. After the burning, he lived in his coal barn and cut hair in a folding chair set on the sidewalk, because life went on, no matter how terrible it could be. Townsend Jackson cut hair in his tent on Cincinnati, grieving for his son, the doctor. Young Robert Fairchild, Dick Rowland's old buddy, shined shoes downtown. Professor Hughes taught his classes at Booker T. Washington High School, which became a school again when the injured people were moved into a little hospital built by the Red Cross on Hartford Avenue. H. A. Guess hung his law shingle in his family's tent, assuring his wife and two daughters all along:

"Don't worry, girls. I'm gonna build you a nice new house, better than the last one." Within a few months, he did.

A few days after the burning, Bill Williams and his parents had walked to Greenwood Avenue because their car was burned up or stolen, and they saw for the first time that the Dreamland was a pile of rubble with only a couple of walls standing, and the Williams Building on the corner was in the same condition. They found Loula Williams' safe lying open in the middle of the street, empty of course. Loula cried for a few minutes that day, clinging to her husband's arm as she looked at their property. But then her tears dried and John and Loula Williams plowed forward, as they had since the first day they were married.

They started rebuilding with the savings they had in a white bank downtown, and by September, the family was able to move from their tent along Greenwood Avenue to the second floor of the new Williams Building, which was almost exactly like the one before. Crowds stood in line to get into Williams' Confectionary the day it opened, desperate for Greenwood life as it used to be. People congregated around the soda fountain, and young men resumed their confectionary marriage proposals. The Dreamland also came back to life that autumn, but half of the seats sat empty for many months, except on the nights when Loula Williams decided to show movies for free.

John Williams rebuilt his engine shop, too, and within a few weeks, the rich white men brought their cars back north across the tracks so he could work on them. A few of the whites told John Williams that they were sorry about what had happened in Greenwood, that they felt like the burning had been a very bad thing. But most of John Williams' white customers said nothing at all about the tragedy. They just looked a little sheepish when they walked into the garage with this or that complaint about their cars, wondering if old John could have a look under the hood. Bill's father knew that many of the men who owned those cars were part of the mob that came pouring over the tracks when the whistle blew before dawn on June 1, that many of those same men shattered the windows and splintered the bricks of the Williams Building with their rifles and shotguns. But John Williams fixed their cars anyway, because life went on and that's what Negroes did in America after the Civil War. Whatever other feelings John might have had about such matters, he kept to himself.

By winter, most of John and Loula's neighbors along Greenwood Avenue were back in their buildings, too. Deep Greenwood, in fact, looked almost exactly as it did before the burning, except newer.

Out in the neighborhoods, Negro homeowners sometimes borrowed money from their white employers, and the white lumber and brick dealers donated materials or sold them cheap, so by the end of the year, more than six hundred homes in Greenwood also had been rebuilt. By the spring of 1922, the last of the tents were gone and the only reminders of the burning were the occasional piles of rubble, or the empty shotgun and rifle shells that kept turning up in the dirt like arrowheads, or the thousand-yard stares, or the nightmares that afflicted almost every Greenwood house like a plague from the Bible.

It was workers from the Red Cross who cut the huge spruce in the country and hauled it to the spot outside the Negro hospital on Hartford Avenue, where twenty-seven victims of the burning were still convalescing. A wealthy white businessman named Charles Page, from nearby Sand Springs, purchased lights and other decorations for the Christmas tree, including the huge white cross that was placed on top. It had been Page, the oilman and erstwhile newspaper publisher, who had sold the *Tulsa Tribune* to Richard Lloyd Jones only two years earlier.

Then, on a night shortly before Christmas, Negro families walked across Greenwood and gathered around the Christmas tree in the evening chill. Red Cross workers scurried about, distributing twenty-seven hundred half-pound packages of fruits and nuts to the Negro children, and spools of thread, pillows, children's underwear, and quilts to the adults. The singing began when the last gifts were given, two thousand voices raised to the heavens as Greenwood sang traditional Christmas carols, interspersed with spirituals like "Swing Low, Sweet Chariot." The throng clapped for "Down by the River Side." Men and boys removed their hats for "Standing in the Need of Prayer."

Then, when the singing was over, a black preacher climbed onto the back of a truck and began to speak. He wished the crowd a Merry Christmas and reminded the people that they had much to be grateful for.

"Let us always remember the old Negro tradition," the preacher concluded. "There is no room in our hearts for hatred."

"Amen," some of the men and women replied. Then the crowd began to drift away, dispersing back across Greenwood to new homes in some cases, to tents in others. A few days later, on January 1, 1921, the last of the Red Cross workers who had come from around the nation packed up and left town for good.

He stood at the edge of the crowd that had gathered around the Christmas tree, a head taller than anyone, and maybe the only person in the throng who didn't sing. O. B. Mann had been walking across Greenwood on one of his nightly strolls when he heard the strange noises in the dusk. So he turned toward Hartford to investigate and saw all those Negroes at the Christmas tree, singing and taking handouts from the whites. His blood boiled once again.

O. B. had snuck back into Tulsa only the week before, ending a six-month exile that began the day after the burning, when he happened into his brother McKinley, who was staying with a bunch of other Negroes in an abandoned barn in the country. McKinley had cleaned out the safe at the grocery store before fleeing on June 1, so he handed his brother a stack of bills, telling

O. B. to head north because word was getting around about how many whites the youngest Mann brother had killed during the burning.

"Canada might be a good place for you about now," McKinley said. "I hear Toronto's got a fair number of Negroes."

"I ain't running from nothin' or nobody," O. B. stated.

"Well, suit yourself," McKinley said. "But if you stay in Tulsa, I'm telling you, you're as good as hung."

O. B. Mann didn't have the energy to argue long. He hopped a train to Kansas City. There he bought a rail ticket to Chicago, then to Detroit, then to Toronto, the city that did indeed have plenty of other Negroes, and poor white people from Europe who couldn't speak English, burly men who worked next to O. B. building bridges. O. B. took a bed in a boardinghouse with the bridge builders, and at night wrote to his family in Tulsa. The letters that came back said that the grocery store had burned along with almost everything else in Greenwood, but because of all those days O. B. had ridden his horse to the white bank down-town, there had been plenty of money to rebuild the store. In July, McKinley wrote to say that an indictment at the courthouse had O. B.'s name on it, and that five white deputies had come looking for him at the store. But another letter from McKinley about four months later told O. B. to come on home if he wanted to, because the whites no longer seemed interested in anything that had to do with the burning, including messing with Negro fellows, whether they had been indicted or not. So O. B. rode the train back across the border, from Toronto to Detroit to Kansas City, and finally to Okmulgee, where a friend he knew from the Army drove him into Tulsa in the middle of the night and dropped him off in front of the new Mann Brothers Grocery Store on Lansing.

For weeks after that, O. B. put on his apron and went to work behind the counter, or stocked shelves, or slaughtered chickens. He ventured outside only at night, leery that some deputy might still want to make a name for himself by capturing the giant Negro with so much white blood on his hands. On his evening strolls, O. B. nervously checked over his shoulder as he saw the new homes that took the place of the ones that had burned, and the new brick buildings in Deep Greenwood, and the piles of bricks where Mount Zion Baptist used to be. He heard the Christmas carols on one of those strolls and stood at the edge of the crowd, so much taller than anyone else, fuming. *Sleep in heavenly peace.* How could anyone sleep in peace again?

He almost couldn't restrain himself at the end, when that fellow stood up on the truck and yelled, "There is no room in our hearts for hatred." Where whites were concerned, there was no room in O. B. Mann's heart for anything but hatred. The sight of blue eyes nearly drove him crazy, nearly set him off to find his rifle. But the people of Greenwood, these sorry folks singing their carols, they had been beaten down. They were still slaves. They would keep their mouths shut, except to sing carols, and to keep their heads down to take whatever the whites wanted to give.

The crowd at the Christmas tree began to disperse, hauling away their Red Cross packages, and O. B. Mann went mumbling off into the night, wrestling with a rage that lived until the day in the 1940s, when cancer finally killed him. By then, he and Mc-Kinley had grown rich with their grocery store. Nephews remembered Uncle O. B. coming for visits to Southern California in a chauffeur-driven limousine. This huge man climbed out of the backseat and handed out candy and dollar bills to the children, and paid his nephews handsomely for washing his long car. But there was always a menace about him, too—the long silences when Uncle O. B.'s eyes darkened and his teeth ground together, and his fits of temper over the smallest things. Even the adults in his family were afraid of him.

Back in Oklahoma, O. B. Mann grew into a Negro legend from one end of the state to the other. The stories were told of how the giant Negro veteran killed all those whites during the great Tulsa burning of 1921, stories that grew more spectacular with each passing decade. That was one Negro who made the whites pay for their sins. But no one dared raise the subject with O. B. Mann directly for fear of what would happen if his rage boiled over. Once, a young nephew noticed the pale scar that ran the length of Uncle O. B.'s little finger.

"What happened to Uncle O. B.'s pinkie?" the boy asked his father, who was one of O. B.'s older brothers.

"Have you asked your uncle about that scar?" the father replied.

"No," the boy said.

"Good," the father said. "Don't."

CHAPTER 15

WHAT DO YOU SAY NOW?

The Greenwood teenager named Don Ross flunked most of his high-school classes, achievement befitting a loud, skirt-chasing youngster who generally found the meaning of life at the end of a pool cue. Ross, in fact, probably would have had much in common with young Dick Rowland decades before. History courses were the exception to Ross's shoddy academic record. Captivated by the past, he usually aced them. He also had a knack for stringing words together on paper, which partially explained his presence that day in the 1950s for the first meeting of the yearbook staff at Booker T. Washington High School. Ross also figured that yearbook work was a good way to meet girls.

The faculty adviser that year was a history teacher named Bill Williams, a graying man of about fifty who had been around Washington High longer than dirt. Mr. Williams began the meeting that day with a speech, something about the class yearbook being more than a chronicle of one year in a school. The yearbook also described the community at that time, he said, because school and community went together like mother and child. Then the teacher digressed.

"When I was a junior at Washington High, the prom never happened because there was a riot and the whites came over the tracks and wiped out Greenwood," Mr. Williams told the students. "In fact, this building was one of the few around here that wasn't burned, so they turned it into a hospital for colored folks. In those days, there were probably Negroes moaning and bleeding and dying in this very room. The whites over yonder burned Greenwood down, and with almost no help from anybody, the Negroes built it back to like it was. That's one of the things I mean when I say 'the story of a community'. "

Don Ross was daydreaming at his desk in back until Mr. Williams began talking about the burning. The boy's older relatives had never mentioned a word about anything so terrible, and Ross saw nothing about the place that gave the slightest hint of such carnage. Thriving entrepreneurs still lined Greenwood Avenue in the 1950s. Some of the world's finest blues and jazz musicians had gotten their start in the neighborhood. The nightlife at Greenwood and Archer was celebrated in song. So why would this teacher, a man held in such high regard by so many at the Negro high school and in Greenwood generally, tell such a ridiculous lie to a roomful of high-school students? Before he could catch himself, the impetuous teenager leaped from his seat.

"Mr. Williams, I don't believe that," Ross said. "I don't think you could burn this town down and have nobody know nothing about it. My people have been here since twenty-four and they never said a word about no riot."

"Sit down and shut up," Mr. Williams responded.

Ross immediately did as he was told, regretting his act the minute his fanny touched the seat. That was not an era when a student stood up and called his teacher a liar, at least not without the most severe consequences. Those students were taken to the coatrack and whipped for their transgressions, then sent home to be whipped again by their parents, and Ross figured he would get it at least that bad for what he'd said to Mr. Williams at the yearbook meeting.

But Ross never received a whipping, at least not for that. Mr. Williams glared at him, sure enough, but otherwise never said a word when the teenager walked from the classroom that afternoon. It was the next day, after the yearbook meeting, when the other students started to leave, that Mr. Williams finally spoke to him.

"Fat Mouth," the teacher said. "You stay here."

Ross's heart started pounding, anticipating the sting of Mr. Williams's belt on his rear. But when the other students had gone,

Mr. Williams pulled a thick scrapbook from the top drawer of his desk and handed it to the boy.

"Take a seat and see for yourself."

Ross sat down at a nearby desk. His head began to spin the minute he opened to the first picture, which showed white men standing over the remnants of a charred body lying prone in the dirt. The next photograph was just like it. Then came another picture of Negro corpses stacked on trucks; another of Negroes marching down familiar streets with their hands in the air, guarded by armed white men in civilian clothes; another of flames shooting out of little homes and from big brick businesses along Greenwood Avenue; another photograph of a huge wall of black smoke. There were dozens of images in all, each of them more awful than the last. By the time the boy closed the scrapbook, his stomach was spinning just like his head. Mr. Williams had been watching from his desk.

"What do you say now, Fat Mouth?" the teacher said.

For maybe the first time in his life, Don Ross had no reply.

But Bill Williams's lesson, his private tour through the darkest days in Tulsa history, had just begun. That same night after supper, Mr. Williams collected Ross in his car and drove him to the Greenwood home of another longtime history teacher named Seymour Williams, an older fellow, widely known as the taskmaster of the Washington High football teams.

"So this is the boy who doesn't believe in the riot," Seymour Williams said, smirking.

"Says it never happened," Bill said. "Says nothing like that could have happened because he'd never heard about it. Ain't that right, Fat Mouth? You hear about everything around here."

Ross just shrugged.

"Well, sit down next to me on this porch swing," Seymour Williams said. "And we'll tell you about something that never happened."

The two men talked for hours that night. Both were gifted storytellers who made a world from long ago come alive in all its sights and smells, down to the striped green awnings of the red-brick buildings along Greenwood Avenue. Bill and Seymour Williams at first described the magical era when Greenwood was transformed from a lonesome patch of prairie into a colored world within a world, a Negro paradise with its own doctors, lawyers, druggists, hotels, restaurants, grocery stores, funeral parlors, roller rinks, and movie theaters. Remember the Dreamland Theater, the big old place on Greenwood Avenue? Well, Bill Williams' parents owned that movie house, and a huge confectionary down the street, and an auto garage, too. Hundreds of colored folks bought tickets to the movies each night, and bought sodas in the confectionary, and strolled up and down Greenwood Avenue, singing, flirting, and carrying on. Tulsa, Oklahoma, was the best place for a Negro in America. Can you believe that, Fat Mouth?

"But that made the white folks jealous, didn't it?" Bill Williams said that night on Seymour's porch. "They figured the Negroes in Greenwood were getting too uppity, and if there was one thing a white couldn't tolerate then, it was an uppity nigger. Then one night the whites got their excuse to do something about it. The police charged this Negro boy, this fellow named Rowland, with raping a white girl. In fact, the boy's momma still runs a boardinghouse on Archer. A white lynch mob tried to get him at the courthouse, which happened all the time in those days, at least in other places. But Greenwood's finest men, and my daddy was one of them, weren't going to let that happen here. I'm telling you, Tulsa Negroes were a proud bunch. So they drove down to the courthouse to stop the lynching, and a shot was fired, and all hell broke loose, and the next thing you knew, thousands of whites came over the tracks, blazing away with their guns.

"I was a boy about your age when it happened." My dad stood in the window at Greenwood and Archer as they came over. He was a crack shot, got a bunch of them as they crossed the tracks. I was standing right next to my daddy as he fired, and I saw the white hoodlums fall. I figure more white folks died than coloreds. We were winning the riot until the airplanes came.

"Yes, Fat Mouth, airplanes that roared in over Greenwood firing down at the Negro folks as they tried to run. Some of those planes dropped explosives onto the Negro buildings and that's what finally turned the tide against us. The Negroes knew they were licked when those airplanes showed up."

So the white mobs had their way, marching right up to every house in Greenwood, including Seymour Williams's place on Detroit. Seymour said he planned to fix the mobsters when they arrived at his door, because he had a military .45 and damn sure knew how to use it. But that morning, his wife and her friends tripped him on his way to the door and stole his gun, or else he probably wouldn't be sitting here, rocking on his front porch on a cool September night thirty-some years later.

"Instead of killing me, which they would have done if I had tried to get tough, those whites took me away and put me in jail, and I watched from the jail window while everything burned," Seymour Williams said. "And I mean everything. Isn't that right, Bill?"

"Every damn thing," Bill Williams said. "Look around you, Fat Mouth. Everything you can see, for as far as you can see, was nothing but a pile of ashes when those whites finished with the Negroes down here."

Bill and Seymour Williams rocked faster and faster on the porch swing as they talked, and as they did, it was as if ghostlike demons flew up out of their insides and into the cool night. Their spoken recollections seemed to lighten the burden on their souls. It was the same way the next night, when Bill Williams introduced Don Ross to the city worker named Robert Fairchild, who told his own terrible story. The night after that, Ross met George Monroe, that skinny fellow who delivered sodas, and who was only five when the mobster stepped on his hand as he hid beneath a bed in his home. Ross met an undertaker named Jackson, and Wilhelmina Guess Howell, and dozens of others in time, wondering how in the world so many folks could have kept such a terrible secret.

"Because the killers are still in charge in this town, boy," Bill Williams answered as they drove to meet another survivor. "Now you understand why anyone who lived through that once damn sure doesn't want to have to live through it again. You ask a Negro about the riot, he'll tell you what happened if he knows who you are. But everyone's real careful about what they say. I hear the same is true for the white folks, though I suspect their reasons are different. They're not afraid, just embarrassed. Or if they are afraid, it's not of dying, it's of going to jail."

In 1946, a white Chicago native named Nancy Feldman moved South to take a job teaching sociology at the University of Tulsa, and not long afterward met a warm, intelligent Negro man named Robert Fairchild. When they met, Feldman was moonlighting as a sociologist at the Tulsa Health Department, while Fairchild, one of a handful of black municipal employees, organized recreation programs for Tulsa youth. The two quickly became friends, and Feldman was highly curious about Fairchild's life as a Negro who had grown up in Tulsa. So it wasn't long before the Negro man began recounting his days of shining shoes with the notorious Dick Rowland and of Rowland's ultimate misfortune, and the cataclysm that happened because of it. Feldman was stunned as she listened. The way Fairchild described what had happened, the burning of Greenwood surely ranked among one of the nation's worst racial atrocities, yet the young scholar could not recall a single mention of the catastrophe in any of her history texts.

Not that Feldman doubted Fairchild. Not at all. There was something in his manner that convinced her it had happened just the way he described it. She was so sure of it, in fact, that she decided to introduce the Negro's horrifying recollections to her classroom. What better topic for Tulsa sociology students than the historic example of hatred's handiwork that had occurred so close to home?

Feldman also was eager to get her white students' perspective on the affair. But on the day she repeated Fairchild's story in class, she was dumbfounded by the response. The students seemed surprised, or defensive, or they greeted her words with uncomprehending stares. None admitted to knowing about the burning, and a few argued that it was impossible that such a terrible thing could have happened in such a prosperous and tranquil city. To prove it to them, Feldman invited Fairchild to repeat his story to the students in person. He did so, but they remained stubbornly disbelieving. Many of Feldman's students mentioned the classroom debate to their parents, who insisted that the burning was nothing but a lie. Not long after that, Feldman's dean encouraged her to drop the subject entirely, a suggestion the new professor promptly ignored. She insisted on inviting Fairchild back to her class the next semester, but her students then were just as oblivious.

Where the burning was concerned, oblivion was a Tulsa-wide contagion, though it took some time after the event before the affliction fully set in. In the immediate months and years afterward, postcards depicting burning Negro homes and businesses and charred Negro corpses were bought and sold on Tulsa's downtown streets, and white participants openly boasted about notches on their guns, earned during Greenwood's obliteration, which initially was a widespread source of civic pride.

But by modern necessity, the events of 1921 became an embarrassment, something better forgotten. Tulsa much preferred to promote itself as a thriving city with an impressive skyline, tree-lined neighborhoods populated by spacious mansions, new art museums, and a growing degree of sophistication that belied the lawlessness of the early days. The burning was like an ugly birthmark in the middle of Tulsa's cultural forehead that would forever disfigure the place. Unless, of course, it was covered up and forgotten. Those who could not forget meanwhile, consoled themselves with the notion that the burning had been the Negroes' fault—the whites had merely acted to put down an uprising of uppity and lawless blacks.

Thus Tulsa's remarkable conspiracy of silence was born. Communities across the nation had struggled mightily to sweep their racial atrocities under the carpet, but in no other city were the horrors as great and the cultural amnesia so complete as in Tulsa. The burning would later be compared to the pogroms of Europe, or to ethnic cleansing. One scholar termed the burning the American *Kristallnacht*, referring to the night before World War II when the Nazis overran and terrorized Jewish neighborhoods. But the American *Kristallnacht* was not mentioned in an Oklahoma history book until 1941, and that first mention came in a single paragraph. Texts in the years to come generally described the catastrophe in passing, a footnote to what were described as greater historical events of the day.

Though it had generated front-page headlines around the world in the days after it happened, the tragedy also disappeared from Oklahoma newspapers, particularly those in Tulsa. On June 1, 1936, in its regular feature called "Fifteen Years Ago Today," the *Tulsa Tribune* of Richard Lloyd Jones recalled that on the day of the burning, "Miss Carolyn Skelly was a charming young hostess of the past week, having entertained at a luncheon and theater party for Miss Kathleen Sinclair, and her guest, Miss Julia Morley of Saginaw, Mich." The burning was not mentioned, nor did it come up in the paper on the event's twenty-fifth anniversary.

That paper's chief local rival distanced itself just as aggressively. In the spring of 1971, after seven months of research, a local writer named Ed Wheeler submitted his account of the burning to Russell Gideon, editor of the *Tulsa World*'s Sunday magazine. Wheeler had previously published several articles in the *World*'s magazine, but this time, Gideon told Wheeler that the newspaper needed to pass.

"This is a hell of a good article," the editor told Wheeler then. "But there is an unwritten rule at this paper that we don't touch this subject with an eleven-foot pole."

By then, of course, Wheeler was not surprised.

Earlier in that spring of 1971, Ed Wheeler felt a tap at his shoulder one day while walking in downtown Tulsa and turned to see a white stranger, a man in his forties dressed in coveralls.

"Don't print that article," the man said before turning and walking casually down the street.

The phone calls began coming to Wheeler's home at about the same time. There was no secret about what he was up to, interviewing scores of blacks and whites about the one topic in Tulsa that remained taboo. Many white Tulsans cringed when they heard about Wheeler's work, envisioning a blow to the city's reputation, or worse—overdue indictments for murder. Hence the threatening encounter on the street and the calls to his home, each of them with a similar message. "Don't write that article," the callers would say, always anonymously. "You have no business sticking your nose into that. Leave it alone." Wheeler generally sniffed and hung up on those calls, which came increasingly in the spring of 1971. But Wheeler's wife Marcia was not nearly so sanguine. On several occasions, she had been home alone and answered the telephone only to hear an ominous male voice at the other end. "Tell him not to write that article," the callers said, causing Marcia Wheeler to shudder at the implied threat of what would happen—to her husband, or to her, or, most frighteningly, the couple's two-year-old son—if Wheeler proceeded.

Then, on a day in early May, Ed Wheeler finally became concerned himself. That morning as he left his home for work, he found a message scrawled in soap across the windshield of his car:

"Best look under your hood from now on," the words said.

Wheeler fumed while he quickly erased the scrawl before his wife could see it. He was a veteran of several dicey operations as a Military Intelligence officer in Vietnam, a hulking fellow who, over the next twenty years, attained the rank of brigadier general in the Oklahoma National Guard. In other words, Ed Wheeler did not frighten easily. But now the bastards had crossed the line.

Wheeler would never back down. He would not be intimidated, and if anything, the threats only made him more determined. But he could no longer dismiss the threat to his family. That night he moved his wife and son across town, into the home of his wife's mother, subsisting himself for the next month on canned food and frozen dinners while completing what became Tulsa's first detailed account of the burning in fifty years.

The assignment had begun innocently enough in a casual conversation between Wheeler and Larry Silvey, editor of Tulsa's Chamber of Commerce magazine. That night the two men had run into each other in the Tulsa Press Club and proceeded to discuss Wheeler's popular local radio show, called *The Gilcrease Story*, named for the prestigious local museum that sponsored the program. Five days a week, Wheeler used radio sound effects to recreate moments in U.S. history. The show also occasionally depicted events from black history, which had earned Wheeler a large audience on the north side of Tulsa.

That night at the Press Club, Silvey wondered if there was a piece of history that Wheeler would not dare tackle.

"I suppose there is," Wheeler said after thinking for a moment. "I wouldn't want to do a story on the Tulsa Race Riot. I'd be afraid I might create another Orson Welles effect."

Silvey could see Wheeler's point, but quickly thought of an alternative.

"Would you be interested in doing it for print?" he asked.

Wheeler, who had written several articles for local newspapers, was intrigued with the idea, especially when Silvey kept talking. The fiftieth anniversary of what was known as the Tulsa Race Riot rapidly approached, and in Silvey's estimation, a story about the event would be a positive thing, demonstrating the city's progress in race relations. Who could object to something like that, especially a half-century later?

Wheeler thus agreed to embark on a long and surprising odyssey, realizing within weeks that the horror of what had happened in 1921 transcended anything that had been publicly discussed in Tulsa for decades. He knew this after the first few interviews with black survivors in meetings he was able to arrange because of his visibility in the Negro community. Their fear remained palpable, even five decades later. None would allow Wheeler to use their names in his story. Most insisted on meeting only at night, in the sanctuary of their churches and with their pastors present. Wheeler was glad to agree.

As winter turned to the spring of 1971, he became a familiar sight in Greenwood, crossing over the tracks night after night to meet another aging survivor who was always waiting in the pews with his or her family and their preacher when Wheeler arrived. Grandchildren accompanied some of the survivors, and the white writer knew by the shocked look on their faces as they listened that the young people were hearing the story of the burning for the first time.

Word also quickly spread to the white side of town about Wheeler's work, about his interviews with Tulsa whites, and about the hours he spent in the public library poring over old newspapers. Like the blacks, Wheeler's white sources insisted on anonymity. Among them were two remorseful Klansmen who said they had merely tried to teach the Negroes a lesson, a lesson that had gotten out of hand. A third Klansman whom Wheeler interviewed said his only regret was that more Negroes weren't killed, that more Negroes' buildings had not been destroyed. The anonymous phone calls to Wheeler's home intensified; then came the overt threat on his windshield as the writer stubbornly plowed ahead to finish what he had begun.

"This is the story of a race riot," read the first sentence of Wheeler's story. "It is not a pretty story, and it is not told for its shock value or to reopen old wounds. It is presented because it happened fifty years ago to another generation whose story is pertinent to this generation.

"The blame for the riot was heaped upon 'Negroes of the lower class—gamblers and bootleggers and a group of Negroes who had been worked upon by a lawless element of white agitators, reds and bolshevists.' But this was hogwash," Wheeler wrote. "Prejudice, suspicion, ignorance and hate caused the riot. Intolerance, anger, rumormongering and fear fanned its flames. Such elements were prevalent in abundance on both sides of the racial fence."

They were courageous words for a white writer in 1971 Tulsa. But by the standards of stories printed two decades later, the piece that followed was restrained and understated. After estimating the death toll at three hundred, and describing the internment of thousands of homeless blacks, Wheeler recounted the tragedy hour by hour, beginning with Dick Rowland's arrest, followed by the outbreak at the courthouse and the attack on Greenwood by thousands of armed whites. The report seemed based more on 1921 newspaper stories than on the writer's own interviews. No white or black participants were implicated by name.

Wheeler's restraint no doubt contributed to Larry Silvey's delight when he read Wheeler's article for the first time. Silvey immediately made plans to publish the piece in the Chamber magazine opposite an essay on local race relations written by one of Tulsa's black ministers. The Chamber's general manager, Clyde Cole, however, was much less enthusiastic.

"This article will start a race riot," Cole told Wheeler. After seven months of work without pay, Wheeler's story was rejected.

A few days later, Wheeler pitched the piece to Larry Gideon at the *Tulsa World*, but with the same result. Wheeler began to realize that his only hope of salvaging the months of work that had brought such pain and dislocation to his family was a print outlet in the black community, desperation that spawned an unlikely alliance between Wheeler—the white military officer, radio personality, and freelance writer—and a black magazine publisher named Don Ross.

Ross was the same Greenwood pool shark whose life had been transformed in the 1950s by Bill Williams' grim history lesson. He had joined the civil rights movement a decade later and by the spring of 1971, had begun publishing a black magazine called *Oklahoma Impact*, a publication he hoped would someday tell the real story of the Tulsa burning and who was to blame. He could scarcely believe his good fortune when Wheeler walked into his office on an afternoon in May 1971, completed manuscript in hand. Ross's opportunity to wrest the burning from the shadows of history had come sooner than he could have dreamed, and there could be no more credible writer than a man like Wheeler, who went around town in his captain's uniform of the Oklahoma National Guard, a man who was a celebrity with whites and Negroes alike because of his radio show.

In 1971, the cover of the June/July edition of *Oklahoma Impact* was a wreath of flames around the large headline: PROFILE OF A RACE RIOT. Wheeler's story took up most of the pages inside; the article was wrapped around grisly photographs of the burning that were published for the first time. The magazine printed five thousand copies, twice its normal press run, which were swept up by black Tulsans the moment they hit the newsstands. Within hours, Negro readers flooded Ross and Wheeler with calls of congratulations. The secret of the burning was finally out. Copies also made their way across the tracks to white Tulsa, where they were passed from hand to hand and read surreptitiously, and some of those who called to compliment Wheeler were whites. Other white Tulsans grumbled, chastising Wheeler particularly for what they believed was his inflated estimate of the dead. But for the most part in white Tulsa, the article was publicly ignored. Wheeler had not named names, which was a relief, and the threatening calls to his home ended. Two weeks after publication, his wife and son returned home. Wheeler stuck his notes into a file cabinet and returned to work on his radio show.

Remarkably, the event, which had briefly escaped the shadows, was immediately allowed to return to limbo. The white press, both in Tulsa and around the nation, ignored Wheeler's article and the historic nightmare it described. The burning remained deprived of its place in contemporary history books. In the years to come, only occasionally would white or black writers attempt to continue the process Ed Wheeler and Don Ross had begun.

Among them was Ruth Sigler Avery, the same person who, as a little girl, had watched Klan members torture a Negro man in a hilltop cross-burning ceremony, the woman who would never forget the face of the dead boy whose body was piled with the others on the truck that rumbled past her window on the morning of the burning. By the 1970s, Avery had taken on the burning as her personal crusade, spending much of that decade interviewing black survivors and white witnesses for what she envisioned as a book that would finally tell the whole truth of what had happened. Avery's book was never published, but transcripts of her interviews became a crucial resource for journalists, authors, and historians a quarter-century later.

By the mid-1970s, a white college student named Scott Ellsworth had also begun his own long investigation into the event; it consumed much of his life for the next two decades. Ellsworth, who was born and raised in Tulsa's white, middle-class neighborhood, remembered hearing about the burning as a teenager from black busboys and waiters, his coworkers at local restaurants. Later, while attending college in Oregon, he chose the burning as his topic for an undergraduate thesis, astounding professors with what he had written, first in Oregon, then at Duke University, where he was a graduate student in history. In 1982, with the encouragement of his teachers, Ellsworth published *Death in the Promised Land*. The book drew on the young scholar's own interviews with survivors such as Bill and Seymour Williams, Robert Fairchild, and Wilhelmina Guess Howell, plus a thorough review of court records and contemporary newspaper accounts from around the nation. What resulted was the most withering indictment yet of the racial climate of the time, and of white Tulsa's role in Greenwood's obliteration, a book that remained definitive on the topic for most of the next two decades.

But *Death in the Promised Land* enjoyed only modest sales and generated only occasional feature articles in the national press. Once again, white Tulsa endeavored to ignore the reminder of its dark past. Surprisingly, as the decade of the 1980s drew to a close, the city remained safe with its terrible secret.

CHAPTER 16

THE VEIL LIFTED

They are very old now, all seven men and women who gather in the Old Capitol Building of Tallahassee, Florida, standing nervously while surrounded by family and friends and the daunting glare of television lights and the gaggle of journalists. It is such a public spectacle after all those decades of hauling their horrors around in private, remembering the gunshots and the deaths and the fire of that first week in January of 1923. The seven had been children then, and after all these years, if they can trust their eyes and ears as they stand together in the Capitol on May 4, 1994, there will finally be a measure of justice, paltry amends maybe, when you considered what had happened to their little village so long ago, but amends just the same.

The seven African American survivors of the massacre at the place called Rosewood are dressed in symbolic red and white: white for Rosewood's innocence, red for the blood of innocent people that was spilled then. Seated before them is Florida Governor Lawton Chiles, ceremonial pen in hand. Television cameras prepare to capture this historic moment, the first time any state has compensated the survivors of racial violence. Chiles tells the television cameras that the bill before him will help disperse the "shadow of shame" that had lingered like a fog over his state for eighty-one years.

It had begun on New Year's Day of 1923 with the accusations made by a white married woman named Fannie Taylor, who told her neighbors that an unknown black man knocked at her door that morning and beat and robbed her when she answered. Little matter that Taylor's Negro laundress saw the woman's white paramour come and go from the house around the time of the supposed attack. Truth was always a relative thing, especially in those days when whites across the state, across the whole nation, really, didn't need much of an excuse to give ruthless vent to their racial hatred.

Just three years earlier, whites snatched four Negroes in the Florida town of McClenny, lynching them for the alleged rape of a white woman. Five more Florida blacks killed and a black community at Ocoee destroyed in a dispute over voting rights. Another Florida Negro lynched in Wauchula for yet another alleged attack on a white woman. Still another Florida Negro burned at the stake in Perry for allegedly killing a white schoolteacher. On New Year's Eve 1922, the Ku Klux Klan celebrates the holiday with a huge march in Gainesville, while the next day, forty miles away in the little place called Sumner, Fannie Taylor weeps hysterically, saying a black man is responsible for the bruises on her face, and the specter of the knuckle-dragging Negro buck appears once again.

So angry white mobs gather in that rural part of Central Florida, clean out the local hardware store of its ammunition and set off into the woods with their guns and dogs in search of a Negro felon who supposedly has escaped from a nearby chain gang. The mob encounters one Negro man who is shot to death and hung from a tree when he isn't quick enough to cough up the fugitive's whereabouts.

The mob inevitably moves toward the place called Rosewood, home to a few dozen black families and a general store, a sugar mill, a one-room school, three churches, and a nifty baseball team called the Rosewood Stars, which plays on the field by the Masonic Lodge. Many of the Rosewood people work in the white sawmill nearby, or as domestics for white families in Sumner, then come home to what is a uniformly tranquil place hidden in the pine woods, at least until the mob comes looking for Fannie Taylor's assailant and tries to force its way into the home of a Negro woman named Sarah Carrier. Sarah's son is a proud man named Sylvester, who greets the intruders with a cloud of buckshot as children in the house flee into the woods. Sarah, her son, and two whites die in the exchange, which newspapers around the state trumpet as a full-fledged race war, making the Negroes seem like the aggressors.

So whites converge on little Rosewood, seething, many of them drunk. One Rosewood woman named Lexie Gordon is sick with typhoid fever and unable to flee with the others, so she stays in bed until flames consume her house, then is shot dead by the mob when she tries to stagger out the back door. Another Negro reportedly is ordered to dig his own grave before the mob shoots him down. The local sheriff and the Florida governor look the other way while the mob sets about finishing its business in Rosewood and does not stop until there is nothing left to burn.

Six Rosewood Negroes are dead by the end of that week, yet a state grand jury cannot find enough evidence to return a single indictment, and the people of Rosewood are scattered forever, keeping their dark secret until 1982, when an enterprising newspaper reporter from St. Petersburg catches wind of the atrocity in the woods that had happened so many decades before. Thus the secret is finally out. A year later, the Rosewood survivors are telling their stories on national television, and by then, it is fashionable for the nation's whites to express their abhorrence at what had happened. The survivors' descendants begin insisting that the state of Florida make good. Some of them are surprised when the government decides to do just that.

"The long silence has finally been broken and the shadow has been lifted," Governor Chiles says on that day in May 1994, as seven old people stand around him, dressed in white and red. "This legislation assures that the tragedy of Rosewood will never be forgotten by generations to come."

The governor does not mention the nasty legislative fight that had led up to that moment, or that the first proposal had called for seven million dollars in reparations to Rosewood's survivors, a figure pared by more than two-thirds during a legislative debate that brought racial politics to a full boil. But the backroom deals had finally been made, the votes taken, and in front of Chiles that morning is a bill that will pay Rosewood survivors up to two million dollars and provide college scholarships for twenty-five minority students. The room erupts in applause when Chiles affixes his signature.

Minnie Lee Langley was one of the seven survivors who stood there and watched. To think that she would be here before these television cameras, behind the governor himself, all these years later. She was just nine years old in those days of 1923 when all the crackers came walking up the railroad tracks by the hundreds, guns in their hands and evil in their hearts, causing Minnie Lee and so many others to scatter into the woods. Now, here she stands in the Old Capitol, where the governor signs the papers and reporters ask how she feels.

"I never lost my faith," Minnie Lee Langley replies. "It's been a long way to go."

Fifteen hundred miles west, another state legislator celebrates the Rosewood triumph. By that spring day in 1994, Don Ross, the same man his history teacher once called Fat Mouth, the one-time crusading magazine editor, is now among the senior members of the Oklahoma House of Representatives, serving the place on the north side of Tulsa that is still called Greenwood. He has kept a close eye on the situation in Florida and has spoken on several occasions with lawmakers who had led the Rosewood reparations fight, because he knows that someday the same battle awaits him.

The more he learns, the more Ross is amazed by how much the story of Rosewood resembles the horrible tales he's been hearing from Greenwood folks since he was a teenager. But there is at least one crucial distinction. The whole community of Rosewood would have fit into one small corner of the sprawling, thriving community that was black Tulsa in 1921. If Florida saw fit to make amends, to coax its own horrors out of the closet,

Oklahoma would have to do so as well. The moment Ross had been waiting for since that day in the high-school yearbook meeting was growing near.

The horrible tremors could be felt at the Oklahoma State Capitol a few miles away. In an awful millisecond on the morning of April 19, 1995, a truck bomb reduced the Alfred Murrah Federal Building in downtown Oklahoma City to a pile of rubble and a dollhouse-like skeleton of twisted steel. The images of that moment were forever seared into a nation's consciousness, and journalists groped for awful superlatives to describe what was called "the worst episode of civil violence in America since the Civil War." One hundred sixty-eight people were killed, so many of them children. Television crews were on the scene within seconds to capture the images of dazed, blood-splattered survivors and the grim rescue workers who carried the lifeless forms of babies from the rubble.

But what if television crews had been present a hundred miles east as the sun came up on June 1, 1921? What if the cameras had recorded Negro families racing from burning homes in their nightclothes; or Negroes screaming as they were burned alive; or Negroes shot dead by the mob because they didn't empty their pockets fast enough; or truck after truck piled high with Negro corpses; or the surreal landscape when it was finally over, the vibrant Negro community reduced to nothing but rubble and ash; or the sea of despair in the detention camps where thousands of homeless Negroes were forced to congregate? What then? That's what Don Ross and so many others in his community wanted to know. Yes, what had happened at the Murrah Building had been an unthinkable tragedy, but the media was mistaken. The explosion was not the worst thing that had happened in this country since the Civil War. That dubious honor also belonged to Oklahoma, but to the city a hundred miles east. It's just that television cameras weren't around in Tulsa on that morning of 1921 when the whites came pouring over the tracks. And most of the victims were black, so instead of days of national mourning and the race to build a fitting monument, the world got out a big broom and swept the obliteration of Greenwood under a huge carpet.

It became known as the Tulsa Race Riot Commission, an eleven-member appointive body made up of whites and blacks—scholars, businessmen and women, and state legislators. In the greatest tradition of American government, before any money could be spent in reparations for the Greenwood survivors, there had to be a study first. Don Ross knew as much when he introduced his bill in 1997, the one demanding five million dollars in reparations for Tulsa's burning. "Reparations for what?" Oklahoma legislators would ask, because at the time, only a handful of them had any notion at all that the catastrophe had ever happened.

So the reparations demand was just to get the political juices flowing, Ross knew, a headline grabber that would begin a long process. Oklahoma legislative leaders proposed a compromise to Ross, the promise of a state-funded commission to undertake a thorough study of what had happened in Tulsa and suggest an appropriate remedy.

Thus the veil was lifted, an exhumation that struck like a thunderclap. In newsrooms around the world, reporters and editors read wire stories about a new state commission created to study the incident in Tulsa, Oklahoma, where up to three hundred people had been killed and mobs of whites had wiped out what had been called "the Negro Wall Street of America," a uniquely prosperous community of ten thousand blacks. In the months and years to come, *The New York Times, Washington Post, Los Angeles Times, The Economist, London Daily Telegraph, The National Post of Canada,* and scores of other newspapers and magazines arrived to remedy the historic oversight and undertake extensive coverage. Film crews from prestigious American TV programs such as *Nightline* and *60 Minutes II* converged on Tulsa with those from Australia, South Africa, and Sweden.

The stories detailed the commission's search for mass graves and the already heated debate over reparations that continued on Tulsa talk radio and in the barrooms and coffee shops. "Why should we pay for something that happened eighty years ago?" went the arguments on one side. "How can we not?" said those on the other. Most of the stories from around the world also reflected something else; the pervasive incredulity that something so horrible could have remained a secret for so long.

No longer were the Greenwood survivors afraid. No longer was it necessary to speak about the burning only at night, in their churches, with their pastors seated nearby as witnesses and protectors. Many survivors, in fact, became minor celebrities in newspapers, magazines, and television, particularly those with the most horrifying memories. Dozens were also videotaped while telling their stories to Riot Commission investigators.

And for the first time ever, white Tulsans spoke out in numbers. A commission investigator named Dick Warner logged hundreds of telephone calls, some of them made anonymously but most of them not, from whites who were children at the time of the burning, or who had heard stories passed down from parents or grandparents. One elderly man told Warner of going to a young friend's house just after the burning and seeing a photograph of fifty black bodies piled on a truck, an image that had stayed with him all these years. Dozens of others had similar recollections, or told stories of black bodies dumped into trenches out in the country, or into the Arkansas River, or into abandoned mines. A white nurse called to describe caring for an elderly white man who bragged of shooting blacks during the burning, insisting that he would do it again if he had the chance. Another man called to say that some Negroes were still moaning when his father, a trucker for a local firm, hauled them to a mass grave near Dawson Road. The trucker always cried when he drove by the place in years to come, and began to drink heavily, and years later, confessed to what he had done to his black coworkers. "Mr. Earl, the police made you do it and it shouldn't bother you," the blacks told him.

Caller Number 35 was a man named Clyde Eddy, an elderly Tulsan who said he knew precisely where some of the black bodies were buried. Eddy had been a boy of ten when the burning happened. A few days later, he and a cousin were walking by Oaklawn Cemetery when they noticed several men digging a large pit. A group of big wooden crates sat nearby. The boys grew curious and snuck up to have a look. Peeking under the lid of the first crate, they saw that it contained the bodies of three Negro men. They saw four more black bodies piled in the second crate before the grave diggers saw them and shooed them away.

Among the last to call was the old man named Lee Cisco, who had lived in Southern California for most of his life. He had seen local television reports about the burning in Tulsa and the subsequent attempts to cover it up, but it never had been a secret to Cisco, who still occasionally woke up drenched with sweat from the Tulsa nightmare. He, too, was a boy when the burning happened, living with his family next door to Tulsa's Convention Hall. He watched whites drag black corpses down the streets behind their cars and stack them in ugly piles just a few feet from the boy's front porch. When the burning was over, Cisco's father drove his family through what was left of Greenwood. "This is what happens when people start hating each other and it gets out of hand," the father said. A few weeks later, Lee Cisco's father loaded his wife and children into the car and headed to California because he didn't want his family to live in a place that hated like that.

By February 28, 2001, those recollections had been folded into the Riot Commission's final report. On that cold, rainy day in late winter, the report, which called for reparations similar to those received by the survivors and descendants of Rosewood, was formally presented to Oklahoma Governor Frank Keating, Tulsa Mayor Susan Savage, and state legislative leaders.

"We accept this report with an open heart," Keating said that

day in an ornate room of the Oklahoma Capitol. Three riot survivors sat before him in the audience, wearing buttons that said
REPARATIONS NOW! "I do not know what the legislature will do,
but I assure you that something will be done."

Representative Don Ross, his work almost done, stood in the
wings while the governor spoke. Whether reparations were paid
or not, there was now no escaping the truth. In the spring of
1921, Greenwood had been destroyed by an act of evil worthy of
Nazi Germany.

"We told these people to lift themselves up by their bootstraps," Ross told reporters afterward, nodding to the three aging
survivors. "And they did, by forming the most successful black
community in America.

"And once they had lifted themselves up by their bootstraps,"
Ross went on, "we destroyed them for it."

John and Loula Williams would know their building today, three
sturdy stories of red brick at the corner of Greenwood and Archer,
the same place they rebuilt within months of the burning. But
today the confectionary is gone, replaced by the offices of the
Greenwood Chamber of Commerce and a women's clothing store.
The Dreamland Theater is long gone, too. State offices have settled into the other old buildings on the same block. There's a
place that rents medical equipment, and there are a few restaurants, but otherwise the area is quiet during the day and deserted
at night. A short distance away, the once-fine neighborhoods of
Detroit and Elgin Avenues are just empty, grassy hills in the
shadow of Tulsa's skyline. The black neighborhoods now lie farther north, stretching away for miles into the rolling hills where
Negro refugees once hid. Only that one historic block of Deep
Greenwood is all that remains of the way things used to be, those
familiar buildings now tucked into the shadows of a freeway over-
pass. For most visitors, it requires a great act of imagination to
envision what the place must have been like all those years ago,

when you had to push through the happy throngs, especially on a Thursday, the maids' day off.

But some still remember. Each year, their numbers dwindle, but more than a hundred of those people remain. They live in nursing homes, or in small dwellings on the north side of the railroad tracks that still divide white Tulsa from black. They are generally warm, gracious people who have spent much of the past eighty years trying not to hate, because they have seen, more than almost anyone else, what hatred can do.

A nurse's aide wheels Wilhelmina Guess Howell from her room in a nursing home into the brightly lit lobby. Wilhelmina is well into her nineties on this sunny morning in the summer of 2000, and most of the past is very fuzzy to her. But the mention of Dr. Andrew Jackson's name still causes her to beam. "He was my favorite," she says.

The previous spring, the elderly widow named Eldoris Ector McCondichie grieved the recent loss of one of her children, but she still consents to discuss the burning, and her own mother's frightening words on that rosy morning so long ago. "Eldoris, wake up! We have to go! The white people are killing the colored folks!"

The life of Otis Clark is a book in itself. Otis went to Hollywood as a young man and butlered for Clark Gable, Joan Crawford, and Charlie Chaplin. But before that, he was a Greenwood teenager.

"Oh, child, we had what you might say a little city, like New York or Chicago," Otis says one day in his apartment, the skyline of modern Tulsa looming in the distance. "We had two theaters, two pool halls, hotels, and cafés and stuff. We had an amazing little city. Williams Confectionary was on the corner of Greenwood and Archer. We'd go there to get ice cream and sodas." He pauses and winks. "And at the same time, we'd slip in a little whiskey."

Then came the burning, the morning when Otis saw one of his friends shot by the snipers in the mill, the day his stepfather disappeared without a trace. But this afternoon in his apartment, still vital and dapper at age ninety-six, he is without a trace of rancor, a man who flirts unabashedly with a pretty white photographer.

"Come here," Otis says to her. "Gimme some sugah."

He grins broadly when the photographer kisses his cheek.

George Monroe has been cutting his grass on this warm summer night near the end of the century, but he agrees to interrupt his evening chores to tell his story once more. He is a courtly, painfully thin old gentleman with a gray mustache, the same fellow who, as a little boy, hid beneath the bed in his home while that mobster stepped on his hand. George tells many other stories from his long life, tales from his time as an American soldier in the Battle of the Bulge, or working as a deputy sheriff, or as Tulsa's first black deliveryman for Coca-Cola, or as the keeper of a popular saloon, or as the still-grieving father of a fine boy, Michael, who was murdered in Chicago a few years ago after earning an MBA. But George Monroe is a survivor above all, one among the thousands of people in Greenwood whose life was forever defined by those hours in the late spring so many years ago when the whites came marching up the street with their guns and their torches. Some days now, George Monroe wears a remarkable souvenir from that day, a pendant made of dimes that were melted together when his family's home burned. And he still wonders how people could be so mean for no good reason at all.

In all these years, no one has been able to answer that for him. The best folks can do is to listen to his story and join in with his remembrances. Now he takes a sip from a beer, rises from his chair and disappears into a back room of his home. In a minute, he returns holding a blackened penny, one of hundreds his family extracted from the ruins of their place so long ago.

"That's a penny you can keep," he says, handing it over. "Keep that penny as a reminder."

CHAPTER NOTES

PROLOGUE

I first heard the story of Eldoris McCondichie from Eddie Faye Gates, a member of the Tulsa Race Riot Commission, and it was Gates who arranged my interview with Mrs. McCondichie on a cloudy morning in the spring of 2000. The elderly burning survivor had lost a son to cancer only a few weeks before, but was patient, poised, and gracious during our talk in the living room of her home. And her statement about the burning, made while grabbing tissues from a box on her bookcase, testified to the fact that old horrors and heartbreak also remained vivid.

CHAPTER 1

My account of Townsend Jackson's address at the First Baptist Church in Greenwood is drawn from the *Tulsa Star* of May 30, 1913. Front-page coverage of the meeting of the United Brothers of Friendship, a leading black fraternal organization of that time, was no doubt written by editor Andrew J. Smitherman himself. In addition to describing the duet of the Rollison sisters and the attire of the men and women in attendance, Smitherman's paper also provided a complete text of Jackson's speech, which "went deep into the hearts of those who heard it," the *Star* reported. That fawning coverage was typical of Townsend Jackson's early years in Tulsa, when he was something of a media darling, at least in the *Star*. Two months after his speech at First Baptist, another story in the *Star* announced that the Oklahoma governor had appointed Jackson a representative to the National Negro Education Conference in Kansas City. Other stories regularly promulgated Jackson's political views, articles that ran beside the increasingly familiar portrait of the handsome middle-aged Negro man in a starched white shirt.

In 1914, the *Star* published short profiles of black Tulsa's leading citizens, including John Stradford, John and Loula Williams, O. W. Gurley, and Barney Cleaver, articles that were invaluable sources of information on those prominent individuals and their community. Townsend Jackson's odyssey from slavery to the Battle of Lookout Mountain, to Memphis and Guthrie, and finally to Greenwood, was described in one of those newspaper profiles.

My descriptions of life in Memphis and Guthrie and the insights I gained into that time came from several sources, including Joseph H. Cartwright's *Triumph of Jim Crow: Tennessee Race Relations in the 1880s* (University of Tennessee Press, 1976); *Crusade for Justice: The Autobiography of Ida B. Wells*, edited by Alfreda M. Duster (The University of Chicago Press, 1970); Shields McIlwaine's *Memphis: Down in Dixie* (E. P. Dutton and Company, 1948); and *Guthrie: History of a Capital City 1889–1910*, by Lloyd C. Lentz III (Logan County Historical Society). The classic work of historian John Hope Franklin, *From Slavery to Freedom* (McGraw Hill, 1994), is essential reading for anyone trying to understand the experience of American Negroes in the century after the Civil War and to learn how men such as Booker T. Washington and W. E. B. Du Bois led efforts to transcend decades of horror and injustice.

The description of O. W. Gurley's journey to Tulsa was drawn largely from the aforementioned profile in the *Tulsa Star*, as were passages describing the achievements of John and Loula Williams. My description of early Greenwood was synthesized from many sources, including *Black Wall Street: From Riot To Renaissance in Tulsa's Historic Greenwood District* (Eakin Press, 1998), by Hannibal Johnson. The story of the Williams family was also regularly told by Bill Williams in his later years. A recording of the retired teacher's interview with historian Scott Ellsworth is included in the race riot materials at the McFarlin Library at the University of Tulsa. Bill Williams also discussed the lives of his parents, his own childhood, and the origins of Greenwood in an interview with *Oklahoma Impact* magazine in the early 1970s, and with Ruth Sigler Avery on November 29, 1970.

Details of Sophronia Jackson's death and her husband's bedside vigil were drawn from Andrew Smitherman's *Tulsa Star* editorial in February

1914. From the intimacy of his reporting, it was clear that Smitherman himself was among those attending Sophronia's passing.

My description of the deteriorating racial climate and racial violence in the years after World War I was based on several sources, including but not limited to John Hope Franklin's *From Slavery to Freedom; The Unknown Soldiers: Black American Troops in World War I*, by Arthur E. Barbeau and Florette Henri (Temple University Press, 1974); Wyn Craig Wade's excellent book *The Fiery Cross: The Ku Klux Klan in America* (Simon and Schuster, 1987); Scott Ellsworth's groundbreaking *Death in the Promised Land, The Tulsa Race Riot of 1921* (LSU Press, 1982); the Tulsa Race Riot Commission Report written by Scott Ellsworth and John Hope Franklin, and by numerous newspaper articles from that time.

CHAPTER 2

On October 8, 1939, the *Tulsa Tribune* commemorated the twentieth anniversary of the paper's purchase by Richard Lloyd Jones with several long articles, prominent among them a long essay written by Jones himself. The publisher's piece traced the arc of his remarkable life—from his early love of writing to his frustrations as an aimless young adult, his success at *Collier's* and the purchase of the Lincoln birthplace, followed by his entry into newspapers and his eventual purchase of the *Tribune*. Other biographical details, and those of his prominent father, the Reverend Jenkins Lloyd Jones, Jr., were taken from Richard Lloyd Jones's obituary that ran in the *Tribune* in December 1963.

The infamous missing editorial of May 31, 1921, the piece so widely blamed for precipitating the burning, may be gone forever. But *Tribune* stories and editorials that survive offer a clear window into the editor's opinions about race, including the front-page piece of February 4, 1921, that announced the KKK's intention to expand into Oklahoma, and the *Tribune* editorial on June 4, 1921, that declared, "A bad nigger is about the lowest thing that walks on two feet."

In an August 19, 2000, telephone interview with Jones's son, Jenkins Lloyd Jones told me the story of how his father housed Booker T. Washington when the famous Negro could not find lodging in Madison, Wis-

274 · CHAPTER NOTES

consin. But the younger Jones was also surprisingly candid about his father's shortcomings, conceding that father and son did not have a close relationship. "He was very opinionated and argumentative. We often clashed," Jenkins Lloyd Jones said. "Or he would run over people. It's hard to describe that as a clash. He had a strong temper. You can never out-argue people with a strong temper."

Jenkins Jones was my source for his father's Wisconsin confrontation with Robert La Follete, an enmity that led to Richard Lloyd Jones's move to Tulsa in 1919. Jenkins Jones also provided descriptions of the *Tribune* Building, details of his father's office, and described his father's habit of pacing and gesturing while dictating his editorials. The publisher's grandson, Jenkins Lloyd Jones, Jr., told me about listening to his grandfather's tales of meeting Jefferson Davis and Ulysses S. Grant, and of flying with Orville Wright. Jenkins Lloyd Jones, Jr. also possessed valuable knowledge concerning the life of his great grandfather, the Chicago Unitarian Minister and Lincoln devotee.

My depiction of early Tulsa history was based on several sources, including *Tulsa: Biography of an American City*, by Danney Goble (Council Oaks Books, 1997); Angie Debo's *Tulsa: From Creek Town to Oil Capital* (University of Oklahoma Press, 1943); *Death in a Promised Land*, by Scott Ellsworth; and the report of the Tulsa Race Riot Commission.

Ellsworth's work was also crucial to my attempts to place the burning in the ugly context of the times. Other sources that described the rampant paranoia, nativism, the Red Scare, and the rise of vigilantism were *The Fiery Cross: The Ku Klux Klan in America*, by Wyn Craig Wade; John Hope Franklin's *From Slavery to Freedom*; and Frederick Lewis Allen's *Only Yesterday: An Informal History of the 1920s* (Harper and Row, 1931).

My description of the kidnapping and torture of the Tulsa members of the I.W.W. was based largely on Scott Ellsworth's *Death in the Promised Land*, and on accounts in both the *Tulsa Tribune* and *Tulsa World*.

Tulsa attorney John R. Woodard would have conceded that he was not the most objective source where Richard Lloyd Jones was concerned. In fact, Woodard clearly was numbered among Jones's most bitter Tulsa enemies. But Woodard's account of the scandal surrounding Jones and his affair with Amy Comstock, one recounted in the attorney's self-published book, *In Re: Tulsa,* was substantiated with transcripts of sworn legal depositions taken from private investigators who had their eyes to the keyhole in the Tulsa Hotel. I also read the testimony of local businessmen recruited by the investigators to observe Jones and Comstock, transcripts I obtained from Dick Warner, an investigator with the Riot Commission.

CHAPTER 3

Damie Rowland was eighty-seven years old when Ruth Sigler Avery interviewed her on June 22, 1972. "She was a tiny, wrinkled black woman wearing a white, dotted-swiss cap over her gray hair," Avery later wrote. "In her apartment she proudly showed me the ring her husband had given her the day they were married. Then she began to tell me the story of the little boy, Jimmie Jones, whom she had raised."

My account of Dick Rowland's life is drawn largely from the transcript of Avery's interview with the shoeshine boy's caregiver—beginning with his appearance at Damie's door in Vinita, continuing through the tragedy in Tulsa, to Dick Rowland's eventual death on the West Coast.

Ruth Avery mentioned her childhood memories of the hilltop crossburning and torture of the black man in one of our first conversations. She also wrote about the event in her unpublished account of the Tulsa burning.

My description of the origins of the Ku Klux Klan rely heavily on the text of Wyn Craig Wade's *The Fiery Cross.* The invention of the Klan's name by the Pulaski six and the order's early days are recounted by Wade on pages 32–38. Wade covers the KKK's descent into terror and its subsequent banishment by the federal government in Chapter 2. The author's description of *Birth of a Nation* and its role in the Klan's rebirth in 1915 begins on page 119, while William Joseph Simmons, father of the modern Klan, first appears on page 140. It is on page 165 that Wade tells the story of Warren G. Harding's initiation into the KKK, one that took place shortly after Simmons's testimony before Congress.

"A five-member 'Imperial induction team,' headed by Simmons, conducted the ceremony in the Green Room of the White House," Wade wrote. "Members of the team were so nervous that they forgot their Bible in their car, so Harding had to send for the White House Bible. In consideration of his status, Harding was permitted to rest his elbow on the desk, as he knelt on the floor during the long oath taking."

My description of the Klan in Tulsa is based on several sources, including my interviews with Philip Rhees and Richard Gary, two Tulsa whites who were boys at the time of the riot and who remember watching the Klan parades with their fathers; transcripts of Ruth Avery's interview with Klansman Andre Wilkes; and Avery's interviews with other whites knowledgeable about the KKK's influence in the city at the time.

CHAPTER 4

A description of the events inside the *Tulsa Tribune* on the afternoon of May 31, 1921, came to me secondhand, but from two excellent sources. In the 1960s, a senior writer with the *Tribune* told the story of what went on at the paper that day to a highly respected Tulsa historian. That historian passed the account on to me on the grounds that I would not divulge his name.

My description of Sheriff William McCullough and McCullough's reluctant role in the hanging of a young black man in 1911 comes from a 1954 profile in the *Tribune*. McCullough was in his eighties when reporter Toby LaForge wrote about the ex-lawman. McCullough's involvement in the burning of 1921 was never mentioned in that story, which focused on McCullough's lingering regret about the 1911 hanging, the only execution over which he presided.

Descriptions of the Tulsa County Courthouse and the fourth-floor jail were taken from interviews that Ruth Avery conducted with former members of the Tulsa County Sheriff's Department.

My description of the escalating tensions on both sides of the tracks that afternoon was drawn from several sources, including Scott Ellsworth's *Death in a Promised Land*, the report of the Tulsa Race Riot Commission, and newspaper accounts in the *Tulsa Tribune* and *Tulsa*

World. In interviews with Scott Ellsworth conducted in the 1970s, Greenwood residents Robert Fairchild and Bill Williams described the scene along Greenwood Avenue late that fateful afternoon and early evening. Fairchild also recounted his friendship with Dick Rowland, and the statements of the Greenwood pool sharks who vowed retaliation should whites attempt to lynch a Tulsa Negro.

Veneice Dunn Sims told me the story of her new blue dress when we spoke at her home in the winter of 2000. I am glad to report that in the spring of 2000, Mrs. Sims, then well into her nineties, was the honorary prom queen at Booker T. Washington High School, an event she attended in a blue dress much like the one she had hoped to wear in 1921.

The story of Wilhelmina Guess's love for her Uncle Andrew, her bout with scarlet fever, and the last time Wilhelmina saw her uncle alive, came to me from several sources, including interviews with Jack and Don Adams, Wilhelmina's nephews; Wilhelmina's speech at the Tulsa Community Center in the fall of 1989, a recording of which resides among Scott Ellsworth's materials at the McFarlin Library of the University of Tulsa; and a brief profile of Wilhelmina in *They Came Searching: How Blacks Sought the Promised Land in Tulsa*, by Eddie Faye Gates (Eakin Press, 1997).

CHAPTER 5

It was my great good fortune to make the acquaintance of Obera Mann Smith, the daughter of O. B. Mann. Mrs. Smith's recollections of her father were sketchy, but she provided me with an outstanding photographic portrait that itself gave me an insight into the towering veteran of World War I. Obera also pointed me toward John D. Mann, O. B. Mann's nephew, who now lives in Michigan and is well versed in his remarkable family history. It was John Mann who told me about the birth of O. B. Mann's mother to the white slaver from Texas, about O. B.'s notorious temper, and his role in attempting to fend off the white attack on Greenwood.

My descriptions of the experiences of black soldiers in World War I and German propaganda directed toward them were taken from *The*

Unknown Soldiers: Black American Troops in World War I (Temple University Press, 1974), by Arthur E. Barbeau and Florette Henri. Mann's loud appearance in the Dreamland Theater on the night of May 31, 1921, was based on several sources, including the testimony of Dreamland projectionist Henry Sowders and interviews with Bill Williams, who was in the theater that night. A few days after the burning, Mann's role in what was happening in Greenwood was also described by O. W. Gurley in the *Tulsa Tribune*.

"The real leader of the gang was a tall, brown-skinned Negro named Mann," Gurley said. "This boy had come back from France with exaggerated ideas about equality and thinking he can whip the world."

In 1924, William Redfearn, the white owner of the Dixie Theater on Greenwood Avenue, went to trial against an Oklahoma insurance company, seeking payment for losses incurred on June 1, 1921. The insurance company had refused to pay, arguing that the policy had been voided because the fire that destroyed Redfearn's theater occurred in the course of a race riot. Redfearn, who lost the case at trial, appealed all the way to the Oklahoma Supreme Court, losing there eventually, too. But the defeated property owner left a grand legacy for future researchers and writers. Transcripts of testimony in his case are among the richest veins of information I found anywhere.

O. W. Gurley was among those who testified in the Redfearn case. My depiction of Gurley's actions on the afternoon and evening of May 31, 1921, are taken largely from transcripts of that testimony. The tense scene as described in the *Tulsa Star* that evening is also based in part on Gurley's later interview with the *Tulsa Tribune*, one that did little to endear him with his brethren on the north side of the tracks. "I entered the *Star* office about nine o'clock and found activities far advanced," Gurley was quoted by the *Tribune* as saying. "Men were coming singly and in little groups in answer to the call to arms. And guns and ammunition were being collected from every available source, and many of the men were making open threats and talking in the most turbulent manner." Jonathan Z. Larsen's excellent article in the February/March 1997 issue of *Civilization* magazine also describes the volatile meeting that night in the *Star*, quoting from the unpublished memoirs of John Stradford in which Stradford vowed to go to the courthouse alone if the need arose.

In describing the escalating tensions at the courthouse and the blacks' first trip to the courthouse, I consulted Tulsa newspaper stories of the time, Scott Ellsworth's *Death in a Promised Land*, Gurley's court testimony, the *Tulsa Tribune* story in which he is extensively quoted, and later interviews with Bill Williams.

The whites' rush for weapons at the National Guard Armory was recounted in Major James A. Bell's duty report for that night.

My account of the fateful attempt by the old white man to disarm O. B. Mann comes from several sources, including newspaper accounts, Scott Ellsworth's interview with Bill Williams, and my own interviews with Mann's descendants. Gurley's interview with the *Tribune* was helpful once again. "This fellow Mann fired the first shot," Gurley was quoted as saying. "That brought calamity."

It is here that I will state my debt to a late World War II veteran named Loren Gill, who returned from Europe to attend the University of Tulsa and picked the burning as his topic for his master's thesis. Any investigative journalist would have been proud of Gill's work. He interviewed dozens of witnesses, most of them white, studied newspaper accounts of the time, Red Cross records, and government documents to produce a history of the burning invaluable to me and essential to anyone attempting to understand what happened.

CHAPTER 6

It was my good fortune that Henry Sowders was among the witnesses in the Redfearn case. His remarkable story about events in Greenwood on May 31 is contained in transcripts of that case. The stories of Helen Donohue and W. R. Holway are based on interviews the two white Tulsans gave to Ruth Avery in the 1970s. The account of Tulsa grocer Hugh Gary is based on my long interview with Gary's son Richard, at Richard Gary's Tulsa home in the summer of 2000.

My description of events immediately after the first shots were fired at the courthouse were again drawn from the writings of Scott Ellsworth, from newspaper accounts, and on the fairly voluminous after-action reports written by the Tulsa members of the National Guard.

The story of the old black couple murdered while kneeling in prayer was first told by Walter White, a black writer from the East Coast who arrived in Tulsa hours after the burning was over. White was a light-skinned black who moved freely among the Tulsa whites. He said he based his accounts of the atrocities on statements made to him by top law-enforcement officers in Tulsa.

Choc Phillips's compelling story of those hours comes from the Riot Commission's Report. I also gleaned a few details of Phillips's story in an interview with Tulsa resident Ron Trekell, a friend of the late Phillips, who described for me how the teenager and his barbershop quartet were practicing on the steps of Central High School as the black platoon came marching downtown.

The story of Negro officer H. C. Pack is also contained in the transcripts of the Redfearn case.

CHAPTER 7

Young Bill Williams was one of those who heard the whistle at 5:08 A.M. on the morning of June 1, and decades later continued to speculate as to its origin, though no one had any doubt as to its intent.

The dreadful story of what young Walter Ferrell witnessed came from Ferrell's interview with Ruth Avery on March 3, 1971. "I've never forgotten that horrible sight, and knowing what was happening to my friends," Ferrell, a maintenance worker for the Tulsa school district, told Avery that day. "That's all I can tell you of my personal experience. It is just too terrible to talk about even decades later."

The story of John Williams and his son Bill, and what happened to the Williams family on the morning of June 1, is taken from the previously mentioned series of interviews that Bill Williams conducted in the 1970s. My description of the plight of O. W. Gurley and his wife Emma derives from Gurley's testimony in the Redfearn case and his appearance as a witness in the July 1921 criminal trial of Police Chief John Gustafson.

The story of Green E. Smith, who watched the mob march up Greenwood Avenue to set the Dreamland Theater on fire, was also contained in the Redfearn transcripts.

CHAPTER 8

No one can testify more dramatically to Tulsa's conspiracy of silence than Ed Wheeler, whose life was threatened while he researched the burning for a Tulsa magazine article published in the spring of 1971. Wheeler is the magazine writer to whom the three Klansmen spoke, two of them with regret, one without the slightest remorse.

The official position of Tulsa authorities was taken from newspaper accounts of that time, from books and other articles written about the burning, and through numerous interviews with Tulsans, including some who continued to try to minimize what happened.

The testimony of Fire Chief R. C. Adler was contained in the Redfearn documents, as were the stories of several other Tulsa firefighters who said that their superiors prevented them from combating the Greenwood conflagration. I found the account of Van Hurley among newspaper accounts collected by the Tuskegee Institute. The statements of Thomas Higgins and V. B. Bostic were contained in the report of the Tulsa Race Riot Commission, as was the story of the white policeman who changed out of his uniform, then hurried to Greenwood to join the looting. The story of the Tulsa detective's daughter passing out chewing gum came from my interview with Philip Rhees, a Tulsa white who lived near the girl. Laurel Buck's story came from his testimony at the criminal trial of Police Chief Gustafson.

My description of the white mob's modus operandi derives from several sources, including Scott Ellsworth's book, newspaper and magazine articles, and interviews with witnesses.

The story of the blind beggar dragged off down the street is another of Ruth Avery's contributions. In 1971, Avery heard the horrible account from a man who said he witnessed it, E. W. Maxey, formerly a deputy sheriff for Tulsa County. In the interview, Maxey said he was present when Roy Belton was hung in 1920, and insisted to Avery that Klan members were among those responsible. Less than a year later, about

8:00 A.M. on June 1, 1921, Maxey and another teenage friend were downtown when they saw the white thugs race up, tie the beggar to the car and start off. "He was hollering," Maxey told Avery. "His head was being bashed in, bouncing on the steel rails and bricks. They went at all the speed that the car could make, about fifty or sixty miles an hour; a new car with the top down, and three or four of them in it, dragging him behind the car."

Stories of the Negro survivors came from several sources. I first read of Kinney Booker's experience in Brent Staples' *New York Times Magazine* article of December 19, 1999, titled *Unearthing a Riot*. I heard George Monroe's recollections firsthand during one of several interviews with Monroe at his Tulsa home in the spring and summer of 2000. The stories of Callie Rogers, Susie Williams, and the wealthy Negro woman who lived on Detroit Avenue were found in *Race Riot 1921: Events of the Tulsa Disaster* (Out on a Limb Publishing, 1998), an amazing little book written by Mary E. Jones Parrish. Parrish was a young mother who fled Greenwood with her daughter when the white mobs attacked; then, in the months and years afterward, she was among the first to write down what had happened. Seymour Williams's story was based on an interview the old coach did with Scott Ellsworth in the late 1970s. A recording of the conversation resides at the University of Tulsa's McFarlin Library.

The murder of the paralyzed old man was among the anecdotes contained in the Riot Commission Report.

CHAPTER 9

Reverend C. Calvin McCutchen preached his first sermon at the Mount Zion Baptist Church on October 20, 1957, and he still leads the historic church today. In our telephone interview, he described much of Mount Zion's history, told me about Pastor R. A. Whitaker's oratorical gifts, and traced the congregation's long odyssey to rebuild, efforts that were not completed until the 1950s.

My description of the battle for Mount Zion was drawn from several sources, including Choc Phillips's account published in the Riot Commission Report, Tulsa newspapers of the time, and an article in *The Crusader*, a publication of The African Blood Brotherhood. The article, which was written by a Tulsa Negro and published in July 1921, described the casualties taken by whites who attempted to charge the church held by a "handful of ex-soldiers, fifty to be exact. . . . Five times they came against it in mass formation, and five times were they repelled with deadly loss. However, what they had not valor enough to accomplish by force, they treacherously achieved. Under cover of a white flag of truce, several of them sneaked forward and set fire to the sacred building. As the fate of the church was recognized, the Negro heroes, who had given such a good account of themselves and had held it so valiantly, determined not to die like rats in a hole, and taking up their few wounded comrades, intrepidly charged through the mocking foe, suffering severely, but nevertheless breaking through the enemy line to safety. Ten heroes were left behind, however, stricken to death. Upon these the white barbarians vented their wrath by further riddling their bodies and kicking the lifeless clay after they felt sure that no spark of those heroic lives remained."

O. B. Mann's part in the battle of Greenwood Avenue and his dash to Mount Zion were part of my discussions with John D. Mann, the Negro fighter's nephew.

Ruth Avery's account of that morning is taken from her own writing, and from our interviews.

Events at Central High School were variously described by whites interviewed by Avery decades later. References to the "Nigger Day" sign and the weary man's hand-off of gun and ammunition to the boys came to me via the research of Scott Ellsworth.

CHAPTER 10

Dr. Andrew C. Jackson has long been described as one of the burning's most tragic figures, a man whose death symbolized both the larger atrocity and the state of race in America at that time. Thus I was fortunate to discover the recording of the speech Wilhelmina Guess Howell made in 1989, Eddie Faye Gates' profile of Wilhelmina in the book *They Came*

Searching, and to track down Jack and Don Adams, Wilhelmina's nephews and keepers of the family stories. It is through those sources that my portrait of Andrew Jackson emerges.

Because of the court testimony of John Oliphant, I had access to a contemporary and highly detailed account of the Negro physician's death. Transcripts of Oliphant's testimony at the criminal trial of Police Chief Gustafson rank among the most chilling descriptions anywhere of the burning.

CHAPTER 11

As part of my research, I contacted many of the people who had called Riot Commission investigator Dick Warner with their memories of the burning or to share stories of the event that had been passed down through the years. Only a small percentage of these conversations produced relevant information for me, so my expectations were low on the afternoon I called Margaret Anderson at her Tulsa home. Nearly two hours later, I possessed an account of the burning and its aftermath that still causes my stomach to stir. Her name had been Margaret Dickinson then, the young daughter of Tulsa's most successful builder. I was astounded not only by the story she told me, but by the small details she was able to remember. Clearly, her experiences during the burning have been much on her mind over the years.

My description of the Negro exodus derives from several sources. It was Red Phelps, son of Merrill and Ruth Phelps, who told me of how his parents ran what amounted to a stop on an underground railroad in the days after the burning. Red Phelps still lives in the house where his parents gave shelter to the fleeing Negroes.

Details of Hugh Gary's trip with his boys to survey the destruction of Greenwood, and the subsequent observation of the truckload of bodies in the country, were obtained in a long interview with Hugh Gary's son Richard.

S. M. Jackson discussed with Ruth Avery in the early 1970s his work embalming Negro victims.

CHAPTER 12

It's worth noting that Faith Heironymous was the only reporter of the *Tulsa World* to receive a byline in the paper's coverage of the burning. Hers was an excellent and haunting piece that brought the misery of McNulty Park into multisensory focus. It was abundantly clear from her writing that she had been deeply affected by what she saw. The pathos of her words provided a dramatic and telling contrast to the stories that appeared after the burning in the *World's* rival, the *Tulsa Tribune*. The *World's* coverage, with the Heironymous story as the most dramatic example, was full of remorse. *Tribune* stories reflected a mood that was almost celebratory.

CHAPTER 13

Most sources here are self-evident—*The New York Times* and other papers around the nation, and the coverage of the burning's aftermath in the local papers. Within hours, Red Cross volunteers were on the scene, and the precise records kept by that agency also provided much insight into the scope of what happened.

We will never know exactly how many were killed during those terrible days in Tulsa, but Ed Wheeler's assessment is bound to be closer to the truth than the ridiculously low figure promulgated by official Tulsa.

A list of indictments and the grand jury's report are part of the public record. O. W. Gurley's name appears prominently on the list of witnesses, but not among those who were indicted. Based on his interview with the *Tulsa Tribune* and his other public statements subsequent to the burning, there is no doubt that Gurley was among the most damning witnesses where the Negro fighters were concerned, and no doubt he was considered a traitor to his people.

CHAPTER 14

The account of Dick Rowland's exoneration, his last visit to Tulsa, and his life and death on the West Coast were part of Damie Rowland's interview with Ruth Avery in the 1970s.

Descriptions of the rebuilding of Greenwood are based on several sources, including interviews with Bill Williams, the work of Scott Ellsworth, Hannibal Johnson's *Black Wall Street*, and Mary E. Jones Parrish's *Race Riot 1921*.

It was John Mann who told me the story of O. B. Mann's flight to Canada and his return to Tulsa after six months, just in time for the Red Cross Christmas party in Greenwood. An account of that hopelessly bittersweet moment was written by Maurice Willows, who led the Red Cross efforts to assist the blacks, and whose name still evokes reverence among black Tulsans today.

CHAPTER 15

Oklahoma State Representative Don Ross was nothing but helpful from the moment of our first telephone conversation. Becoming his friend has been one of the great pleasures of this work. Of course, Ross is also one of the key characters in the story of the burning and how it came to be restored to its proper place in history. Over several long conversations, Ross told me about the day in the yearbook meeting with Bill Williams and the impact it had on his life. It was no accident that Ross was the editor of *Oklahoma Impact*, the black magazine that published Ed Wheeler's account of the burning, or that Ross should be the legislator whose work led to the creation of the Tulsa Race Riot Commission. The horror of 1921 Tulsa has seemed to follow Ross around all of his adult life.

Nancy Feldman's experience at the University of Tulsa is taken from the Riot Commission Report.

Scott Ellsworth coined the term, "the American *Kristalnacht.*"

I learned of Ed Wheeler's chilling adventures during a long interview in Wheeler's home and in several follow-up conversations on the telephone.

CHAPTER 16

My description of the ceremony where Florida Governor Lawton Chiles signed the Rosewood reparations law was taken from the May 5, 1994, edition of the *Miami Herald*. Details of the 1923 attack on the Rosewood

Community were drawn from *The Rosewood Report*, a 1993 study led by Professor Maxine D. Jones of Florida State University. The linkage of the Rosewood reparations, the bombing of the Murrah Building, and Ross's legislative efforts to exhume the Greenwood tragedy were explained to me by Ross in several conversations.

The accounts of Clyde Eddy and Lee Cisco are based on my interviews with both of those men, who were children at the time of the burning.

My description of the presentation of the Riot Commission's Report to Governor Frank Keating, Tulsa Mayor Susan Savage, and legislative leaders is based on the reporting of Randy Krehbiel in the *Tulsa World* and on a *New York Times* article of March 1, 2001.

For several weeks in the summer of 2000, I drove the north side of Tulsa, searching for relics of the burning—buildings or places that might look the same as they did in 1921. With the exception of that one block of Deep Greenwood, few remain. But many people remember. *Fort Worth Star-Telegram* photographer Jill Johnson and I were charmed during our visit with survivor Otis Clark. Wilhemina Guess Howell, though her memory failed her for the most part, was radiant when I visited her in the waiting room of her nursing home. And I will always treasure the burnt penny George Monroe placed in my palm during my last visit to his home.

INDEX